# A PATTERN
# OF
# MADNESS

# A PATTERN
# OF
# MADNESS

*Neville Symington*

KARNAC
LONDON        NEW YORK

First published in 2002 by
Karnac Books Ltd.
118 Finchley Road, London NW3 5HT

A subsidiary of Other Press LLC, New York

Copyright © 2002 Neville Symington

Reprinted 2002

The rights of Neville Symington to be identified as the author of this work
have been asserted in accordance with §§ 77 and 78 of the Copyright Design
and Patents Act 1988.

**British Library Cataloguing in Publication Data**

A C.I.P. for this book is available from the British Library

ISBN  978 1 85575 279 5

10 9 8 7 6 5 4 3 2

Edited, designed, and produced by Communication Crafts

www.karnacbooks.com

*In memory of Bob Gosling
a True Friend
in whose warmth, honesty, and courage
it was a privilege to be included*

# CONTENTS

PREFACE                                                    ix

Introduction                                                1

PART I
The pattern of sanity                                      13

  1   Ontology                   25

  2   Freedom                    37

  3   The person                 45

  4   Narcissism and the struggle for survival        49

  5   Emotional action           56

  6   The internalizing act      66

  7   Roy Schafer's action language   70

PART II
**The pattern of madness**                                          77

8    The jelly                                                      83

9    God                                                           91

10   Acts of God                                                  109

11   The quality of attachment                                    114

12   The worm                                                     122

13   Perversions                                                  128

14   Trauma                                                       131

15   Psychiatric diseases                                         141

16   Psychoanalytic schema of narcissism derived
     from psychiatry                                              150


PART III
**The subjective experience**                                      159

17   Human dilemmas                                               163

18   Guilt                                                        175

19   Generation of perception and belief                          183

20   Self-knowledge versus self-consciousness                     188

21   Technique                                                    191

22   Reverse perspective                                          206


*APPENDIX*
     Principles of action                                         215

*REFERENCES*                                                       219

*INDEX*                                                            225

# PREFACE

In a book of this nature I have many people to thank; it is the product of a lifetime's research, so it must begin with my parents, for whose undoubted love, even when I tested it to the limits, I am eternally grateful. This debt of gratitude to my parents then spreads out to my brother and sister and then to my numerous aunts, uncles, and cousins, who had such a formative influence upon my life. Without that background of support, I cannot imagine that I should have been able to search out some meaningful solutions to the mad chaos I found within myself and others and whose outcome is largely encompassed within the pages of this book. This book attempts to find the core pattern that underlies all the different manifestations of madness. The result is an amalgam of my own academic study and personal experience, and the latter component requires me to thank people from my earliest years.

Joan Smith was an extremely important figure in my childhood. She came to us as governess when I was aged two and left us just before my sixth birthday to finish her studies in Social Work at McGill University in Montreal. She later occupied the Chair of Social Work at St. Louis University and has continued her interest and encouragement down to the present time.

My educational journey in the exploration of madness has been a long one, and there have been many people who have helped me to develop an understanding of it. George Ekbery is one of the most important people in that development. His lectures in Ontology when I was in my early twenties laid a foundation upon which I have been able to build many subsequent understandings. He gave me more than intellectual understanding because I sensed that what he taught had become integral to his character. I believe he lived his intellectual understanding. When he taught me, I grasped intellectually what he was communicating, but it is only in recent years that it has become also an emotional foundation that has guided me in my exploration into madness. An understanding of madness requires a grasp of sanity. It was the latter that George Ekbery communicated. There is a foundation stone upon which sanity is built. I think I can safely say that all my subsequent learning was secondary to this. It was not that George taught me, because what I am talking about can only occur through a personal act of understanding, but he lit the flame that allowed this to occur. My gratitude to him is inestimable. I only regret that I was unable to communicate this to him while he was still alive.

From George Ekbery I came to understand unity in the diversity of reality while studying Philosophy. From Charles Davis I came to grasp the unity within the diversity of Christian culture while studying theology, and Hubert Richards supplemented this in his imaginative exposition of Scripture. To these three men I owe a great deal, but I regret that only the last one is still living and able to be thanked.

I owe special thanks to John Klauber, who was my analyst when I was doing a psychoanalytic training in London. There was a great deal that he did not understand, and there is much in this book that does not owe anything to him directly, but indirectly I owe a great deal. I think he "believed" in me. He saw through the chaos into something that he believed was worthwhile and would persevere. That act of "belief" was crucial in my exploration of madness. He had another quality that I have come to value greatly in recent years: he had the view that there was in me something trying to find a healthy solution, even if I mistakenly went down the wrong path in trying to find it. He was never negativistic, which unfortunately many analysts are, and, as will appear in this book, I believe that this attitude is in itself a feature of madness. So he kindled the healthy in me, and I am grateful to him for this, and again I am sorry he is not alive to hear me say it.

The psychoanalyst from whom I learned most in a continuous sense was Herbert Rosenfeld. Six years of fortnightly supervision seminars illuminated for me the inner world in a way that was remarkable. He opened perspectives that were quite new to me. He was limited, however, in his vision to the particular perspective of psychoanalysis, shutting out other avenues of understanding. I am certain that mental life cannot be understood by psychoanalysis alone, by philosophy alone, by religion alone, by literature alone, but only by a synthesis of all of these. This narrowness of perspective distorted, I believe, his understanding quite considerably, but I learned from him a great deal about madness, despite that limitation.

I attended several workshops taken by Wilfred Bion, which had a huge influence. I also went twice to supervision with him. I learned more from those two than from any number of supervisions from others. He had that simplicity of soul that cut through to what was most essential. There is no one within the psychoanalytic world who understood madness better or realized the extent to which it applied in institutions and cultures in the wider world. I felt with him that same resonance of soul that I felt with George Ekbery—that sense of "Oh, thank heavens to find the voice I have been looking for, for so long." That particular quality shared by Bion and George Ekbery is something that transcends any particular discipline of thought. It is an attitude of heart and soul that comes I know not from where, but I am certain it is not the product of any particular educational system or discipline. It is as difficult to account for as genius.

Conversations and correspondence with Elliott Jaques have been important, in particular his decision theory, and I have come to see the paralysis of decision-making as one of the symptomatic signs of madness. His continuing research into human functioning unabated by age is inspiring, and his sustained interest in my communications has been an encouragement.

More important, however, than any psychologist, psychoanalyst, or formal teacher, was a patient who forced me out of my complacency. I saw her on the National Health Service in Britain, and, because vacancies for treatment by the psychoanalytic method that I was employing at the time were so rare, she knew she had to make do with me. I was not adequate for her needs. She had to shake me and make me into what she needed in so far as that was possible. Through her instrumentality I came to understand subtle emotional processes that I had not even suspected existed before. Her knowledge of my internal mental processes was alarming but, at the same time, a revelation. It radically changed my understanding of human communication and mental life. Confidentiality prevents me from mentioning her name, but, in the way a wreath is placed on the grave of the unknown soldier on Armistice Day, I wish to place a garland of flowers upon her head. She deserves from me all the tributes that are granted to the unknown soldier. She is the unknown patient. Since that time, other patients have been responsible for adding to that knowledge, but she gave me that first shake without which the rest would not have followed, and I am profoundly grateful to her.

I should like to thank various members of the Sydney Institute for Psycho-Analysis for allowing me to try out some of my theories on them and for their perceptive comments.

I should like to thank my two sons, Andrew and David, with whom I have had many conversations about matters concerning the human condition that have contributed greatly to my understanding.

Lastly, I should like to thank my wife, Joan, for tolerating the demands of this ever-present book.

# A PATTERN
# OF
# MADNESS

# Introduction

I was well aware that the so-called helper—that is, myself—
could not help them [patients] unless he knew their fantasy
material from his own direct experience, and that at present all
he possessed were a few theoretical prejudices of dubious
value.

C. G. Jung, *Memories, Dreams, Reflections* (1983, p. 203)

I have become convinced that narcissism is the core pathology in our contemporary world, the elucidation of which illuminates what we mean by madness. Narcissism is a self-centredness, a solipsistic pathology that affects individuals but is also one that has staggering social repercussions. Behaviours that look entirely different originate from the same core pathology: the greed and corruption of someone like Mobutu, the murderousness of the serial killer, the coldness of a mother who refuses warmth to her children, the hypocrisy of the moralist who preaches one thing but does the opposite all stem from the same narcissistic source. It is also responsible for medical conditions such as cancer, endometriosis, or low-back pain and for psychiatric conditions such as

1

schizophrenia, manic-depressive psychosis, borderline pathology and obsessional neurosis. It is because it is the core of all pathology, that I have entitled this book *A Pattern of Madness*. It sets out to understand nothing less than what it is that constitutes madness. Psychiatric textbooks give us some of the symptomatology of madness, they pick out some of the classical manifestations, but they do not grasp the inner factors that generate it. They therefore fail not only to illustrate the structure of madness but also to cover the phenomenology adequately. A great deal of madness goes unrecognized for this reason.

The aim of this book, therefore, is to produce a sketch of the structure of madness whose core I have called narcissism, but this word has unfortunately attracted to itself a pejorative overtone. Self-centredness, egoism, solipsism are all synonyms for what I am talking about. Also, I believe that autism is another variant of the same condition, and I think that what differentiates autism from narcissism is not the phenomenology as such but, rather, the descriptive accounts of its aetiology. Whereas narcissism has been seen as being due either to a preponderance in someone of the death instinct or to an early fixation point, autism is seen to be the result of an early trauma that occurred to the individual when he was still an infant.

I believe that ignorance of the structure of madness has led to sterility in psychotherapeutic practice. I hope to try to demonstrate in another book the way in which so much of the modern *malaise* finds its origin in this core and in the thought processes and ideologies that issue from it. However, the task here is to outline the inner structure of madness itself with the greatest economy of language possible and thereby to bring the kernel of it to consciousness. I have struggled to do this over some years. I have called this core of madness "narcissism", but as I come to define what I mean, people may want to give it a different name. What might be called healthy self-confidence is called "narcissism" by some writers. This is not what I mean by it. When I use the term "narcissism", I refer to something pathological, however widespread it may be. The fact that it may be almost universal does not mean that it is thereby sane. Pathological conditions of a severe kind are woven into the very fabric of cultural life.

Narcissism and consciousness are mutual contradictories. It takes a big emotional effort to bring the narcissistic structure to consciousness. This book alone will not be enough, but my hope is that it might begin to light up a path for those who seriously want to tackle it, both in themselves and in the culture. I would like to be able to say that psychoanalysis, psychotherapy, or interventions by a wide range of clinicians reduces the power of narcissism in the personality, but I think a patient would be extremely lucky if he achieved this outcome. There are several reasons for this: the resistance to giving up the narcissistic way of being is very great, and the road to achieving it is full of terror. There is no utilitarian advantage to be gained. The desire for freedom that the endeavour involves has to be something that a person thinks is worth striving for. The other reason is that the majority of psychoanalysts and psychotherapists are themselves very narcissistic, and they pass on this viewpoint and psychopathology to their patients. It is like a contagious disease. There is no guarantee against this, but if the pattern of narcissism is clear, then the chances of it being understood are enhanced. An architect's plan is no guarantee that a house is going to be built, but without it there is no chance of it happening at all. Psychoanalysis and psychotherapy, as well as the social sciences more generally, are rooted in presuppositions that are narcissistic in themselves. It is for this reason that I think it necessary, in order to understand madness, to go back to the fundamental assumptions that underlie our thinking about mental life and the world in which we live.

At the beginning of *The World as Will and Representation* Arthur Schopenhauer (1969) says that his book is the exposition of one thought alone, but he goes on to say that in order to be communicated, it has to be split up into parts, and these form an organic unity. It is only, therefore, when the end of the book has been reached that the single thought has been communicated. Hence the parts being read at the beginning cannot be properly understood until the end. When the thought has been grasped, then, in order to understand the way in which the sections are an organic part of the whole, the book needs to be read a second time, and this is exactly what Schopenhauer recommended. Taking my cue from him, this is also what I recommend. To bid the reader to read this book twice is a big request, but I believe that the single thought and its ramifications won't be understood on a single reading. Solipsism as the core of madness is a single entity, but it is made up of interlocking parts. To grasp the unity in diversity, a second reading is necessary. I may know one of these parts or another, but what I am aiming to communicate is the whole, of which these are organic components. I am less concerned to communicate knowledge than to bring a human reality to consciousness.

Some years ago I wrote a book on narcissism (Symington, 1993), but at that time I had only partly understood it. This was because I focused on the aetiology of narcissism at the expense of its structure. My endeavour this time has been to sketch out the structure as adequately as possible and then to attend to the aetiology, and in doing this I came to realize that the way I had previously conceptualized it was biased and one-sided. I think that had I handed in my previous essay to be marked by my professor of social sciences, he might have given me 13 out of 20 and put in red ink at the end:

"A good effort with some original thinking, but the whole topic is being seen through moralistic spectacles and consequently the organic interlocking nature of narcissism has been almost entirely missed. What I want to see is a *psychological* understanding of narcissism."

If I were asked how I have come to a richer understanding of it now, I would have to answer that I am a bit further freed of the narcissistic condition. Although in that book I spoke of "narcissistic currents" in the personality, yet I tended to divide people into those who are narcissistic and those who are not. This was a categorization that was altogether too wholesale and too concrete. That way of conceptualizing is itself the product of narcissism.

A consequence of narcissism is that you cannot understand it when you are completely in the grip of it. It is not something that can be understood intellectually. You can know about it, speak about it, even write about it (!) but to have it as an object of consciousness is only possible through emotional intuition. The different parts have to be seen as part of the organic whole, otherwise there is no consciousness. It is necessary to see it in oneself, but to do this one has to be freed of it to some degree. It has to be a discrete entity within the personality. It has to have a fence around it, so to speak, and other parts of the personality have to be free of its influence in order that consciousness of it can emerge. Consciousness of narcissism can only be arrived at through an intellectual and emotional struggle combined with a quasi-religious pursuit of integrity.

I am professionally a psychoanalyst, and for many years I saw patients, had a post in a prestigious clinic, taught students, wrote a book (Symington, 1986) that was well received not only by mental health professionals, and yet I know that all the interpretations that I gave to my patients, the lectures that I gave, and the articles that I wrote were distorted through the influence of narcissism. I am not saying that everything I said to my patients, to my students, and to my readers was rubbish. I can recognize good things but because of narcissism the significance of the good things, was not sufficiently recognized and therefore lacked any principle of coherence and was not part of a comprehensive understanding. Then there were things that were quite misunderstood by me, and a rewriting of that book now would require me to structure them differently. Although I am a psychoanalyst and have until now conceptualized narcissism in the language forms of my profession yet I do not think understanding of it has come about principally through psychoanalysis. Psychoanalysis was part of a search for understanding, but it was ever an instrument subserving a higher purpose, and I have learned a great deal about narcissism through other experiences. It is rarely understood, but when it is, the person may be in one of many fields of human enquiry. It was understood by Tolstoy (for example, in *Anna Karenin*); it was certainly understood by the philosopher John Macmurray (1932, 1936, 1949) and also by the religious mystic, Caryll Houselander (1952), and by George Eliot (see, for example, *Middlemarch*, 1989, p. 702) and also by Marion Milner.[1]

I am hoping, then, in this book to present the core of narcissism in a language that will be accessible to all who want to pursue it.

---

[1]In 1934, before either becoming a psychoanalyst or being analysed, Marion Milner wrote a book called *A Life of One's Own*, in which, in order to achieve happiness, she realized the need to tackle narcissism. She did not call it this but used terms such as "self-interest" to describe it (see Milner, 1934).

The question is, therefore, "what language?" The language I have chosen is a combination of ordinary language and what might widely be called religious language, although the latter is comprised entirely of words that have passed into common usage. The reason for this choice is twofold. In the first place, I know of no other language that describes as well the interior phenomena that we are trying to understand, and, secondly, it has a greater emotional impact than words derived from the psychologist's armamentarium. I know that if I say to someone:

"You have a devil inside you",

it has a much greater impact than if I say:

"There is an internalized bad object in you."

It has a much greater impact on a patient if I say:

"When I said to you yesterday that I thought you had stayed in the waiting-room after the session because you wanted to stay physically close to me, you now believe that God has forbidden you to use the waiting-room at all",

than if I say:

"When I said to you yesterday that I thought you had stayed in the waiting-room after the session because you wanted to stay physically close to me, then, because I am an omnipotent object to you, you now believe that you are forbidden to use the waiting-room.

In my book *Emotion and Spirit* (Symington, 1994) I used the word "virtue", and it provoked an antipathetic reaction in many people. I am sure that if I had used the word "emotional potency" or "reparation", it would have passed without comment. Of course, I know that for many people, schooled in the worst of Christian pietism, any word associated with that child nightmare has to be immediately banished. I had an option, therefore, of either adopting new words or using traditional words but reinvesting them with their proper meaning. My project here is the same as that of D. H. Lawrence, who tried in *Lady Chatterley's Lover* to use sexual words as they are supposed to be used. In this case Lawrence was wanting to use the word "fuck" as it should be used rather than as a swear word. Richard Hoggart illustrates this with the following quip:

> A soldier on leave from abroad was charged with assaulting another man. He explained why he had done it: "I come home after fucking years in Africa, and what do I fucking find?— my wife in bed, engaging in illicit cohabitation with a male!" [Hoggart, 1961]

Just as Lawrence wanted to reinvest sexual words with their proper meaning, so I want to do the same with religious words. Another reason why I use this language is precisely because I think that many of the symbols in the Judeo–Christian mythology are projections of inner realities, and it is to these that those symbols properly apply. I am implying that much of the apparatus of the Judeo–Christian religions finds its origin in narcissism. In fact, I believe that it would be a worthwhile project to separate out those aspects of the Judeo–Christian religions that originate in narcissism from those that are the true objects of our healthy emotions.

I believe, for instance, that the social analysis of Michel Foucault is faulty in that he does not make this distinction in the structures that govern our lives. In his view, they are entirely imprisoning. These institutions, like the Judeo–Christian one, have been fashioned by human beings, and therefore they have some aspects that have their origin in narcissism and some that do not. The more we are able to be conscious of narcissism, the more we shall be able to make an accurate diagnosis. One of the effects of narcissism is that, under its influence, we split good from bad according to concrete agglomerations rather than according to mental tendencies that run through the activities of all institutions, whether political, aesthetic, or moral. Making a proper diagnosis—doing the job properly, in other words—requires much more work than making divisions according to agglomerative entities. When I use the word "work", I do not principally mean conscious activity, but the pursuit of emotional goals that are not usually conscious. Freud, for instance, referred to "mourning" as "work". It is goal-directed but unconscious. I am using the word "work" principally in this sense.

Readers may wonder what thinkers, teachers, or schools of thinking have influenced this work. I have no doubt that within the field of psychoanalysis the most influential clinician has been

Wilfred Bion. My wife and I wrote a book on him (Symington &
Symington, 1996). Chapter 1, on ontology, and Chapter 2, on freedom, both owe Bion a debt of gratitude—particularly the latter.
Next to Bion the clinician, the person who has influenced me most
has been one of Bion's analysands: Frances Tustin. Her works on
autism make complete sense to me and have the ring of authentic-
ity. Another clinician and theorist who has been influential for my
thinking has been Erich Fromm. More recently, I have been inspired by Marion Milner's early works. I have studied, of course,
many other analysts, such as Freud, Jung, Ferenczi, Ernest Jones,
Melanie Klein, Fairbairn, Winnicott, and Balint, but none of these
have made as deep an impression on me as have Bion, Tustin,
Fromm, and Milner within the psychoanalytical tradition or of the
other writers and thinkers whom I am about to mention.

I have been influenced by a wide range of thinkers and writers.
Within psychology, Brentano's *Psychology from an Empirical Standpoint* (1973) influenced me considerably when I was reading psychology as well as while I was doing my psychoanalytic training.
Piaget's book on the *Moral Development of the Child* (1932) had a
great influence when I first read it, long before I started formally to
study psychology. Later, Vygotsky's *Thought and Language* (1962)
was equally arresting. Arthur Koestler's *Act of Creation* (1975) was
an important study into the factors present in scientific understanding and the place of creative insight at its centre. Another
important influence has been the decision-making theory of Elliott
Jaques (e.g. 1982). Bernard Lonergan (1954), who based himself
almost entirely upon Newman's *Grammar of Assent*, has also been
influential.

Within psychiatry, I have derived most from Bleuler's *Textbook
of Psychiatry* (1924). Psychiatrists may complain that I have not
been better schooled in this subject. I have come to believe that
understanding of mental life and madness has been far too "informed" by psychiatry. I should perhaps explain what I mean by
this. The attempt to understand the mind via psychoanalysis has
been dominated by the psychiatric categories of thinking, and as
psychoanalysis has influenced our culture in the West so greatly,
this psychiatric imprint has left its mark far and wide. Abnormali-
ties in mental processes can only make sense against a backdrop
of sane mental functioning, but both the former and the latter are

understood through acts of understanding directed towards these very processes. These acts of understanding reveal the inner processes that enable us to distinguish the normal from the pathological, whereas the categorizations familiar to us since the time of Kraepelin are a particular set of outer symptoms, and only a very restricted set at that. The fact that psychoanalysis and all those disciplines that it has influenced have been framed according to these psychiatric categories has greatly impoverished the understanding of those who have been trained according to them. These categories have, I believe, so structured the way we think that it takes a great effort to free ourselves of their baneful influence. In particular, they have framed our terms of reference according to particular sets of symptomatic constellations. Also, many of the dogmatic modes of expression within psychiatry have passed straight into psychoanalytic language and onwards into our culture. After outlining my own schema for an understanding of the pattern of madness, I have devoted a chapter (Chapter 15) to the current psychiatric categories and tried to show how they are manifestations of a basic pattern. I hope by this that this deeper pattern will structure our thinking rather than a surface symptomatology.

A book that was very illuminating in the breadth of its understanding was Ellenberger's (1970) classic study of the history of the Unconscious. This study puts the whole development pathology and its remedies into its historical context in the most scholarly way.

Within philosophy, I have been much influenced in recent years by John Macmurray. He has been as influential within philosophy as Bion has been within psychoanalysis. In my early years I was deeply influenced by the Russian philosopher Vladimir Solovyov (Soloviev) and by Maurice Blondel. More recently, an understanding of Kant and Schopenhauer have helped to bring precision to a constructive psychology. Collingwood's *Metaphysics* (1969) has clarified my thinking considerably. Within theology, I have been inspired by the writings of John Henry Newman—in particular his *Grammar of Assent* (1888) and *The Idea of a University* (1927). Teilhard de Chardin, C. S. Lewis, and Bonhoeffer have also been strong influences. I have also derived considerable understanding from a study of Buddhism and Hinduism and from some study of the mystics, particularly Teresa of Avila and John of the Cross. Aldous Huxley's *Perennial Philosophy* (1980) has been a *vademecum*.

Isaiah Berlin—in particular his studies of Vico and Herder (1976)—has been a major influence in the sphere of the history of ideas. Berlin's stress on choice and human freedom have, for many years, been music to my ears, in particular his collection of essays, *Against the Current* (1979).

Within sociology, Max Weber has had a big influence, in particular his *The Protestant Ethic and the Spirit of Capitalism* (1971), but also his studies on the religion of China, the religion of India, and Ancient Judaism. Durkheim's *Suicide* (1952) and *The Elementary Forms of Religious Life* (1915) have been important.

Another new science, the history of mentalities—in particular the studies pioneered by Philip Aries (1976, 1981 1986, 1987)—has been extraordinarily illuminating.

Within literature, Tolstoy, Dostoevsky, George Eliot, and Emily Brontë have been major influences. It is difficult to convey how large has been the impact of these authors. I remember well trying to understand psychopathy when doing prison work, and what a revelation it was to come upon Emily Brontë's depiction of Heathcliff: I was left staggering like some drunken man after reading *Wuthering Heights* and George Eliot's profound insight into Lydgate's agony in *Middlemarch* was an important milestone on the journey into the heart of narcissism. And, as I said in my book on narcissism (Symington, 1993), Tolstoy's *Anna Karenin* furthered my understanding immensely. The idea that profound psychological understanding is the preserve of psychologists and psychoanalysts is extreme professional arrogance—a point that has been cogently made by Aldous Huxley (1980, p. 152).

The reader may ask: "Well, what bearing do these explorations into philosophy, literature, sociology, theology and science have on the subject of an understanding of madness?" There are two answers to this. The first is that into any problem there are different mental axes that are, as it were, tools for elucidating a problem. Imagine a carpenter making a table: he will require a saw, a plane, a chisel, and sandpaper. If he lacks one of these tools, the finished product will be blemished. So, with a subject like madness, one needs more than one "tool" to form a comprehensive understanding of the topic. To understand madness, we need many tools:

psychoanalysis, psychology, philosophy, sociology, science, economics, theology, psychiatry, history, and literature. A broad sweep through all these disciplines is necessary for the study of any nodal element in the human condition, such as motivation, madness, sex, war, creativity, religion, destructiveness, love, cruelty, and so on. The specialization that so typifies education today cannot by its very nature grasp the central determinants of mental life in human beings.

The second answer is that it is only through comparison that clarity of understanding is achieved. I only understand my own language when I start to translate into another; I only understand psychoanalysis when I begin to study behaviourism; I only understand religion when I begin to study science; and so on. The comparative method is the acutest instrument for understanding. One of the reasons why the illuminating new insights of an emerging discipline become ossified into a hardened orthodoxy (Koestler, 1975, p. 225) is through the loss of the comparative method, I want to make it clear that when I speak of the comparative method I am not speaking of dialogues between psychoanalysis and religion, or psychiatry and literature, or art and economics, which are frequently the substance of conferences or symposia. It is rare that these are true attempts to inquire into the human condition as a yet undiscovered entity; usually they are complacent, self-satisfied eulogies on both or more sides. I believe it would be rare for someone to come away from such an encounter and say to himself:

"My God, I believe that the basic assumption that I have been wedded to for the last forty years is fundamentally flawed."

We resist as strongly as we can going back and becoming children and starting all over again. But the comparative method, if taken seriously, challenges us to do exactly this.

However, what has driven the exploration into all these areas has been an overwhelming need to solve a fundamental problem in life. I have never seen these different areas of knowledge as dissociated categories but, rather, as the accounts of people who are struggling to understand the problems of living from different angles. It has been this self-exploration that has illuminated for me the subject matter of this book. All these thinkers and writers have been teachers, shamans, or psychoanalysts for me, and what they have written have been interpretations to myself. Slowly through this process I have found myself, and the theories that appear in this book have crystallized out of this journey. The fundamental idea is that madness in all its forms has its root in a constellation of elements that I describe as narcissistic, self-centred, solipsistic, or autistic.

At a critical time in my life I went and had an analysis that rescued me from acute sickness but did not free me from madness. That is something I have had to do for myself, with the aid of many different teachers, thinkers, and disciplines of thought. Psychoanalysis was like the emergency department in a general hospital where a patient is brought in grievously damaged and pouring blood in all directions following a serious car accident. I was sewn up with stitches and my life was "saved" by psychoanalysis, but true healing has come about through a lifelong convalescence that has required doctors [the "learned"] from many different quarters to allow the repair to occur. To be sane, it is necessary to be able to "stand outside oneself", and this can never be done within one discipline of thought or ideology.

It is mad to destroy the bases of human fulfilment and happiness. All the authors and thinkers I have mentioned have struggled to separate what is constructive from what is destructive of human fulfilment. This book is an attempt to distil what I believe to be the core of the matter.

# PART I

# THE PATTERN OF SANITY

A fatuous passivity towards the present springs from an infatuation with the Past.

Arnold Toynbee, *A Study of History* (1962, p. 261)

To be mad is to do something that destroys happiness, restricts freedom, and prevents emotional giving. Madness is mad because it is self-damaging. There are diverging views on what happiness consists in. There is the utilitarian view that happiness consists in forging a path that achieves the maximum degree of pleasure and the minimum of pain. Freud's view on this has governed very largely the outlook of most schools of psychoanalysis and psychotherapy, but also of psychological understanding more generally. The quote at the start of this chapter is an invitation to rouse ourselves into a state of renewal. In other words, I am inviting those in the social sciences to consider a different basic assumption: to consider that the utilitarian view might be wrong. A stark exception is *logotherapy* as devised by Victor Frankl (1959). Another exception is Wilfred Bion, though this has not been generally recognized. The other view is that of Kant, who believed that our duty is to pursue the "just act" and that happiness, should it arrive, is a fortuitous by-product. I disagree with both these views. The first is based too heavily upon what may be called a sensual or contingent estimate of happiness, and the second is not sufficiently rooted in the individual's own creative capacity to produce happiness. Although Kant stressed the mind's creative function so emphatically, yet when he crossed over from "pure philosophy" into the field of ethics, he invoked the "categorical imperative", which is a philosophical euphemism for "act according to God's commands". In other words, once you cross into the ethical arena, just do what you are told and don't use your own creativity.

In this first part, therefore, I have found it necessary to attend to the very foundation out of which I believe human beings, the animate world, the inanimate world, and the whole universe are constructed. I have tried to outline this in the first chapter, which I have entitled "Ontology". In the second chapter I have put forward my contention that what human beings aspire to is freedom, and that madness is an obstacle to its achievement. The third chapter concerns the nature of emotional acts. These three chapters form a background illuminating the motivational principles of all emotional behaviour. One might see them as the light against which madness, as a darkness, is silhouetted.

*Sanity*

While going down a slope, Zorba kicked against a stone, which went rolling downhill. He stopped for a moment in amazement, as if he were seeing this astounding spectacle for the first time in his life. He looked round at me and in his look I discerned faint consternation.

"Boss, did you see that?" he said at last. "On slopes, stones come to life again."

I said nothing but felt a deep joy. This, I thought, is how great visionaries and poets see everything—as if for the first time. Each morning they see a new world before their eyes; they do not really see it, they create it.

Nikos Kazantzakis, *Zorba the Greek* (1972, p. 140)

The pattern of madness is sketched out in Part II. If there is a pattern of madness, then what about a pattern of sanity? I shall try to sketch this out in this first part.

In the most general terms, the sane person is the one who is in touch with the real world, whereas the mad one is divorced from it. Therefore the real seems to be the touchstone that separates the mad from the sane. It is the diagnostic indicator. But, at the same time and for reasons that, will, I hope, emerge in this account, madness is destructive to the individual's life and development, whereas sanity enhances it.

For some reason,[1] when people talk of "the real world", they usually think first of the non-human and even the non-living world. Only after some thought may there be some readjustment

---

[1] I think the reason is that concepts are of their nature static, and therefore when a phrase like "the real world" is used, it conjures up an image of a lifeless inanimate world.

of sights so that the human world comes into focus: a human world with all its variety and changeableness. We take the view that judgements of human beings like:

"He is a real person."

Or:

"She is genuine."

Or:

"I have never known her not to be truthful."

Or:

"He is a very caring person."

Or:

"She is very loving towards all her children."

Or:

"He is a man of great courage . . ."

are primary. They are the first emotional judgements, and they are the template through which we see the inanimate world. This view is the opposite of that held by determinists and those scientists of a positivist disposition.

So, just as there is a constellation of madness, so there is also one of sanity. The sane constellation is made up of the Real and Truth, of which the following elements are components:

goodness
love
acceptance

Again the *principle of inclusion* (see Appendix) applies in that in each are included all the others. As sanity and madness are distinguished according to what is real, then this is the factor that needs to be understood. The first thing to realize is that when we say that someone is in touch with reality, we do not mean that there is a something out there that the person perceives but, rather, that he has constructed things in a way that leads us to say that he is in touch with reality. If a person comes and says that his parents hate him but within a few sentences he mentions that his mother had sacrificed a holiday in order to look after him when he had 'flu, then we might question whether he is in touch with reality. In other words, his statement that his parents hate him does not seem to represent what is really the case. We must, then, declare his judgement to be delusional or mad. In a judgement there is a scale of madness, but here we consider just the two categories, without their intensity. We need to examine which qualities require us to name the judgement or perception to be mad rather than sane.

This matter is also covered in Chapter 6, so some of what is said here is repeated there but in a different context and therefore changing it somewhat. When the person says:

"My parents hated me . . ."

he describes his persecuted state. This statement, which is treated as an unchallengeable fact, is persecuting and restricting to him. Schematically, let us say that there are two sets of feelings about this person's parents:

1.  a good feeling imbued with warmth and affection.
2.  a bad feeling imbued with hatred and bitterness.

In both cases the mental outlook has powered a selection of memories that support the feeling. The good feeling selects memories of parents being kind and loving; the bad feeling selects memories of parents being cruel and negligent. Let us say that the Real demands that the psyche embraces an apprehension of both sets of memories. The question, then, is: what is the feeling that governs such a state? The answer to this question is that it is not governed by a feeling but by an emotion that generates acceptance. The apprehension of the Real demands a psychic act, whereas the two stated perceptions rest upon a fundamental selection that requires only a passive registration. Frequently the good feeling imbued with warmth and affection hides the bad feeling that is imbued with hatred and bitterness. I have written about the way a psychotherapist may be seduced into changing the patient's attitude from mode one into mode two (Symington, 1996, pp. 110–115). In such an instance, the psychotherapist has not wrought any change at all.

The Real, then, requires the psychic act of acceptance. This needs a bit more explanation. It is the view that a statement like:

"My parents hated me . . ."

restricts emotional growth and derives from a selection and implosion. In Chapter 6 I differentiate between what I referred to as an introjection that is "photographic" and one that is creative. It should be clear from what has been said above that both modes one and two are different manifestations of the "photographic", and that neither is true because they are based on a selection that obliterates a series of memories that do not conform to the philosophy of that selection—like the editor of a Communist newspaper who selects only those facts that support his ideology.

What is being claimed here is that the Real requires a psychic act of acceptance, whereas madness results from an act of condemnation. What drives the statement:

"My parents hated me . . ."

is a condemnation that is legitimated through the memories selected to support it. The sense of it is:

"My parents hated me, and this justifies my condemnation of them."

What is being said here is that the presence of persecutory figures within that restrict the growth of the ego and strangle creativity is consistent with a mentality that condemns, and therefore this latter psychic act is what fashions madness. Condemnation spawns madness, whereas acceptance generates sanity. Condemnation issues from an ego that is under the direction of god. Condemnation that always includes expulsion of parts of the self is inherently destructive because parts of the self that are necessary to enable creative functioning are not available as a resource within.

It needs to be said here that when I refer to the act of acceptance, it is fundamentally an act that is tolerant of an entity in the self that enables the self and the parents to be seen as they are. So either the statement that my parents were bad and cruel or the statement that they were loving and good or both are false.

The diagnosis of what is mad as opposed to what is sane rests upon a value judgement for which there is no rationale. It arises out of a basic human conviction. It is as basic to the structure of the human sciences as the statement

"The shortest distance between two points is a straight line"

is basic to geometry. What we know is that madness and sanity are differentiated according to the two processes of condemnation and acceptance but why the latter is valued whereas the former is sanctioned can never be explained. Attempts to explain in terms of either a contract theory or the survival of the individual ultimately fail because we have finally to ask why is the maintenance of this communal structure is so valued. As the human community has put such weight upon this distinction, I want to examine the architecture of these two emotions.

The core difference between condemnation and acceptance is that in the former the negative qualities in the personality are hated and expelled from it with violence. The entity is expelled violently into a receptive host within either the micro-social or sometimes the macro-social environment. Acceptance, on the other hand, receives the negative quality, and through that very act the quality becomes endowed with a positive valence and becomes a source of strength in the personality. It is a principle that anything that stays in relation to all others is good, whereas if it becomes separated or isolated, it has a corrupting effect upon the personality. The strange paradox is that an envy that is hated damages the personality, whereas an envy that is recognized and accepted becomes a source of strength in the personality. According to the *Zohar*, moral evil is always either something separated or isolated or something that enters into a relation where it does not fit (Scholem, 1995). Sanity, therefore, consists in the acceptance of all parts of the personality, and madness consists in hatred and non-acceptance of large parts of the personality. What needs to be emphasized is that in the act of acceptance it is the act itself that structures both our system of perception and our beliefs. When the inner act is one of acceptance, we call our perceptions real and our beliefs sane; when the inner act is one of condemnation, we call our perceptions delusional and our beliefs mad. The claim here is that the inner act structures our perception and our beliefs, and this needs further examination.

* * *

We turn our attention first to the perceptual system. We are saying here that the perceptual system is driven, as it were, by a template of inner emotional acts, and therefore when the act is one of condemnation, it selects what we see, hear, and touch according to that act. So when I see or hear loving acts in parents whom I hate and condemn, I obliterate the sight and sound of them and intensify my sight and hearing of cruel acts. The judgement that follows is mad in that it is based on a perception of certain facts and on the obliteration of others. On the other hand, if the inner emotional act is one of acceptance, then cruel acts *and* loving acts are perceived and a judgement follows that we call in touch with reality or sane. What has been said about the perceptual system also applies to memory.

Contrary to the usual view that we perceive the inanimate world as if it were being processed through a perceptual system divorced from emotion, our view is that the templates that govern our perception of the human world also colour our perception of the non-human world. I had a striking example of this. A young man realized that he had never committed himself to any project, whether it be wife, children, or career. He said:

"That is an awful thought—it's so basic; it's such a basic thing not to have that capacity in me."

I had a conflict in myself at that moment. I was tempted to say that this was a thought he could not bear, but I realized that I would be repeating what he had said and also that it would reinforce a negative perspective, whereas this realization was proof that a capacity was coming to birth in him. So, struggling between the dark and the light, I said to him:

"You are building that capacity for commitment now."

There was a silence, and then he said:

"A most extraordinary thing happened when you said that a few moments ago. When I came into your room, I looked at the branch of the tree outside your window and was struck by the fact that it was bare. When you said I was building the capacity for commitment a few moments ago, I suddenly saw that the branch had leaves on it . . ."

I think that the negativity that I was tempted into was in him, and that it was responsible for his perception of the branch of the tree without leaves. I believe that at the moment of my interpretation, the inner template changed, altering his perception. What the template now included within it was the building of commitment that was at work. The leaves were young ones in late winter, on a deciduous tree. I believe that this is a dramatic instance of a perceptual process that is much more widespread.

We turn now from the perceptual system to beliefs. When outer facts are structured according to an inner template, we refer to this phenomenon as a belief. The belief is the inner correlate of the human value judgement. Why we value love rather than hate is mysterious. Although I believe that it is profoundly reasonable, yet that reasonableness is inextricably linked to a belief. The belief and the reasonableness are partners. One has what the other lacks. Belief motivates me to act, whereas reasoning makes sense of the act. Belief always requires reasoning to support it, so a sane belief and a mad belief will always have the support of reasoning. In the former case we call it "reasoning" and in the latter "rationalization". However, the belief is the engine that drives the machine, as it were. The key to the reasoning that underlies the sane belief is contained in Chapter 1. The concept of existence as a unity includes all reality and excludes nothing. The act of acceptance, the integrative act, is the template that underpins the sane belief, whereas the act of condemnation, the hated expulsion of parts of the self, underlies the belief that is mad.

The integrated self is able to fashion a perception that we call real or a belief that we call true. A damaged self, however, does not have this capacity and is only able to fashion a perception or belief that is faulty or what we would call delusional or mad. The real and the true, then, are determined by the state of the functioning self.

A good action as well as a loving one is the sane action as experienced by an outer person. The true, the real, and the sane, then, are bound into the object world by bonds that are described as good and loving. The constellation of sanity, is made up of these components: the Real, the True, the Sane, the Good, and the Loving, which includes Acceptance, Trust, Freedom, and the Absolute. The constellation of madness has the negative function of smothering this sane constellation.

The capacity to test reality is, then, dependent upon the degree to which there has been a comprehensive act of acceptance. Our psyche is the inner instrument capable of apprehending reality. This instrument's capacity to be capable depends upon this inner act of acceptance. Sanity finds its root, then, in an inner decision; madness lies in its rejection.

### Creative decision making: the hallmark of sanity

I have stressed the inner act in this chapter. The hateful act generates madness, and the act of acceptance creates sanity. There is a profound difference between these two acts: the one is reactive, whereas the other is a personal creation. We might call the hateful act instinctive and the accepting one personal and creative. Therefore the ability to decide, to choose, and to create are the prime manifestations of sanity. The man who is acting sanely is the one who thinks rather than reacts. A thought is an inner creation. And, as has been said, creative acts structure our perception, our memory, and our judgement.

As will become clear in Part II, the pattern of madness makes decision making impossible. There is a very fundamental level at which someone gives him- or herself to the project of life itself. This fundamental decision manifests itself particularly in personal relationships but also in a person's involvement in their vocation and working life. The degree to which the *intensifiers* (see Part II) are present is the degree to which this fundamental decision is handicapped in its operation, but their transformation is possible through creative acceptance.

Acceptance is a creative act. The person is made up of an array of disparate elements, all of which are taken up in the creative act of acceptance. Acceptance is a creation. Creation can occur and does occur as all the parts are loved. It is this very primitive creative act that fashions the person. What society judges as sane is, then, a relation to the self, which is a creation that is inseparable from acceptance. What society judges to be mad is emotional hatred in which parts of the self are expelled and in which there is no act of creation.

# CHAPTER ONE

# Ontology

> I celebrate myself, and sing myself,
> And what I assume you shall assume,
> For every atom belonging to me as good belongs to you.
>
> Walt Whitman, "Song of Myself" (1986)

Ontological reflection is necessary in order to arrive at a coherent theory of the personality. The perspective adopted here is that the structure of personality reflects the ontological composition of reality.

Existence in itself just is. If we ask ourselves, "Why is it?" we don't know. We cannot say that the world and the universe do exist but they might just as well not have existed. Therefore necessity is elemental to the structure of existence. Those with a particular form of religious belief might say that existence is but could not have been or need not be because it has been created by God, but that places this elemental necessity into a portion of reality that is named "God". Such a believer would not say, "Oh, well, God exists but just as well might not exist"; such a statement would be denying godhood to god. This form of belief already makes an assumption about the way the whole of reality is structured. Before any such assumption is made, I want to say that existence is necessary in its very essence. This is the ground-rock that confronts the mind as true. The human mind says that it cannot be otherwise. Reality or existence is a "must". This is its elemental character.

As the fundamental necessity of existence confronts the mind, so also does its unity. Parmenides realized this, but then, as he observed through his senses the changeable nature of the world, he was confronted with a contradiction, and he solved this contradiction by favouring the act of understanding and saying that the world of change and movement must be an illusion. Aristotle believed that he had solved this problem by separating reality into Pure Act and Potency, but this only named in a different way the problem that Parmenides had posed. The religious mode is to honour the contradiction but to state that our minds are limited in their capacity to understand it; the contradiction is a mystery—the central mystery of existence. It is something that is clearly so: reality is a unity, yet our senses tell us it is diverse; a reconciliation of this contradiction is not possible. The statement of mystery is an act of humility—a declaration that the human mind is limited, that it cannot resolve this contradiction.

This contradiction runs right through our analysis of the animate and inanimate world. It is elemental to our understanding of human beings as well as of the rest of the universe. The universe is one and yet diverse; an alternative description is that it is at the same time both necessary and contingent. It has to be; it could not not-be, and at the same time it exists in forms that are changeable, contingent. So we say that it is necessary and yet contingent.

Mental life, like all reality, is also necessary and contingent. The *narcissistic constellation* described in Chapter 3 (p. 46) on "The perception of persons" shows that this form of mental life is proper to contingent existence. The human task is to allow necessary existence to permeate contingent existence so that the two realms interpenetrate. Just as biological survival is the aim of the instincts, so human reality's essential nature is freedom of choice. The instincts limit its realm. Freedom of choice is the defining element of human life. Our lives are also determined, limited, and changeable, but we avoid in this analysis the philosophical solution of

Parmenides. We are autonomous free agents *and* determined by antecedent causes. The interpenetration of these two so that they are also a unity is a mystery. I think that the philosophical position that states that we are determined and do not have freedom of choice fails to do observational justice to the way human beings behave and speak of each other, just as Parmenides' statement that all change is an illusion fails to do justice to the convictions and sense of nearly all human beings in the conduct of their affairs. So also the extreme existentialist position, which states that we have total freedom of choice and are not determined, is mistaken for the same reason. Humans are a composite of these two. There are areas where the one predominates more than the other, and in any analysis of human behaviour it is necessary to respect this. What frequently happens, however, is a missionary attempt to categorize all human behaviour under one rubric or another. The point of intertwinement that seems to run through the whole of human activity to a greater or lesser extent needs constantly to be respected and deferred to.

These two facets of existence are the source in human beings of two forms of actions: alpha and beta activity. I have taken these two terms from Wilfred Bion (1962b). One can think of beta elements as the deposit in us that determines the direction of our being and of alpha activity as our creative autonomous existence.

Alpha activity exists between two poles, one of which is constructed into a subject and the other into a created object. Beta activity exists between two poles: an it and a deformed object. The object is deformed through the activity that is a discharge.

These two forms of activity are mutually exclusive and therefore do not exist at the same time. There can be a switching from one to the other from one second to the next. The locus of these activities is in interpersonal communication but also in intrapsychic communication.

There are entities in the personality—pain, guilt, grief, joy, conscience, and contentment—but their existence is manifested differently in the personality that is guided by alpha function and in the personality guided by beta functioning. In beta functioning, pain, guilt, and grief are manifest in paranoia and aggression. That is their form. A person functioning in this way does not suffer pain, experience guilt, or sustain grief, which are all proper to alpha functioning—that is, creations of alpha function. Conscience is also a creation of alpha function, as are generosity and contentment.

These two mental manifestations of existence in human beings reflect the necessary and contingent nature of existence. It needs to be emphasized that these are not two modes of existence but two perspectives on one reality. The unity of the two is mysterious to the human mind. We could conjecture that the contingent is a free creation of necessary existence, which is the Judeo–Christian view. The other is to say that the contingent and necessary are the way of formulating existence, but it remains mysterious how these two can coexist as one due to the limitations of the human mind. We are a duality and yet not a duality. It seems a contradiction and yet is not.

As necessary existence is in its nature absolute, it cannot be perceived, but it can be grasped through an act of understanding, which is, then, mediated through images. The images do not correspond directly to the reality within existence, but they have an analogical relation to it. For a blind man, the colour scarlet may be represented by the blast of a trumpet. The blast of the trumpet is an analogue; so also are the images drawn from contingent existence to represent necessary existence. This is the basis of symbolism. What is necessary can only be grasped through an act of understanding; what is contingent is perceived through the senses. These two different ways of apprehending reality are united through an act of faith. This is not the same as faith as understood in Judeo–Christian teaching. How did Helen Keller suddenly grasp that the letters W–A–T–E–R being spelt into one hand by her teacher, Ann Sullivan, represented the liquid trickling through the fingers of her other hand? Through an act of faith. It is also through such an act of faith that I unite in my mind what I grasp through an act of understanding and what I perceive with my senses.

The link between the absoluteness of existence and freedom can be established in this way. We attribute the quality of goodness to absolute reality. The fact of existence confronts the mind as necessarily good. "Good" is a judgement made upon the fact of absolute existence. That is its only possible quality. "Why not bad?" you might say. There is the suggestion in "badness" that it should not be or that it would be better if it weren't, but we have already established that existence *is*, so to be suggesting that perhaps it would be better if it weren't is to misunderstand its nature. Is there anything bad in existence? It seems that we must say "yes", at least when we come to the human domain, and again how that is possible is mysterious for the same reason that we cannot grasp the real as one yet diverse, determined yet free, and now good yet bad. These are the antinomies of existence. It is difficult not to associate the bad or evil with the contingent mode of existence, and it is mysterious for just the same reason.

We need to consider life as one form of reality. In the inanimate world the source of movement and action is to be sought outside the object, but in the animate world it is in the living object itself. A satisfactory definition of life would be one where the cause of action is to be found within the object, whereas in inanimate objects it is located outside. In living things the essential necessity of being coincides with this inner cause because existence can have no cause outside itself, and, as we have seen, this is identified with life because chosenness, an inner autonomy, is the form of life— that which distinguishes life from non-life. In the living kingdom there is a hierarchy of absoluteness with a greater representation of it in the living reality of *homo sapiens*. Acting, therefore, in accordance with the absolute is a free act, and this is what man most deeply yearns for as it is the fulfilment of his own being. The relevance of this has been pursued further in Chapter 2. However, as necessity is the hallmark of existence and also unity, then freedom is inseparable from it. Contingency is also present, just as we are also determined by antecedent causes and to this extent we are not free but there is a freedom whose root lies in the fact that existence ultimately must explain itself. This may have been an aspect of the Buddha's enlightenment under the Bodhi tree.

People may think that this level of abstraction is irrelevant to clinical work, but how can this be so if we are looking into the deep structure of our being? To illustrate the link between Freedom, Choice, and Unity in a clinical example: Colin, a schoolboy, was broken into fragments. A fragment was attached to his analyst, a fragment to his French teacher, a fragment to his Maths teacher, a fragment to his Science teacher, a fragment to his History teacher, and a fragment to his English teacher. Then a change occurred. The fragments came together, and he attached to his analyst, but by choice rather than through necessity. Prior to this change, he had been a passive dreamer; after it, he became decisive in the management of his life.

Various philosophers (such as John Macmurray and Isaiah Berlin), and psychologists and psychoanalysts (for instance, Roy Schafer—see Chapter 7) have stressed the need to replace Freud's mechanistic metapsychology with one based on human freedom and choice. I believe, however, that this switch in metapsychology requires a different ontological presupposition. I have said above that the dual nature of reality is something that the mind cannot comprehend, though reflection reveals it to be a fact. The mystery lies in the question: if existence is necessary, then how can it, at the same time, be contingent? There have been two different ontological solutions to this problem, one the Judeo–Christian one and the other that which was conceptualized in the West by Spinoza. The Judeo–Christian supposition is that the necessary is concentrated, as it were, in one being and that the rest of reality is contingent upon that one being. The popular expression of this is the statement that there is a being called God who created the universe. In this view, the stress falls on the idea that the presence of the universe is due to an arbitrary wish of God. This view explains the contingent reasonably satisfactorily, but it fails to explain the necessary. If being is absolute, then there cannot be contingent being, or, in popular terms, if God had the fullness of being, why produce the universe? This view is psychologically problematic because it makes the sensible world subject to an arbitrary command, and ultimately the human task is to accommodate to that command. I believe that Kant's categorical imperative is rooted in this ontology and leads therefore to moralism rather than to morality.

Spinoza's supposition is that there is just one reality, one substance, and we are all it. His problem, then, is to explain the contingent. Spinoza called this substance God, but he works hard to bang into our heads that this is quite different from the Judeo–Christian God. He is saying in another manner what I have been saying when I refer to existence as necessary.

Neither ontology is correct. There is a conceptual contradiction the resolution of which cannot be grasped by the mind. Kant realized that the mind was limited in its capabilities, and this is the clearest instance of it. Christian theologians, such as St. Augustine and St. Thomas Aquinas, were correct in saying, within their formulation, that the reason why God created was utterly mysterious. Spinoza, however, as far as I am aware, does not say that the fact of contingent existence is mysterious. He argues that God the Absolute exists in different modes. He falls into the same arrogance as does Parmenides: he does not consider that the human mind may not be able to reconcile these basic and evident contradictions. However, I believe that Spinoza's ontology is more consistent with the metapsychology of human choice and purpose. I will try to explain this shortly, but first I want to show very briefly how the mechanistic view is a consequence of the Judeo–Christian ontology.

As already stated, this ontology declares that necessary being is concentrated in one being that is entirely separate from contingent being but that the latter is utterly dependent on the former. This is what the doctrine of creation asserts. However, all but a tiny minority of thinking Christians, Jews, and Muhammadans think that creation is a past event rather than a description of a present reality (and a past reality). I believe I am correct in saying that this was even Kant's assumption. This metaphysical presupposition is known as Deism. Whereas Aquinas believed that because the Universe had a relation of absolute dependence upon God, therefore He imprints a godlike autonomy into living beings ("breathed into Adam"), Deism, on the other hand, asserted that God had given the first push to the Universe and had then withdrawn into some paradisical anchorage, letting contingent existence tick away for ever like Harrison's chronometer. Descartes expressed this Deistic position and gave it philosophical respectability (such is the powerful influence of a famous philosopher). The result of this divorce between God and the universe was the death of this "soul of God" within it. The world was governed by the properties of matter as expressed in Newtonian physics. Newton's formulations were concurrent with Descartes' deistic ontology. The animate and the inanimate world were governed according to mechanical principles. The clearest expression of this is in the anti-vitalist pact of the *Physicalische Gesellschaft*:

> No other forces than the common physical and chemical ones are active within the organism. In those cases which cannot at the time be explained by these forces one has either to find the

specific way or form of their action by means of the physical–mathematical method or to assume new forces equal in dignity to the chemical–physical forces inherent in matter, reducible to the force of attraction and repulsion. [quoted in Jones, 1972, p. 45]

The signatories to this pact were Emil Ludwig, du Bois Reymond, Ernst Brucke, and Hermann Helmholtz.[1] Once these mechanistic principles were in place, it was then a logical step to deny the existence of God. Whether that occurred or not was in fact irrelevant, because the deistic God was an ontological spoof. The determinist view of the universe is the handicapped child of a spurious Judeo–Christian ontology.

It is possible that an intentional view could prevail with a Judeo–Christian ontology but not with a spurious one; but even correctly formulated contingent existence remains divorced from necessary existence because the notion of godhood in this ontology is essentially separate from it. It is for this reason that I believe Spinoza's ontology is more satisfactory in that it emphasizes that the essential necessity of existence—or what might be called its absoluteness—is inherent in us and in our world and there is nothing outside it. We all are that one substance, though the concept of existence is not one that is arrived at through sense perception but through an inner act of understanding (and not through an act of faith in the religious sense). So in his ontology there is no possibility of our existence being dissolved, because we are it. The pitfall of Spinoza's ontology is that there is a danger of individuality and variety evaporating. It is, however, an ontology to be preferred to the Judeo–Christian one, because it is consistent with the autonomy present in living things. The absoluteness or necessity of being receives more emphasis in his ontology. The meaning of this absoluteness is that you find the explanation for existence within itself and not outside it. Once one says this, then there is no problem in stating that living things have an autonomous characteristic. The problem, then, becomes how to explain that the inanimate does not.

---

[1]Ernst Brucke was Freud's professor and influenced him greatly. Freud also said that Helmholtz was one of his heroes.

The clinician reading this may say to him- or herself:

"This is all hi-falutin' philosophy that has no relevance to me when I am trying to understand patients . . ."

yet I think this is incorrect. In Chapter 2 I emphasize that in the free act I become myself. In a determinist philosophy there is no place for human freedom. The determinist philosophy is underpinned by a radical assumption that everything I do as a human being is caused by an agent outside myself. It denies the possibility of my being the originating cause of anything. It is a philosophical position that is entirely apt for the inanimate world and human beings to the extent to which they share the properties of the inanimate world, but it does not encompass the essence of living things. Although Christian theologians believed in human freedom they quarrelled for centuries trying to reconcile this with their ontology—if God is the Absolute and we are his dependent creatures, then how can we be free?—and, as said above, the determinist philosophy is the handicapped offspring of this view. Spinoza's ontology makes sense of the possibility of a free act.[2] In the free act there is testimony to the Absolute in our nature. The pull against the free act comes from the conditional in us.

My imagined psychotherapist may still say:

"Oh, well, let us admit that achievement of the free act is the goal of psychoanalysis, or the goal of psychological development, but why clog us down with all these abstruse arguments about Spinoza's ontology? Can't we just leave that to philosophers in their academies?"

The answer is "No", for two reasons: We cannot live without an ontology. We already have one, and it needs replacing. The one we have leads to a paper chase full of false trails. Once we have the right trail, we can climb over rivers and rocks with confidence. The second reason is that if we stick with the ontology we have at the

---

[2]There is a weird contradiction in Spinoza in that although his ontology invites an ethics based on a free act, yet he is a determinist in his approach to moral problems. I am arguing here for his ontology and a theory of human action based upon it and not his own theory of ethics.

moment, then we are stuck with false assumptions that find their way right into the subtlest interstices of human communication. It also necessitates splits in the personality, because we have to accommodate statements that are actually mutually exclusive.

At one time, psychology, sociology, and all that is referred to as the human sciences (or social sciences) were part of philosophy. One of the misfortunes arising from the categorization of knowledge within the human sciences is that thinking has been relegated to philosophers, and the rest of us in the human sciences tend to base our propositions on discrete intuitions, feelings, and *"aperçus"* that are all agglomerated, but there is no unity. The example I gave of Colin's disunity is a symbol for all of us. It is worth proceeding on the basis that the pathology of patients is a magnification of our present social diseases.

Philosophy is simply the systematization of all knowledge and thinking that has come in answer to the questions: "Why?" and "How?" Ontology represents the deepest thinking and questioning about the nature of existence. It probes into what is most fundamental. Psychoanalysis—or what is sometimes called depth psychology—probes into what is fundamental in the human mind, but it will fail if it repudiates philosophy. And philosophy will fail if it repudiates psychoanalysis, and the latter will fail if it repudiates behaviourism, and this will fail if it turns its back on psychoanalysis—and sociology, and economics, and history, and natural science, and so on. There is a parallel between ontology and psychoanalysis: they both rely on an act of understanding. Just as Bion said of psychoanalysis—that you just have to go and do it—so also of ontology. Some people, mostly psychoanalysts, think that we hate confronting what is dark in ourselves and refer to it as resistance. However, this is just one instance of the more general principle that the act of understanding whereby we grasp reality directly is always avoided.

Spinoza's ontology also makes sense of symbolism. A symbol is an outer object that can be perceived through the senses being used to represent an inner reality that cannot be seen but can only be grasped through an act of faith. That this element here represents an inner mental reality is arrived at through an act of faith. The whole of culture is built upon this human activity. That one represents the other is something that we believe. It requires an act of faith, but intrapsychic communication rests upon it. A theory of symbolism makes no sense without this ontological assumption. In psychoanalysis, for instance, what are known as "transference interpretations" are symbolic comments that depend upon this ontology.

I was treating a woman in brief therapy who was trying to decide whether to marry Anthony or not. She was speaking like this:

"He is very kind . . ."

"He does help me to think clearly . . ."

"You see I do like looking after him . . ."

I said:

"When you say these things about Anthony, I have a strong sense that you are trying to persuade me of them, and I wonder why you feel the need to do this?"

She answered:

"I think it's myself I am trying to persuade . . ."

So it seems that I stand as a symbol for her own self.

The same patient said in one session that Anthony drank very heavily, and I said:

"You had not told me that before . . ."

"I was not aware of it before."

So the moment of telling me coincided with her own self-awareness. Her telling me equated with her telling herself. I think that I as the Other for her symbolizing her own self makes sense if we posit that we are both together in the necessity of existence.

## *The Absolute is personal*

I have so far painted the distorted aspect of the Judeo–Christian tradition, but I want now to come to its unique contribution to our understanding of existence. It is that this necessary existence, this absoluteness of being, is personal. In the history of salvation in the Judeo–Christian drama we have a revelatory unfurling of a personal god—a god who freely chose this people and entered into a covenant with them. The same truth was proclaimed in the Christian epiphany: the revelation of a personal god. There were, of course, some bad side-effects: in Judaism the tendency to believe that the Israelites were special and superior to the surrounding tribes, in Christianity the belief that Christians alone possessed the fullness of truth, and in Islam that God's eternal law had been revealed through Muhammad and was now enshrined in the Koran and nowhere else. However, this is an unfortunate side-effect: in any attempt to configure this essence of being and its qualities there is always some narcissistic element colouring its expression.

I want here to look through the side-effects to the belief in a god who is personal, to endow existence with this personal quality, and so to say that its presence in us is the source of personal creative life—that this basic substance, this necessary existence, is personal and the source of creativity in the world. So when I say above that the task is to let the necessary permeate the contingent, I am saying something much more direct and relevant: it is allowing the personal to emerge in the personality. This, I believe, is the human task confronting us all. It has always been present but is now so much under threat through the dehumanizing effect of mass media and advertising that it is now a crucial challenge for our age. It is clinically urgent; it is culturally urgent.

# CHAPTER TWO

# Freedom

So hopeless is the world without
The world within I doubly prize—
Thy world where guile and hate and doubt
And cold suspicion never rise—
Where thou and I and Liberty
Hold undisputed sovereignty.

Emily Brontë, "To Imagination" (1844)

What human beings most want is freedom. I have tried to sketch out the rationale for this in Chapter 1. I believe that much psychological theorizing has gone wrong because the central aim of human endeavour has been thought to be either the drive for survival or the pursuit of happiness, and that if you take either of these two to be the human goal, then it is not possible to explain many of the weird paradoxes that confront us once we begin to study human beings in any depth. The instincts that ensure our survival are a necessary given. They are like gravity in the natural order. Without gravity, there would be no stable beings on the earth. Without instincts, animals and humans would not be held together as living entities, but we take this for granted, just as we take gravity for granted. The psychological distress that lands people in a mental hospital, that takes human beings to the psychiatric clinic or for psychoanalysis, is the suppression of their freedom. It is not just what brings a few individuals to seek treatment for their ills; it is THE cause of human distress. The ability to love is concurrent with it. If freedom has been achieved, then physical survival is less treasured. Happiness is consequent upon the achievement of freedom, and it is not therefore the psychological aim of human beings.

Let me start from a practical angle. What the clinician meets is not a hatred of the factors that strangle freedom as such. The narcissistic condition prevents such personal insight, but a figure, institution, or ideology outside is hated, but this is a displacement of the inner *intensifier* (see Chapters 9 and 15) onto the outer reality. A figure who is hated is one of the diagnostic signs of narcissism. The true object of hatred is the *intensifier* within. Hatred of the outer figure occurs through displacement. But the question is: Why?—because it stands as an obstacle to freedom.

I am free when I am able to create. When we use the word "create", we tend to think of artists: a musician who creates a sonata or an opera; a Raphael who paints "The Virgin of the Rocks"; a Michelangelo who sculpts the Pietà; a Christopher Wren who designs St. Paul's. But Darwin's *Origin of Species* is also a creation, as is Newton's *Philosophiae Naturalis Principia Mathematica* as well as Einstein's theory of relativity. However, when it is said of someone that he had a genius for friendship, that is also a testament to creativity. But the most important of all human creation are thoughts. The thought-creation transforms inner events from rigidity to plasticity. It is through thought-creation that qualities of character like sincerity, simplicity, loving kindness, courage, or gentleness come into being. These are not givens, they are not inherited. They are personal creations. They are created in the face of currents that pull the individual in the opposite direction. An individual is pulled towards brutality and brashness, and in combating it he creates gentleness. Another individual is afraid and wants to take flight, and he creates the response of courage. What is combated needs to be thought in emotional terms. These currents that pull the individual in the opposite direction are the "raw material" out of which the creation is fashioned. The purpose of fashioning such a character trait is that it is then able to dissolve the current that pulls us first in this direction and then in another. The created character trait is able to incorporate the feared entities within the newly created trait. Sometimes the raw material is much more resistant than others—like the difference between sculpting a statue out of marble rather than out of Cornish soapstone. Arnold Bennett gives an example in *Anna of the Five Towns* (1969): Anna is terrified of her father who embodies crushing power, but in an act of supreme courage she opposes him. The way in which these admired qualities of character are struggled for are the stuff of psychoanalysis. The point I am making here is that these qualities are creations, and what the narcissistic condition prevents is the capacity to create those character traits that enable us to manage the crises of life.

You may ask: What have these character traits to do with mental health? Let us say that those people who succeed in creating these character traits are then able to withstand the emotional traumata of their lives. People come for psychoanalysis because of deficiencies in their character. This means that something has prevented them from creating the qualities of character that they need for managing their particular life situation. These "life conflicts" are experienced as coming in the form of assaults on the self from outside, but their origin lies in entities from within that fashion the outer incursion on the self.

When I act because I am being pressurized, manipulated, or persuaded, I am not free but a prisoner. I am slave to outer persuasion because of my hatred of the *intensifiers* within. The hatred pushes the *intensifiers* into significant others in the environment, and this then forces me into bondage *to* those significant others. Why? Because there is in me a drive to incorporate back into myself all parts that belong to me. Only when they are back in me am I free. I need all parts of myself available in order to create. To make a painting, I need a canvas, paints, and a brush. If one of these is lacking, I cannot produce a painting. Freedom in action is creating; creating is my freedom. This longing for freedom is what I have called the *integrity principle* (Chapter 14). Therefore the problem is not the presence of the *intensifiers* in themselves but my hatred of them. It is clear from clinical evidence that a mental attitude of *acceptance* rather than hatred changes the nature of the *intensifiers*: in other words, they no longer liquify or solidify, but they endow the personality with strength. Envy is converted into admiration; jealousy into concern; greed into courage. Time is an important factor: the link to tolerance of frustration is obvious. Schopenhauer *knew* that his philosophy was of value and that it would bear fruit, although he thought that it might only be after his death. Personal recognition would be a source of pleasure, but it might have to be foregone. In fact, it came to him in the last years of his life, but recognition was like a knighthood that may or may not be bestowed. Expression of his free understanding was the aim; happiness that came with recognition was a lucky consequence.

My use of the word "hatred" may cause surprise. In all those mental disciplines derived from psychoanalysis we are more familiar with the term "denial", but this does not convey either what the emotion is or its intensity. This dilution of emotion in the psychoanalytic language has led to a reduction in its effectiveness. As a simple example of this hatred: a young man needed human contact desperately, yet he hated this neediness; his hatred of it led him to be enslaved to god embodied in his father, his analyst, and his boss at work. It is the expulsion of the neediness through hatred that manufactures the enslavement. The god is savage in his demands. What he is enslaved to is a needy god, a greedy god whom he must obey on the pain of death.

It is a principle that the creative act can only occur when all parts of the self are contained within an encircling membrane. When parts of the self are roaming around in figures and institutions outside the personality, it is not possible to create. When envy, jealousy, and greed are tolerated and accepted as items in the personality, they cease to liquify or petrify but instead endow the personality with strength. Bion's image of the mother processing the infant's impulses with reverie finds its place here (Bion, 1962b, p. 36).

When I refer to the hatred of the *intensifiers*, I am talking of a primitive hatred of which the person is unaware. It is hatred whose elemental character is the expulsion of the *intensifiers* and God into people or institutions of the outer environment. God is also hated because it is the agent responsible for the expulsion and therefore is a co-conspirator against the possibility of freedom.

This hatred that I am talking about is usually referred to in the psychiatric and psychoanalytic literature as "paranoid" :

> one eventually encounters in the transference paranoid developments, with feelings of emptiness, rage and fear of being attacked. [Kernberg, 1975, p. 234]

I prefer to call it "primitive hatred", conjoined with a sense of betrayal. This is the reason for the chronic depression seen in narcissistic patients. The depression is at the knowledge that God and the *intensifiers* are being expelled, which the person knows to be a futile solution. In psychiatric language the patient is depressed about being paranoid. It is important to distinguish depression in this sense from the "depressive position" as described by Melanie Klein, which is depression through guilt about the expulsion of the *intensifiers* into outer figures, whereas the chronic depression is related to unconscious knowledge and an unresolved state of affairs.

There is much confusion because knowledge and consciousness are thought to be synonymous. In the above scenario there is knowledge of the primitive hatred and there is knowledge that this is a futile solution, but there is no awareness of these two factors. The purpose of this book is to bring to consciousness the *narcissistic constellation* that is already known. Freud said that in a successful analysis the patient will say that he knew all that had been discovered. The same applies to any form of treatment where cure is being sought through insight and understanding. Freud also gave an illustrative example of three different physicians who had knowledge but were not aware that they had it (see Freud, 1914d, pp. 12–14).

Therefore the crucial step seems to be a change of mental attitude towards the *intensifiers*: a change from hatred to acceptance then alters the condition of the personality. The aim of psychoanalysis in particular is to bring about this change. (How this is done is discussed in greater detail in Chapter 21.) Integrity of personality is achieved when all parts of the personality are encircled within its own boundaries through a creative act of acceptance. Once all parts of the self are embraced in this way, the individual is not pressurized from outside. He or she is capable of being a free-acting agent, because there is now an inner spirit that is the source of all activity in the personality. The image of an all-embracing outer membrane is inadequate, because it does not convey the sense of a spirit of purpose integrating and informing all the parts in a direction of development.

We have seen how God, hatred, and the presence of the *intensifiers* causes large parts of the personality to be lodged in figures outside the self. At the same time, the centre of the personality is a jelly. In this situation there is no freedom; much of the personality is imprisoned in outer objects, and within, good qualities are dispersed and interpenetrated with substances that belong outside. The potential elements of freedom are present, but they have to be freed from the *intensifiers* and from God. As explained in Chapters 9 and 22, the mental attitude towards the *intensifiers* has to undergo a transformation. Then, as God's power diminishes, an autonomous agent begins to develop in the personality.

The question is: what is the object of free desire? It is an object that *invites*, that does not exert obligation. It is something that lies at the root of all choices: the voice of conscience. (The creation of conscience in the personality through alpha function is discussed more fully in Chapter 1.) That there is such a presence in the personality is attested by all. There is this very big difference between conscience and God. God commands, demands, and abhors freedom, whereas conscience *invites*. In fact, clinical observation tells us that as the power of God diminishes, so the voice of conscience becomes heard in the personality. Conscience comes into being in the personality as the jelly begins to sort into different realms or faculties and as the power of God diminishes. Of all the faculties, however, conscience is the one that is central for emotional health. In Chapter 1 we discussed the dual composition of the human being: necessary and contingent. Conscience is the evidence of the necessary, and the *formal centre* is the contingent linked to the necessary. Conscience is the presence of the necessary in the contingent. Speaking in intentional terms, we say that the contingent element becomes illuminated through acts of understanding.

Freud equated conscience with a harsh punishing god. This castigating god made himself felt brutally in the personality because a reprehensible act had been committed. This was the view of conscience canonized in Western thinking by St. Paul and was so understood within Christendom throughout the Middle Ages. However, with the advent of the Enlightenment, conscience took on another meaning. It was not only a reproach for acts committed, but an indicator of the right path when the individual was at the cross-roads and trying to decide which road to take. Bertrand Russell expresses this post-Enlightenment view:

> The orthodox view is that, wherever two courses of action are possible, conscience tells me which is right, and to choose the other is sin. [Russell, 1946, p. 190]

However, it would be psychologically inadequate to suppose that conscience is an invitatory voice based on no antecedent occurrence. I believe that the benign conscience that bids the individual to go down Path A rather than Path B is the outcome of a mild reproach for an act that has already occurred. The committed act, however, is a mild emotional one, and the reproach for it signals a different direction for the next act. Choosing, however, to follow its indication is entirely free.

Right and wrong are differentiated according to paths generated by the necessary or the contingent. The contingent has a strong pull—even sometimes an addictive one—but the necessary always sends signals through the complexities of the personality that reach the ego if there is sufficient contemplative space for it to be reached.

The emotional structure that I have been describing is the lens through which we see the world. The world I see through a free structure is very different from the one I see through imprisoned eyes. We perceive the world through the eyes, ears, and touch, but how we view it depends upon the dominating presence of either a free structure or an imprisoned structure. These structures, as we have seen, are dependent upon our response to early childhood traumata.

These structures fashion the way we see the human world. Our thesis is that this mode of seeing determines the manner in which we see the animate and inanimate world. We take here a view that is contrary to the view espoused by most psychologists and philosophers: namely, that we see the inanimate world according to what one might call a neutral perception of the world through our senses. The viewpoint here is that the human world as seen through a free structure also determines the way the non-human world is seen.

On other words, there are two basic ways of seeing the world: in a free manner and in an imprisoned manner. As the free manner implies a free response to conscience, then it implies a choice of something that is essentially good. Our view is that this is also co-extensive with the necessary as defined in Chapter 1.

Although freedom is essentially one, we see it, due to our limited mental capacity, under two modes: "freedom from" and "freedom to". "Freedom from" can be thought of as being free of the constraints imposed by emotionally liquifying forces, whereas "freedom to" is the ability to create. In fact, only in the act of creation is freedom achieved, but subjectively the individual experiences a process where first there is one and then the other.

A man clung to all people in authority desperately, following exactly what they prescribed. Why did he do this? What made him cling so desperately? What was he fleeing from? He was riven by a violent jealousy, which he feared. His clinging was a phobic flight from an inner reality of which he was terrified. The combination of this jealousy and his phobic clinging imprisoned him, so he was filled with hatred at this condition. What he hated, though, was these "admired" people who exercised this authority over him—who entrapped him, as he saw it. However, it was the hatred of the jealousy in him that was the real culprit, the one responsible for imprisoning him.

Answering the voice of conscience, then, is a creative act. A person is called particularly to combat those vicious tendencies that have arisen through the activities of the *intensifiers*. The significant character traits are those that have been created in transformation of the vicious tendencies. Within psychoanalysis and therapies derived from it the clinician's key role is to elucidate conscience, thus enabling free creative acts that reverse the narcissistic state. Great care is needed by the clinician not to embody either god or an anti-god.

# CHAPTER THREE

# The person

Talk rot by all means, but do it in your own way, and I'll be
ready to kiss you for it. For to talk nonsense in your own way is
a damn sight better than talking sense in someone else's; in the
first case, you're a man; in the second you're nothing but a
magpie.

Dostoyevsky, *Crime and Punishment.* (1978, p. 219)

We come now to a difficult question, but one that it is
necessary to solve, at least provisionally. We have put
emotional activity at the centre of our understanding,
but who is the author of emotional activity?

The sense we get from the chapter on the jelly (Chapter 8) is
that there is no integrated author of emotional action, that the
intensifiers are hated and expelled in a reactive way, and that this
is in tandem with an unintegrated state. But this very way of
talking suggests that there is an alternative state where action proceeds from an integrated centre. What has been said about freedom implies a creative act issuing from a centre. Findings from
psychoanalysis also suggest that health and sanity come from re-

integrating split-off parts of the self, the implication being that wholeness of parts is a goal to be aimed at.

Wilfred Bion nominated what he called *alpha function* as being that in the personality which was responsible for thinking. However, it is clear that it is more than just a function—or if it is, then a function of what? A function of the personality? The sense of it is, though, that this is a centre from which elements in dreams are synthesized and from which creative acts issue forth.

What we are positing, then, is that there are two alternative states in a human being: one where there is a jelly or a disintegrated state and one where there is an organizing, creative centre. Solipsism as the core of madness is the unintegrated state, and sanity is associated with the state of affairs where there is a creative centre.

However, there is a semantic issue that needs to be resolved. Are we to call this centre "I"? There is a problem in that activities that flow from the jelly are often designated "I", and reactive and creative actions are both attributed to "I". So this word is problematic. We suggest differentiating personal action from impersonal action: what we call action that issues forth from the "narcissistic constellation" is impersonal, and that which is the creative act of an integrated centre personal.

What constitutes the person, then, is action that is creative and that originates from an autonomous centre. It comes into being through communication with another person. The existence of the person and the free act are interrelated realities. (This perspective has been developed by John Macmurray, 1991.) What the "narcissistic constellation" prevents is the emergence of the person, the emergence of the free act. Paradoxically, it is what is most desired but, at the same time, most feared.

It is probably quite easy for people to see why it is desired, but the reason it is feared is at first perplexing. The reason, I believe, is this: it is free personal action that reveals the self. Awareness comes through the instrumentality of action. If cruel acts have been done, then they come into awareness through the instrumentality of action. As soon as they come into awareness, they are felt and have to be borne. There is a huge burden of guilt or pain to be suffered. It is for this reason that the emergence of the person signals panic.

We have made a distinction between impersonal action and personal action. In impersonal action there is attachment of a glue-like kind to a coalesced entity. Relations to a person, however, occur through a free inner creative act. I will put it even more surprisingly: the person is the product of such an act. A relation between two persons can only occur when such an act has occurred in each.

If the person is the result of a creative act, then the materials necessary to make that possible are all the disparate elements in the personality. If essential elements are left out, then a person cannot be created. Someone who hates any greediness in him has, in that very act of disavowal, chosen not to be a person but to be invisible, to be an automaton. There is a frustrating consequence of this: that he is not recognized, and, although he has good qualities, he is not noticed as someone capable of filling a role that requires those qualities. An essential aspect of being a person is the creative combination of good and bad elements. An individual who hates and therefore obliterates the "bad" in himself is condemned to being largely a non-person. The individual is then forced into being invisible, to hide himself, and usually this is achieved through immersing himself in the imago of another. The individual holds an ideal here: one of perfection, one without deficits of character—a sort of saint or Jesus-character—and all the *intensifiers* are disowned into surrounding figures.

\* \* \*

Detachment therefore from the immediate, from reactive self-gratification, allows the personal to permeate the personality. And this godhead is creative in its nature; its creativity is only prevented through the presence of the "narcissistic constellation". This process of detachment from gratifying support starts with mother's disillusionment of her child (Winnicott, 1971). In detachment is aloneness. The need to cling to avoid this is very powerful. What it is that makes it possible for someone is difficult to say. It must somehow lie in the possession of an inner substance. I suspect that this is present in most people, and knowledge of its presence is the source of confidence and emotional robustness. The individual who does this flings him- or herself away from immediate sensuousness into this unknown void of a disembodied reality—real as real but only grasped through an inner act in the darkness. How this is possible, and how it is that some people do it and others balk at, is mysterious. It cannot be explained in terms of prior good experience or lack of it. Here is mystery.

What are the external conditions, though, that facilitate the birth of the person, the reintegrating of split-off parts? It is through the emotional engagement with a person. The person in the other demands the split-off parts to enter the forum. The person in the other refuses to be treated as the product of the other's assumption, which is fashioned out of a belief structured upon a broken psyche. The individual with the broken psyche believes the other to be structured similarly; someone under the dominance of the "narcissistic constellation" believes the other is the same as himself. This is according to the *principle of reciprocity*.

One person's narcissism, his madness, attempts to persuade the other of his point of view in order to maintain the false assumption, rooted in the "narcissistic constellation", that is only sustainable through ballast from without. It is because it is essentially jelly-like that it can only be sustained from outer ramparts, from joint-ecstasy. If it meets resistance in the unique construction present in the person of the other, then the "narcissistic constellation" collapses. This collapse favours the dispersed elements to return into connection with each other, making thought and creation possible. This is a brief summary of the process by which the presence of a person facilitates personal integration in the other.

# CHAPTER FOUR

# Narcissism
# and the struggle for survival

It is unworthy of man to be merely a means or an instrument of
the natural process by which the blind life-force perpetuates
itself at the expense of separate entities that are born and perish
and *replace* one another in turn. Man as a moral being does not
want to obey this natural law of *replacement* of generations, the
law of *eternal death*. He does not want to be that which replaces
and is replaced. He is conscious—dimly at first—both of the
desire and power to *include* in himself all the fullness of the
*infinite life*.

Vladimir Solovyov, *The Justification of the Good* (1918, p. 138)

I n Chapter 1, on ontology, I posit that materialism is the fated
outcome of the ontological assumptions that lie behind the
Judeo–Christian theology, and of the belief that the human
mind is capable of understanding the fundamentals of existence. I
believe that the mind's capacity to grasp the basic antinomies of
existence is limited. Mature religions (Symington, 1994, pp. 14–21)
have preserved in their traditions the belief that ultimate questions
concerning the nature of existence itself are beyond the capacity of
the human mind to grasp.

The repudiation of mystery leads to the belief that all can be understood through scientific enquiry. One tributary of this huge river is the idea that the struggle for survival is the ultimate motivating force in humans and animals. It is a tributary because inherent in it is the failure to allow any contradictions; everything is to be explained according to Darwin's principle. The idea that some aspects of human behaviour can be so explained and others not confronts us with the need to think harder and work out other principles and their interconnection—it is much easier to put everything under the Darwinian rubric, just as under Christendom everything was explained by God. I have challenged the universality of this principle in Chapter 2, and what is being said here is presupposed in that chapter. However, because it is an unquestioned assumption that all that we do is explicable in terms of the struggle for survival, I have found it necessary to devote a separate chapter to its refutation.

Darwin said that what drove the evolutionary engine was the struggle for survival. Those characteristics that favoured survival were endorsed, and those that did not decayed. The sexual drive, so central in Freud's thinking, is in the service of the survival of the human species. It is important to note that survival applies to the continuation of the species, not of the individual. However, species survival has been applied by social scientists to individuals also. It is this unjustified elaboration that I want to question here, but before doing so, I want to explain why it is so significant in our attempt to understand madness.

If I put my own survival at the centre of my endeavours, then I am narcissistic, but if I am addicted to the assumption that the struggle for survival is the proper motivation for myself as for all others, then how am I to differentiate narcissism from healthy confidence? This is the reason, I believe, why so many psychoanalysts, psychologists, and social theorists are forced to distinguish between healthy narcissism and unhealthy narcissism, or moderate and extreme narcissism, or positive narcissism and negative narcissism or narcissism and anti-narcissism, and so on. Bollas, for instance, refers to the phenomenon of what he calls the "antinarcissist" (Bollas, 1989, pp. 159ff). The result is that the narcissistic condition does not stand out clearly and leads to much muddled thinking on the subject.

Thus, for instance, Otto Kernberg differentiates between a greater and a lesser narcissism:

> Such a "toned down", less grandiose, and more attainable ego ideal permits one the normal narcissistic gratification of living up to the internalized ideal parental images, and this gratification in turn reinforces self-esteem, one's confidence in one's own goodness and one's trust in gratifying object relationships. [Kernberg, 1975, p. 240]

The problem is acute within psychoanalysis and all disciplines influenced by Freudian thinking because the pleasure principle upon which Freud rooted so much of his psychological understanding has been incorporated into Darwinism. The idea that the motivating principles behind human action are the desire for pleasure and the avoidance of pain goes back in the modern era to the utilitarian doctrine of Jeremy Bentham in the eighteenth century, but it has been assimilated into Darwin's motivating principles: that survival is best served by following the promptings towards pleasure and avoiding pain. It is not difficult to see how the motive of self-interest is also served well by this clinical outlook and how it legitimates egoism. What we have here is a doctrine that is narcissistic. When the falsity of the underlying assumption is not recognized, then clinicians have the greatest difficulty in grasping what narcissism is, and, if my contention that all mental disorders flow from narcissism is correct, then mental illness itself is neither seen in diagnostic assessments nor understood. Evidence for this last point is to be found in the failure of psychiatry to pinpoint the core of mental disturbance. Psychiatry defines mental disturbances according to symptoms but does not elucidate the processes that generate them. This means that there is no understanding of the processes themselves.

The survival of the species is, in the individual, located in the sex drive, and therefore the individual carries within himself a species-survival element. However, in the human species, sex serves many other purposes: it may be used to discharge rage, to provoke jealousy, to alleviate loneliness, or to foster love between two people. The use of sex for species survival is a very limited function. In fact, contraception shows that sex is used by human beings for reasons other than species survival; in fact, Freud himself drew specific attention to this (Freud, 1905d), but he did not thereby question his assumption that survival is the motivating principle behind all of human action. The individual turns an instrument for species survival into a usage that pertains to his own personal life. Just as the hand can be used to gather food but also to paint a picture, so sex can be used for species survival but also for the purposes just mentioned and for many others. In this regard, sex assumes a different usage in human beings from the rest of the animal kingdom. The point being made here is that survival of the species is just one element in the life projects of the individual, and therefore all human motivation is not reducible to it.

An argument against what I have said here may be put in the form of a syllogism:

1.  that psychological treatment is mounted against the suicidal in the patient;

2.  that suicide is against survival;

3.  therefore the motivating principle behind psychological treatment is the survival instinct.

The short answer to this is that the minor premise is incorrect because suicide is not against species survival, any more than normal death is against it. But the major premise is also faulty because "the suicidal" relates not only to physical death, but also to a mutilation of a person's emotional and mental talents. One could define suicide as an attack upon the good resources within the self; physical death through suicide is only one of its manifestations. A person could take his own life, and it might not be suicide—the instance of Captain Oates at the South Pole is always quoted in this regard. So also someone can be suicidal in the extreme without ever actually killing himself, as Herman Hesse has pointed out:

> . . . it must be said that to call suicides only those who actually destroy themselves is false. Among these, indeed, there are many who in a sense are suicides only by accident and in whose being suicide has no necessary place. Among the common run of men there are many of little personality and stamped with no deep impress of fate, who find their end in suicide without on that account belonging to the type of the suicide by inclination; while, on the other hand, of those who

are to be counted as suicides by the very nature of their beings are many, perhaps a majority, who never in fact lay hands on themselves. [Hesse, 1972, p. 58]

In fact, looked at in this light, what emerges supports my contention that survival is not the motivating factor underpinning all human purpose. What becomes clear is that what motivates human beings within civilization is the desire to create. Create what? It almost matters not what it is that is created, as long as it is understood to refer to the fashioning of the good, the beautiful, the loveable, and not to the meaning of "create" when we say:

"He created a huge confusion."

I would contend that this is a misapplication of the word "create", and the word "effect" would be more appropriate. Art, music, architecture, literature, an educational system, a government, an agricultural economy, an industrial economy, friendship, religion, a humane welfare system, and so on could be thought of as some of the artefacts created by individuals within civilization. We are born into a society where these artefacts have been created before us, and each new generation refines and improves, according to changed circumstances, but it also destroys.

When civilization breaks down, more primitive forces come into play that would support the view that struggle for survival is the ultimate motivating force. It may look like that, but, if that is so, wherefrom the desire to create civilization? For civilization is itself a human creation. Is it not that human beings, in the most primitive part of their being, have a creative desire for civilization and all its artefacts; that an essential aspect of being human is the use of "survival instruments" for a higher purpose; That instruments that have been inherited through our animal nature for the purposes of survival have been "taken up" to serve a different master?

Once we establish that the desire to create is an important motivating factor, then it is necessary to expel into outer darkness the view that the struggle for the survival is the only determinant of human behaviour. It will not be difficult to see the connection between what is being said here and what I have said in Chapter 2. The capacity to create and freedom are one thing seen from two different angles. The point being stressed here is that if we hold obsessively to the idea that the struggle for survival is only the motivating principle of human behaviour, then it is not easy to perceive narcissism in a distinctive way. One might almost put it this way: the tenacious attachment to the survival theory of motivation legitimates the ruthless self-interest inherent in narcissism. But even without putting this interpretation upon it, which is open to question, the presence of this motivational theory as a fundamental assumption makes it difficult to delineate narcissism as an entity separate from it.

This seems the right place to raise Freud's introduction of the death instinct into his schema. He formulated this theory on encountering people who had dreams of a traumatic event that had occurred to them (mostly in the First World War). This went counter to his view that dreams were the fulfilment of wishes and therefore contrary to the pleasure principle. He also had experienced patients who destroyed emotional progress that they had achieved. This seemed contrary to the survival instinct. The important point here is that Freud recognized that the survival instinct did not fit with his clinical findings in these two instances, and that therefore some other principle must be at work. His solution was to formulate the idea of the death instinct. Freud recognized that something that contradicted a motivation based upon Darwin's struggle for survival was at work. Petocz (1999, p. 221) has pointed out that whereas Freud's definition of instincts was by their source, yet in the case of the death instinct it is defined according to aim. I think one could stretch this further and say that Freud has introduced a motivating principle here that is not an instinct at all.

What happened is quite clear. In the First World War, Freud stumbled upon clinical phenomena that did not fit the premise that survival is the motivating factor in human behaviour; he therefore introduced a new motivational principle, but he did not carry his re-casting far enough. The instincts that he had enumerated until then were components of the more general instinct for survival. He now introduced a different principle—but was it correct to call this an *instinct*? As Petocz has noted, it is certainly not instinct in the same sense as he had used the word until then. What I believe Freud failed to do was to detach human behaviour from its instinctual base by invoking the principle of plasticity, whereby human beings are able to take up an "animal instrument" and use it for purposes of creative communication. However, Freud, by calling this anti-developmental principle an instinct, hoped to keep the survival instinct intact, although it was logically inconsistent.

* * *

Human behaviour can be understood to be the outcome of a blend of the survival instinct and the desire to create civilization; we will have a distorted picture of human beings if we universalize one or the other. It is necessary to incorporate into our conceptualizations a blend of both. This foundation-stone is essential if we are to grasp the essence of madness.

# CHAPTER FIVE

# Emotional action

> A strong egoism is a protection against falling ill, but in the last
> resort we must begin to love in order not to fall ill, and we are
> bound to fall ill if, in consequence of frustration, we are unable
> to love.
>
> Sigmund Freud, "On Narcissism" (1914c, p. 85)

There are two kinds of activity in human beings: motor action and emotional action. Motor action refers to all those activities that occur on the two axes of space and time; emotional action refers to activity that does not occur on the space–time axis but whose effects are registered on those axes. This does not seem to make sense, yet if the act were on the space–time axis, then it would be possible to detect it. It is easier to understand this if we take time first, and to do this we need to formulate one of our principles of action.

The presence of an emotional state indicates that there has been an emotional act responsible for it. So, for instance, Rufus is in a bad mood. The reason for its presence is to be sought in an emotional act, which is itself not detectable either by the subject or by an observer. It occurs out of time and also out of space. The principle, though, is that an emotional state is evidence that an emotional act has occurred. We call this the *principle of sedimentation*.

Because emotional action does not occupy space, it cannot be directly seen, heard, or touched, but it is either responded to with feeling or registered in actions of various kinds. To the extent to which narcissism—the core of madness—is present in the personality, to that precise extent is emotional action registered not in feelings but in events. So, for instance, the registration might be a stomach pain, a friend getting angry with me, a car crash, a sexual impulse. In these latter registrations there is no consciousness of the emotional action that is responsible for them.

I need to emphasize that although the emotional act is generated outside time and space, yet it is registered in it. But this formulation is not accurate, as it suggests that the sphere of the necessary is divorced from the contingent, but expression is necessarily limited. The solution of this problem lies in the paradoxical nature of being, as discussed in Chapter 1. In brief, one aspect of being is registered by the senses and another through an act of understanding. Feelings, in so far as they are registrations of emotional activity, are judgements-in-the-senses of the emotional activity.

Emotional action is of two basic kinds: *integrative* and *liquifying–petrifying*. The consequence of the latter is that the self is fragmented and damaged. In the former the self integrates and expands. The agency governing the latter is an alliance between the *intensifiers* and god. The agency governing the former is an alliance between the *formal centre* and conscience. Actions are either out-going or in-coming. When they are *intensifying*, they are expulsive and implosive; when they are *integrative*,[1] endowment is substituted for expulsion and receptivity for implosion.

It needs to be understood that the primary object of all emotional action is the self. This remark may appear to mean that all emotional activity is narcissistic, but this is not so. In order to understand why this is not so, it is necessary to conceptualize the dual character of the self and its symbolic character. The nature of this duality has also been explained in Chapter 1.

Emotional action that is *intensifying* is only known indirectly through symbolic equivalents. A symbolic equivalent differs from

---

[1]For the effect of these upon perception, belief, and affect see Chapter 19.

a symbol in that the latter refers to creative emotional acts and the former to *intensifying* emotional acts. These symbolic equivalents are hated because the actions that they embody—emerging, as they do, from the *intensifiers*—prevent freedom. The person believes that the symbols are things-in-themselves. The job of psychoanalysis or any investigation of the mind is to demonstrate in a manner that is entirely convincing that the things-in-themselves are symbols.

These two kinds of action can be observed daily in numerous human encounters. Psychoanalysis is one observation platform available for observing these processes, but there are many others. The observational instrument in psychoanalysis is what is called the "transference". The question is, how this is an effective instrument? The answer to this question is relevant not only to psychoanalysis but to all interpersonal emotional encounters.

The direct person-to-person encounter reveals emotional activities. In the absence of such an encounter, the subject remains unaware of them. It requires a special human effort to speak the feelings that are experienced towards the person about whom they are the response. Why is this so? I think there are two interrelated reasons: (1) because in such a situation I become aware of my own emotional acts, and this is inevitably accompanied by feelings of sadness, regret, or pain as well as of joy and happiness; (2) an act of understanding always requires direct confrontation with the object. A psychoanalyst's task is to use himself as a symbolic object that can throw light upon the emotional acts that otherwise remain in darkness. The way in which this light is thrown is through understanding or an intuitive act. This needs some explaining. Confrontation with the reality itself is avoided in any sphere. The resistance that Freud described as arising in psychoanalysis is part of a much more widespread reluctance, of which the analytic instance is only one example. It brings the subject into an encounter with the necessary essence of existence. This naturally illuminates the unity of existence and, on the human emotional level, the interconnectedness of what seem to be disparate events. Wilfred Bion refers to this phenomenon when he speaks of the particular element that unifies what on the surface look like disconnected events. He calls this particular element the *selected fact* (Bion, 1962b, pp. 72–73).

The person of the "other" is the symbol of the necessary, so the act is a giving of the contingent to the necessary, and the consequence of this is that the necessary permeates the contingent and is understood through an act of understanding. However, there is another aspect to it: that the act is generated as a response to the invitation of conscience and is therefore in itself good. A person only becomes aware of *intensifying* activity when she or he has accumulated some self-worth through integrative emotional activity. As the emotional act that is a response to conscience is good, it makes it possible for the individual to become aware of his/her *intensifying* actions. The bad or the "Shadow Side", as Jung called it, can only be seen when silhouetted against the light.

Every time a person evades the call to expression under the influence of the *intensifiers,* god becomes more punishing. We are talking here of decision-making in the way in which Elliott Jaques uses the term. He emphasizes that at the time of making a decision the person is not aware of it:

> deciding or choosing are always in the final analysis founded upon unconscious processes. The role of protomental unconscious factors in decision-making can be succinctly summed up in the fact that if you consciously know all the considerations that led to a particular choice then you did not make a decision: you were a computer. [Jaques, 1982, p. 70]

The reason why the person is not aware of the decision is that it occurs in a split-second. Even afterwards the person may not be aware of it, but I have frequently pointed out to a patient that it seems as though a decision had been made since the last time I saw him or her. For instance, I have very frequently come across this situation: the time for the ending of the session has arrived, and the pain of it is anaesthetized in a violent act. As the person walks out of the consulting-room, in a split-second he says to himself:

> "To hell with bloody development. I'll go and visit Jonathan . . ."

Jonathan being someone who always encourages him or her to go along the path of least resistance and avoid psychological treatments of any kind. The person does not say to him- or herself what I have just said. I have put a split-moment into words to convey the meaning of it. When questioned about this sort of event subsequently, it would be characteristic for a patient to say:

> "As I was leaving I *did* have the thought that it would be nice to go and see Jonathan, and it's true that he always laughs at my efforts to change and tells me I am wasting my time and money on psychoanalysis."

This thought is the manifestation of the decision, and it is only brought to mind, even subsequently, through searching self-scrutiny and usually with some embarrassment. When I have said that the decision or emotional change occurs in a split second, I do not think that that is the correct way to formulate it. It occurs outside time, but its effect is in time. Because the emotional change is out of time, the effect occurs in a split second of time, so that the event itself cannot be "caught". When we say that a process is unconscious one aspect of that is that it occurs outside the space–time axis.

What has been said about time also applies to space. The emotional act occurs in no place, but it has an effect in space. When Elliott Jaques says that deciding or choosing is founded in unconscious processes, that means that it is not in time or space, otherwise it would not be unconscious. Freud said that there is no time in the unconscious. Another way of putting this would be to say that the emotional source of action is unconscious because it is outside space and time.[2] Because the source of emotional action is outside space and time, it is conceptualized in representative imagery, which, while capturing the form of action, yet distorts it. As there are two basic kinds of emotional action, we conceptualize two sources in representational imagery.

I have distinguished between actions that are *integrative* and those that are *intensifying*. These definitions consider the effect of the actions upon the self. When we think of the effects of these actions on people outside, we call them "projective identification" and "creative communication".[3] *Projective identification* goes on outside, and *intensifying* activity goes on inside. The inside can therefore be visualized as a series of fragments in suspension in

---

[2]This is why Bion formulated the finite and the infinite.

[3]What I have called "creative communication" is, I think, the type of relationship to which Bion refers as "commensal" (see Bion, 1970).

the jelly, whereas *creative communication* is the outer result of *integrative* action. It must be remembered that these are analogical images, as explained in Chapter 1.

When someone is pressurized into acting in a certain way, he or she is being dominated by projective identification in combination with an acceptance of it. Persuasion, as it is used by politicians and religious leaders, is achieved through the mechanism of projective identification. Socrates in the *Gorgias* condemns this form of persuasion and argues that it is morally evil. Alasdair MacIntyre has this to say:

> The idea that techniques of persuasion are morally neutral is a recurrent one in human society. But in order to hold that such techniques are neutral, it is necessary also to hold that it is morally irrelevant whether a man comes to a given belief by reasoning or in some nonrational way. [MacIntyre, 1967, p. 27]

It seems that we have stumbled upon the very foundations upon which a judgement of what is good and what is evil rests. The only matter in MacIntyre's description that needs further refinement is the antinomy between "reasoning" and "nonrational". We equate "nonrational" with pressurized, impulsive action or reactive modes of exchange, whereas reasoning and free choice are interrelated entities. There is a judgement here: that the latter constitutes the good and the former lacks this quality. As the good is a quality of the Absolute, so a lack of it indicates that pressurized activity flows from a situation where the contingent is divorced from the absoluteness of existence.

Anyone familiar with the thinking of Wilfred Bion will see the similarity between what has been described above and his theory of beta elements and alpha elements (Bion, 1962b). The difference lies in the substitution of a pattern of fragments brought together into a whole for alpha elements, which are described by Bion as discrete entities. The other is that this pattern of fragments is what constitutes alpha function. Alpha elements and alpha function are therefore two different ways of describing the same thing— one being the individual elements, the other being the elements brought together into one *gestalt*. The other difference is an elaboration being made here as to how these two sources come to be.

What I am proposing here is that the state of discrete fragments held in suspension comes about through trauma, and the establishment of a pattern of fragments comes about through the coincidence of the *principle of integrity* with an object that is transformational. There is a drive in human beings to repair the ego, which I call the "principle of integrity". Bion (1967b) sees this repair to be the job of the psychotic part of the personality. This may sound confusing in that Bion emphasizes that the psychotic is that part of the personality that attacks mental cohesion. Whether repair or destruction occurs depends upon the way the object functions in relation to the ego. I shall try to illustrate this with an example of a woman who had been in analysis for some years subsequent to a psychotic breakdown. At the outset her capacity to communicate with me was severely impaired. This improved very considerably. So she came in and said:

> "All you've taught me to do is to communicate with the wonderful you. You haven't helped me to communicate with people outside. Oh, yes, I can talk to the wonderful you, but there are few people other than you, you know . . ."

I felt injured but processed her clamour. The next day, having been to visit a gynaecologist, she came in and said:

> "Now I've found someone *really* sympathetic to women. Now I've found someone who I can really talk to and who understands my difficulties . . ."

My blood began to boil, and I was about to point out how she was denigrating what had been achieved since the start of her analysis, but I held it; then, as I calmed down, a thought came to me, which I voiced:

> "So there has been a good development since yesterday. Now you are able to communicate with someone outside this consulting-room. . ."

Had I reacted according to my first impulse, then the *communication thrust* would have been met by an object that would have cemented the fragmented state. Instead, the object, together with the subject, transformed fragments into a pattern. Alpha elements and alpha function were more thoroughly established. What determines, therefore, the outcome of the "communication thrust" is a *quale* existing in the subject, object, and process. The "communication thrust" incorporates these three elements in such a way that they are three separate elements and yet one reality. The Trinitarian doctrine of three persons in one god may be the externalization of this inner psychic reality. Religious myths and doctrines frequently symbolize the emotional activities of the psyche, and this is why they have so powerful an influence on believers. Freud understood this with the introduction of the story of Oedipus as a myth to symbolize neurotic conflict. He did not carry this quest further into the mythology of more developed religions. I suspect that he felt too much "in" the Judeo–Christian tradition to appreciate the symbolic significance of its mythology.

From what has just been said, it is obvious that this *quale* is something crucial for the psychic development of the couple. The question is "What is it?"—a desire for wholeness, a desire to repair the psyche. E. M. Forster said through the character of Dr Aziz in *A Passage to India*:

There are many ways of being a man . . . [Forster, 1974, p. 263]

It requires that this particular way is that the person's inner vocational life is to repair his/her ego. This, I believe, is the *quale* that has a determining effect upon the "communication thrust", making creative communication a possible outcome. Melanie Klein and Bion both suggested that a large deposit of inherited envy is responsible for an over-supply of projective identification. I favour the view that it is the result of infantile trauma.

It should be clear from what has been said here that projective identification is the activity generated by the narcissistic part of the personality and that *embodiment* in outer objects is integral to it. The particular objects that are fashioned in this way we shall name "narcissistic objects" and a particular chapter (Chapter 21) is devoted to them.

There is something that seems, at first sight, to be a contradiction. In the person who is most passive, most jelly-like, there is at the same time the most virulent projective identification. It is an instance of the *principle of the coexistence of opposites*. It is very common for someone who is very passive to be surrounded by people who are exasperated with him. This exasperation is a sign that there is a virulent projective identification in process. For instance, a calm wisdom that may be superficially similar lacks entirely this despair and exasperation in those surrounding the person. So, for instance, the case of Herbert Read, quoted by Graham Greene, is a demonstration of quietness that generates peace and goodwill.[4]

> Certainly my meeting with Herbert Read was an important event in my life. He was the most gentle man I have ever known, but it was a gentleness that had been tested in the worst experience of his generation. The young officer, who gained the Military Cross and a DSO in action on the Western Front, had carried with him to all that mud and death Robert Bridges's anthology *The Spirit of Man*, Plato's *Republic*, and *Don Quixote*. Nothing had changed in him. It was the same man twenty years later who could come into a room full of people and you wouldn't notice his coming—you noticed only that the whole atmosphere of a discussion had quietly altered, that even the relations of one guest with another had changed. No one would any longer be talking for effect, and when you looked round for an explanation, there he was—complete honesty born of complete experience had entered the room and unobtrusively taken a chair. [Greene, 1980]

The exasperation in those around the passive person is generated by intense emotional action. Through what channels does this emotional activity pass? I believe that it is principally through the eyes, but also through gestures, gait, tones of voice, and speech. Wilfred Bion believed that a hallucination is fashioned through projecting a stored image through the eyes, (Bion, 1962a). So the passive person projects with great intensity through the eyes causing thereby frustration, exasperation, or rage. The eyes are the central channel through which such a projective action occurs, but there are also subsidiary channels, such as gestures, gait, words used as missiles, and tone of voice. So the jelly is always accompanied, according to the "principle of the coexistence of opposites", by projective action of high intensity.

### Emotional action structures perception

We have divided emotional action into two types: *projective identification* and *creative communication*. The individual is not aware of either of these two activities, but his perception of the human world is determined by them. Just as Kant held that the objects of the world are determined by the categories of the understanding, so the perception of the human world is determined by these emotional activities.

To illustrate what I mean, I will start with a perceptual distortion that is frequently referred to in psychoanalytic literature: idealization, which means that the person is perceived as faultless and which is therefore a distorted perception. What emotional actions are responsible for this distortion? It is, I believe, a dual process: first there is a splitting of the self into all bad and all good; secondly the good in the self is projected into the other figure, and then this other is perceived as perfect and at the same time the self is seen as worthless. This situation is then hated, and the bad is catapulted into the idealized figure. This latter part of the process was called "envy" by Melanie Klein, but the earlier part of the process, whereby there is the projection of the good, is an integral part of it.

The dual activity can take place only if there has been a coalescence between the two people. Coalescence takes place to the extent to which the *narcissistic constellation* is present. A crucial factor in the "narcissistic constellation" is the lack of an emotionally creative centre. This lack forces the narcissistic individual into coalescence in an attempt to seek a centre of action in the other and thus avoid responsibility and freedom. If we ask why these are avoided, it is because of the presence of unbearable guilt. The ultimate reason for guilt is if someone has enslaved himself. Guilt is not so much for what has been done, but for what has not been done: the person has not freed him- or herself from the constraints of the "narcissistic constellation" and therefore not cared for self or others. And yet the search for causes results in a circular argument that suggests that what we are talking of is a series of interconnecting elements. What brings about the whole system of these interconnections is to be sought in a traumatic situation and its management. This we shall explore more fully when we come to Chapter 14, on trauma.

# CHAPTER SIX

# The internalizing act

If we want really to know what is in a man's mind, we must refer to what he does and not to what he says.

Henri Bergson, *The Two Sources of Morality and Religion*
(1935, p. 119)

I had been going to entitle this chapter "Internalization", but this word conveys the sense of something being done to the individual rather than something that the person does. As "internalization" is an emotional activity of the ego, it could have been subsumed within Chapter 5. However, as this activity is so central to the psychological identity of the human being, it has been given a separate chapter in order to highlight it.

There are two modes of "internalization", which we might call "creative" and "photographic". The model I am initially using here is of two people facing the same landscape: one has a canvas, paints, brushes, and palette, and the other has a camera with a film in it. The painter creates a picture out of the scene in front of him, whereas the photographer, with the aid of light, mechanically impresses the scene onto the film.[1] The painter in the process of creating a picture will know the landscape: he personally knows that which he has created. It was Giambattista Vico who, in refutation of Descartes, said that we only know that which we create. It is a personal possession. In the "photographic act", however, the outer object is not in *me*; it is in a depersonalized system. There is no *me* that knows it; it is impressed upon a passive object.

In the photographic act it is tempting to suggest that the outer object is imploded onto the inner system *as it is*, but we know that this is not the case. As introjected, it is an inner object that persecutes and inhibits freedom. There is no neutral introjection. There is either an internal act that expands and enhances the inner personality or one that inhibits and restricts it. The most typically internalized objects are the parents. When they are inside through a "photographic act", it is asserted that this is how they were. it is not said:

"This is the way I perceived them."

Or:

"Anyhow, this is the way I experienced them . . ."

Or:

"I saw them this way, though I know my brother saw them differently . . ."

But:

"My mother always put me down. She did not want me to have my own life . . ."

Or:

"They both hated children. I know that they did not want children . . ."

Or:

"Neither my mother nor my father could bear us children having fun . . ."

---

[1]No analogy is perfect. A contrast is being made here between a creative act and one that is uncreative. I am acutely aware that taking photographs is a creative activity. There are no pure types within the human condition but the process of reasoning requires that we create them.

When there is some contradiction between an event described and the parental photograph, the contradictory event is quickly made to fit the photographic template, however much it strains logical consistency.

Therefore a restricting, persecuting image has been introjected. A selection has occurred whereby those memories that are persecuting to the self are preserved and those that are loving, generous, and magnanimous are annihilated. Now, an important question arises: if a creative internalization and a "photographic" one are both selections, which is real? It can only mean that real is a value judgement that is very close to the adjective "good". It means that the real image is the one that is loving, generous, and magnanimous, whereas the delusional image is the one that is persecuting because it is mean and restricting of the ego; in fact, it crushes the ego. The creative internalization expands and enhances the ego, whereas the "photographic" one restricts it. It also implies that implosion of this "photographic" nature fashions delusion, the unreal, whereas the creative internal act is what creates the real. Real and unreal are categories fashioned by the mind.

I believe that this distinction and definition of the "real" is of momentous importance as it totally changes the meaning of the real as it has been received in psychoanalytic teaching and tradition. When Freud uses the term "reality-testing", he is referring to the perceptual registration of an event. When I say:

"I know that Joseph Spencer has died. . ."

I know it cognitively. If I am a doctor, I may have signed the death certificate, attended the funeral. In this sense my "reality-testing" is intact. I know that Joseph Spencer has died, but if he is my son, I may know it but, following Freud, will not have worked it through. This means that emotionally it is not real for me. It can and does happen that a death is never "worked through"; it never becomes emotionally real. So what makes it emotionally real or unreal is dependent upon activities of an internal kind. Using the above analogy: if the death is photographed, it does not become emotionally real; if it is painted, it does. Freud says that the work of mourning consists of a detachment of the self from the object. But is this right? I think it misses an essential element.

Mourning consists in the re-creation of changed events. The ability to undertake this work depends upon whether the creative capacities of the individual are functioning. If the "narcissistic constellation" is in full force, it prevents this creative functioning. What I have referred to as the photographic are raw sensations that are either imploded or exploded, and the ego is fragmented and not capable of creative activity. In the case of the event being a death, the raw sensations of which it is composed are imploded and exploded in the emotional arena, so there is a shattered ego incapable of creating—in this case, a creation called mourning: a re-fashioning of raw sensations. What we are talking of here is the emotional activity. At the practical level, where I know that Joseph Spencer has died, this is all motor activity.

I have said above that Freud's idea that mourning consists of detaching the self from the lost object is deficient. We have to look at the form in which the original attachment to the person existed. If the attachment is on the basis of a clinging to god, then, as has been elucidated in Chapters 6, 10, and 12, parts of the self have been lodged in that other person, and so she has to be kept alive. On the other hand, if the person who has died is free from parts of the self being lodged in her, mourning can occur *because* a whole self is able to perform creative acts, and these acts recreate the changed elements into a new configuration. . .

When a death occurs, there is a changed world; there is a breakdown of the sensational world, and the work of re-creation has to begin. This re-creation is what will constitute my inner world; it is the internalizing act. Internalization occurs through re-creation. When I make it myself, then I possess it inside me.

The conclusion forces itself upon us that there are two modes of internalizing: one that is driven by hate and another that is driven by love. It is the latter that enhances the personality and is judged to be "real". This accords with our central thesis that it is the essential nature of existence that is creative that, when it governs our human behaviour, is sane but is mad when it fails to do so.

# CHAPTER SEVEN

# Roy Schafer's action language

Freudian psychoanalysis can no longer afford to maintain
unchallenged the conviction that psychoanalytic propositions
must be formulated in terms of Freud's metapsychology.

Roy Schafer, *A New Language for Psychoanalysis* (1976, p. 3).

Theories of action have been put forward by various social
scientists, but I think the one that is closest to mine is that
elaborated by the psychoanalyst, Roy Schafer (1976). Those
acquainted with his theory may wonder how my theory of action
differs from his and in what ways it is similar.

He has worked out his action theory in a very detailed way, and
I should like first to pay tribute to his goal of putting the intentional
action of human beings at the centre of his project; I believe his
efforts have not received the attention they deserve. I agree entirely
with his desire to disengage the psychoanalytic investigation from
what he calls Freud's "physicochemical and evolutionary biological language" (Schafer, 1976, p. 3) and from the mechanistic metapsychology (p. 349) and also his "positivistically conceived meta-

psychology" (p. 362). Consistent with this, he wishes to abolish all actions that are attributed to impersonal forces. He is therefore in line with Fairbairn, whose model of the inner structure of the mind dispensed with Freud's concept of the id. Schafer (1976) emphasizes that we *do* things, we are not just the passive receptacles of events. He says trenchantly:

> ... interpretation brings home to the analysand the extent to which, and the terms in which, the analysand has been the author of his or her own life, unconsciously and preconsciously as well as consciously; at the same time, it brings home the extent to which, and the terms in which, the analysand has been disclaiming this activity. [Schafer, 1976, p. 8]

That I am in agreement with him about this should be clear from what has been said above (Chapter 5) about unconscious decisions, which proceed from the ego rather than from the id or some supposed non-personal source. It is, I believe, significant that Schafer's words have fallen on stony ground within the social sciences.

However, there are some significant differences between his exposition and mine. Schafer wants to replace the "physicochemical" model with "action language", which is based on choices and intentions. However, I believe that in order to make this substitution meaningful and grounded in the right soil, it is necessary to go back to ontology and lay a different groundwork in the context of which an action language finds it true home. My point here, then, is that a foundation arrived at through ontological reflection needs to be done in order to make Schafer's psychology cohere upon a surer base. I gave a brief historical survey in Chapter 1 of the false ontology that is ultimately responsible for the mechanistic form of explanation against which Schafer is protesting. It is a question of being able to argue for a different position rationally rather than on emotive beliefs alone.

There are, I believe, three errors in Schafer's schema:

1. non-acceptance of ordinary language;
2. failure to distinguish between projective and receptive activity;
3. equivalence of emotions and feelings.

He is against latinized nouns like "identification" and "internalization" because he wants to grasp the action instead of being left with a noun that smothers what has been done. If I say:

"I have thrust my soul into Freud's mind and heart",

this captures what I have done in a much more vivid way than if I say:

"I am identified with Freud",

or even more so if I say,

"I am in identification with Freud."

All such words are attempts to place psychoanalysis within the language of natural science. Schafer wishes to abolish this metapsychological aim of Freud, and it is therefore consistent of him to banish all words that have been chosen in obedience to this principle. I am entirely in sympathy with his desire to replace Freud's deterministic philosophy with one that does honour to intention and purpose. However, I believe that he is mistaken in banishing all nouns. His rationale for this is that they obscure action, and he would therefore want us to say "*I wish*" but not refer to someone having "*a wish*". Imagine for a moment that we are looking at a game of cricket. A fielder throws in the ball and hits the stumps so one of the batsmen is run out, and a spectator says:

"What a superb throw",

but Schafer would want him to say:

"He threw that ball superbly",

and there is something wrong with the second sentence because it does not express precisely the spectator's meaning. When he says:

"What a superb throw",

he is talking of the action of the fielder in relation to an object. What is the actual difference between the two statements? When he uses "throw" as a noun he is emphasizing the action of throwing plus the object that the ball hits—despite the fact that the object is not mentioned. When "threw" is the verb, it is the action of throwing that is marvelled at, and in fact this is not the correct form of language for what he wants to express, precisely because the object is annihilated. The same applies to these two sentences:

"I wished."

"I had a wish."

The latter sentence invites the question "For what?", whereas the former does not.

Therefore I think that Schafer is right to banish nouns that are pseudo-scientific latinizations. I say "pseudo" because they have been invented to sustain the illusion that psychoanalysis is a natural science, and Schafer rightly claims that it is not. I believe that he is mistaken in believing that it is an interpretative art and not a science. This is based on the false premise that science is restricted to those laws governing the inanimate universe, but if we define science, as Collingwood does, as:

a body of systematic or orderly thinking about a determinate subject matter [Collingwood, 1969, p. 4]

then it includes the animate and the inanimate world. If our scientific thinking about human beings is modelled on the libertarian hypothesis, then Schafer's position is entirely scientific but based upon a different metaphysical presupposition. Whether the libertarian or the deterministic hypothesis is the correct one for a science of human beings is a matter to be debated by metaphysicians.[1]

Why do I accept nouns from ordinary common speech while rejecting the pseudo-scientific latinized ones? It is based on an intuition that ordinary common language has been fashioned naturally by human beings to express meaning as exactly as possible, and the cricketing image above is an example. I differentiate "ordinary common language" from the language of an academic, political, or religious speciality, which is frequently fashioned to give expression to an ideology, whereas the purpose of common speech is to express meaning of realities as they exist.

I think Schafer is also wrong in banishing all words that make the active subject passive. He is surely right in his view that we are

---

[1]Not however, I would hope, without the evidence available from psychoanalytic observation.

always active subjects, and so even in receptivity we are active in our receptiveness. We are surely acting beings, but we are also receivers of activity, *including being receivers of our own activity*. He wants, however, to remove all phrases such as:

"Those thoughts keep crowding in on me",

whereas that is the way in which the unconscious receptivity of events is experienced. Because they are emotional acts that are outside the space–time axis or unconscious, they are *felt* to be something that happens to us. This is not how things occur but how they are felt to occur, so the common man's mode of expression is phenomenologically correct—namely, that the subjective receptivity is not experienced because it is unconscious. The mode of expression is faithful to the experience, and this leads naturally into the third critique.

Schafer equates emotions and feelings. Feelings are the register of what happens to us; they do not tell us what we emotionally do. Emotions are the unseen actions, as has been described (Chapter 5), whereas feelings are the registration of these actions. Feelings, however, are subject to distortion. This is because the character of our own emotional activity affects our reception of outer and inner events. This failure to differentiate emotions from feelings leads Schafer to abolish all phrases that indicate that we are the receivers of events. This distorts the truth, because we are in fact the receivers of events, even though we endow them with our colouring through our emotional activity.

I think that there is a failure to conceptualize emotions accurately. Although Schafer says clearly

What we call emotions is one of the things people do or one of the ways in which they do things. [Schafer, 1976, p. 271]

yet he has not conceptualized human action into its two forms—motor and emotional—and I think that what lies behind this is the idea that the mind is a lump of stuff rather than activity. Aristotle had the view that the natural state of things is to be static, whereas Galileo had the view that the natural state of things is to be in motion. This is an analogy for the mind. Schafer has a Aristotelian view of the mind; what I am claiming is that it is Galilean. I am stressing that what is crucial is an understanding that the mind is action that brings about consequences. There is another difference between Schafer's position and my own: I think that emotional action *is* the mind, whereas for Schafer there is an "I" outside the emotions, and then emotions are something that the "I" does. I think that the "I" is made of emotions.

There is a level of emotional action not encompassed by Schafer. It is the unseen emotional action that is partly responsible for the sadistic, exploitative, or oppressive behaviour of someone else towards myself. Schafer (1976, pp. 128–129) gives the example of a man who allowed himself to be dominated by his sadistic wife and submitted to an unfavourable divorce settlement. Schafer attends to his active compliance with his wife's cruelty, but what is not encompassed is the fact that it is the husband's emotional activity that is partly responsible for generating it.

To sum up: the fundamental difference between Schafer's position and mine is my focus upon the inner emotional activity where Schafer's is upon its outer consequences. The coincidence of our two views is in the focus upon the subject as an active agent rather than a passive receptacle.

# PART II

# THE PATTERN OF MADNESS

Nothing outside *his* own self held any significance for him, because everything in the world, it seemed to him, depended on his will alone.

Leo Tolstoy, *War and Peace* (1986b, p. 734)

Madness consists of a pattern of interlocking elements that distort perception, damage the self, and prevent emotional freedom. I hope that, as the chapters of this book unfurl, it will become clear how these elements function in this way. A diagram delineating these elements is shown, for ease of reference, on the cover of this book.

All the essential elements in the constellation of madness are contained in the diagram. These elements are the internal factors that generate madness. It can be seen that those factors in the upper half of the circle are hard and severe, whereas those in the lower half are soft and vulnerable. However, each element in the upper half is paralleled by one in the lower half—or it can be thought of as one factor made up of two poles. Then the degree of hardness or softness is determined by the *intensifiers*, which are shown to be exerting pressure from the middle of the circle. The violence or mildness of the *intensifiers* determines the relative hardness or softness of any of these elements: in the soft elements the *intensifiers* are *liquifiers*; in the hard elements they are *petrifiers*. The word *petrify* embodies the two senses: the process by which a soft substance is made into a stony one and someone aghast or in a state of panic.

The diagram is in the form of a circle because there is no starting point: all these elements are of equal value. If it were not for the limitation of the human mind, it could be seen that these elements are a unity. The intensifiers give quality to the god: so, for instance, the god will be filled with envy, jealousy, and greed; it will be a greedy god, an envious god, a jealous god. These characteristics have been expelled into the god through the agency of hatred. In paranoia, the person is focused on the expelled element, which is located in god.

The book considers all the elements in the circle. Starting with the *jelly*: it moves according to whatever outer stimuli strike it.

There is no source of action from within. Then there is a hard *crust*, which can be thought of as encompassing the *jelly* as an outer membrane or as bits in suspension. The *crust* is similar to the *jelly* in that it reacts in a mechanical mode to outer stimuli but in a stiff reactive way rather than in a passive liquid way. According to the *principle of opposites*, when a *jelly* is encountered, then it can be known that there is also *crust*, and vice versa. This knowledge can help a clinician (or others!) to be forewarned.

The next pair are *god* and the *worm*. At the divine end is a powerful figure that instructs and directs. The object he directs is a worm—an utterly contemptible figure. This god is always embodied in a figure or institution and the worm is also.

Towards this embodied god there is glue-like attachment, while at the same time there is enormous distance. The glue-like attachment is accompanied by intense feelings, but there is no knowledge of the person on whom the attachment settles, so there is immense closeness, but as there is no knowledge, there is great distance.

Also towards this god there is paranoia but at the same time blind spots. The paranoia focuses on one element in the god with hatred, but because attention is thus restricted, the vision is impaired, and there are large blind spots.

I have called this pattern the "narcissistic constellation", and it is the unitary core of madness. I believe that a diagnosis of madness has relied upon theories and models that do not give a true understanding of madness. Madness as "pain unbearable", that prevents giving, trusting, loving, is a structure that protects the individual, and therefore we call it "narcissistic". It is a project designed to protect the self from pain, and it is therefore a self-oriented system. However, as explained in Chapter 1, it only protects the self looked at from the perspective of contingency. Looked at from the perspective of absoluteness, it damages the self. One piece of evidence of the dominance of contingency is that actions are performed with only the short term in view. The passion of the moment rules the day.

The purpose of this book is to try to lay out the principles of action that flow from the single structure in such a way as to make possible for the whole to be seen in the part at any given moment.

## The effect of the narcissistic constellation

I have tried to outline (in Chapters 2, 3, and 6) what constitutes a health in the personality. Within the "narcissistic constellation" entities exist as realities of which there is knowledge but no awareness. Such realities are grief, anger, sadness, and disappointment, which are projected. In the healthy part of the personality these entities are known and felt; in the narcissistic part of the personality they are known but not felt.

***

Madness is made up of a pattern of interconnected elements. If any one element is focused upon to the exclusion of the others, then the mad structure has not been elucidated. If all the elements except one are attended to, the same principle applies: the person's freedom of action is still inhibited. (Each of these elements of madness receives more attention in subsequent chapters.)

In the state of madness, the person is *driven* by a force, a something, and consequently he is not the autonomous centre of his own activity. Two interrelated elements are a jelly and god; the god drives, and the inner state is a gelatinous mass. There is no firm boundary around the jelly, but it pours out into surrounding figures of the environment, and outer figures also invade the jelly, merging with god. This is the inner situation, but outwardly the person may appear stiff with a lobster-shell barrier between himself and others. This is how it looks, but the inner situation is as I have described. The jelly contains a jumble of bits (bits made up of fragments resulting from inner destructive action) that slop around within it. The emotion that characterizes this inner state is shame.[1]

> Shame and remorse are generally mistaken for one another. Man feels remorse when he has been at fault; and he feels shame because he lacks something. Shame is more original than remorse. [Bonhoeffer, 1970, p. 20]

As there is no autonomous centre, there is also no personal taking in. There is no functioning self that is able to process and

---

[1]Consider Dietrich Bonhoeffer:

take in outer knowledge. Knowledge can sit in the personality as an alien body, but it does not become part of the personality. Personal knowledge is acquired through an act, and as this is not possible to a gelatinous substance, it has to resort to a substitute method. The jelly attaches itself to a god figure and ingests knowledge from god by sucking it into himself. This attachment is glue-like.

There is also a worm, to be despised and crushed under foot. Sometimes the person acts in the shoes of god, sometimes he acts in the shoes of the worm. His way of acting is through being in one of the parts in suspension in the jelly. As the whole of the jelly is attached to either god or the worm, it is passive to the object. This is the inner situation. The outer appearance may *look* active, but it is inherently passive.

There are three elements that keep the jelly gelatinous: envy, greed, and jealousy; because of their unified function I refer to them as the *intensifiers*. However, they are all in god, which gives them power. They are the consequence of a trauma—the trauma in transformed mode. God is the transmutation of an accident, the transmutation of chance. This is elaborated more fully in Chapter 22.

So these are the elements: a god, a worm, a jelly, a jumble of bits, the presence of *intensifiers*, a glue-like attachment. This is a single reality that we can only grasp through looking at the parts, but the whole is in each part as in a hologram.

The function of madness is the strangling of sanity. Sanity is the free human act. Madness is that which prevents the free human act.

# CHAPTER EIGHT

# The jelly

*FISH IN A SHOAL*

A wave comes from the left
And that's the way I move,
My tail is a rudder
But currents are a pilot
That decide every heading.
The currents are a pressure
That I'm unable to resist
My tail can only move me
Quicker down their channels
I am their helpless victim.
A tone of voice; a raised eyebrow;
A haughty manner or nose in the air,
A suspicious look or a rude gaze,
These are the currents that drive me
Along life's waterways.
I'm in a shoal with others,
I feel their bodies swish
And I swirl with them all;
They are the currents of my life
With no soul to resist.

Neville Symington

83

I have said that the presence of narcissism prevents the individual from initiating emotional action of a positive kind (Symington, 2000, p. 52). This makes sense when we realize that the centre of the personality is an amorphous jelly. Sometimes people will describe it by saying things like:

"When my girlfriend became angry, with me I was a jelly inside."

Or:

"Although I am speaking to you coherently, I am just a heap of fragments inside."

Or:

"I am a complete mess inside."

Or:

"My husband never generates a move; I always have to give the lead."

Sometimes these things are not spoken, but the character of a person's life is a message in neon lights that the inner personality is best pictured as a messy substance. We often hear people speak in terms such as these:

"His life is in a total mess . . ."

Or:

"She has had a string of different men, keeps moving jobs, is on drugs, and her whole life is in chaos . . ."

Or:

"Old Mr Johnson was completely broken up when his wife died."

Here the sense is that the person inside is in bits. Language fluctuates, then, between images of the person being in bits, in a mess, or a jelly. We shall see that both the image of a jelly and the image of bits or scattered pieces are appropriate.

Picture the personality as a line describing the shape of a sphere; then inside it imagine a gelatinous mass, with no distinguishable forms. I think Wilfred Bion was referring to this when, quoting Milton, he referred to the "formless infinite" (Bion, 1965, p. 151), because the "substance" to which we are referring seems formless.

Someone once described seeing herself as a body with no bones lying on a round bed. The body would be splayed out, with no structure to hold it in place.

Research into the inner life through introspection, meditation, or psychoanalysis can give us some idea of how this gelatinous state comes about. In such a process "forms" begin to be wrested from the morass. However, this can only be done if the "poisonous forms" are exhumed out of this amorphous psychic material. Let us say provisionally that this entity assumes a shape out of the formless mass, and we give it the name of "greed". Now, as soon as we have done this, we begin to notice something: that the person begins to initiate action in a way that she or he had not done before. We formulate this picture therefore: that when we have named this shape that emerges, we have put around it a permeable barrier, and the rest of the personality is protected from its constant inundation.

When the ichneumon fly comes to the chrysalis of a butterfly and injects a poisonous sting into it, the fleshy substance of the pupa turns into a soup-like mess. The presence of this greed in the morass has a similar effect: the whole substance is turned into a jelly. Greed has this contaminating influence on the whole inner personality. We conclude, then, that the presence of this greed has been responsible for the fact that the inner structure of the personality is now (and perhaps always has been from infancy) an amorphous morass. So, according to the simile, the greed is equivalent to the activity of the ichneumon fly, with this difference: that, so to speak, the greed itself also liquifies.

When a psychoanalyst, psychotherapist, or mental health professional is treating a patient who is narcissistic, he will be able to identify the signs of this inner jelly. I have already given some signs, but there are others—for instance, when a patient complains that he or she is being exploited by another or others and seems to be unable to do anything to combat this. It is a sign that there is no centre of action within the personality. Once these signs are sufficiently convincing, he or she can make the diagnosis that the inner parts are jelly-like. In ordinary life, when you see someone who can never speak up for himself, it is a sign that there is a gelatinous mass within.

The job for a clinician assisting someone in this state is to wrest shapes out of the "formless infinite"; but if it is the presence of greed, together with envy and jealousy, that is responsible for this gelatinous mass, then the first forms that have to be "surfaced" from it are those responsible for maintaining it: greed, envy, and jealousy. It can be observed with an assured constancy that once one of these "forms" is wrested from the morass, a potent ego begins to take shape. As soon as this happens, a person will begin to speak of incidents in which she or he was able to manage an emotional event in a way that was not possible before. (I give more examples of this in Chapter 21; here they would lead the reader away from the descriptive thread of the argument being presented.)

Therefore, as greed, envy, and jealousy are exhumed out of the substance, so creative, courageous, and loving acts begin to occur. The person becomes the potent author of his own behaviour. We make, then, the retrospective inference that greed, envy, and jealousy are the hidden agents that keep the psychic reality in an amorphous, jelly-like state.

It would be a bad mistake, however, to draw the conclusion from this that envy, jealousy, and greed are the cause of this aspect of the narcissistic condition. Why these three destructive agents are there needs deeper investigation. We need to consider that when in an analysis these "forms" have been seen, named, and surrounded with a permeable barrier, then, although they are still active, they no longer poison the personality, reducing it to a gelatinous mess; on the contrary, they help to endow the personality with love, creativity, and emotional vigour. So the wresting of the form from the "formless infinite" has a beneficial effect on the personality not only because the rest of the personality is preserved from its poisoning contamination, but because once this form is in its "place" and not outside, it is able to play out its role as a member of the government of the personality. A country is being ruled by a greedy dictator. In a *coup d'état* he is overthrown, but the new administration installs him as Minister of Development and details his province of activity very exactly. He is a benefit to the new administration and no longer a handicap.

A person whose centre is gelatinous relates to people quite differently from one whose centre is *structured in shapes*. The "gelatinous type" merges with his/her intimates. Two "jellies" merge and mix together, each controlled by the other. She or he cannot disentangle from the other while at the same time hating the other. John and Mary are merged, and this limits the freedom of each; for this reason John hates Mary and Mary hates John, each believing the other to be responsible for their imprisoning chains. This merging can only occur with another individual who also is in the same condition, whereas two people who are "structured in shapes" relate freely to one another.

This jelly-like morass at the centre is responsible for an obediential surrender to gods outside. To the extent to which someone is narcissistic, he or she ingests the views of others. The person can internalize these thoughts and talk "intelligently" but is quite unable to generate thoughts him- or herself. Such people frequently become "executors" of other thinkers and the authentic interpreters of their hero. In the same way they frequently follow the current fashions of thought and make ample use of all the "buzz" words, but they do not think for themselves.

There is another feature of this gelatinous morass. As the inner constituents are formless, so they interpenetrate. For instance, envy, jealousy, and greed interpenetrate, as do also god and these poisonous three as well as god and the devil. In the gelatinous state these all interpenetrate, and this interpenetration of the different parts I call the "principle of inclusion".

Because these three sources of action—greed, envy, and jealousy—interpenetrate, it is a mistake to consider that any one exists without the other two. We are really speaking of one entity that is defined differently according to the subjective experience of an outer figure. I believe that it is a clinical error therefore to consider any one of these three to the exclusion of the other two. It is a certain principle that where one is, so are the other two. The three are one entity seen from different perspectives. It is more appropriate, then, to refer to these three in their joint inner activity as *liquifier* or *liquifiers*. I shall refer to them as *liquifiers* when considering the gelatinous consequence of their activity. However, the superordinate term is *intensifier*. The *intensifier* liquifies in one direction and petrifies in the other.

As the topic of this chapter is the jelly, it is the liquifying factor that is engaging our attention, but this is subordinate to the intensification function where the jelly is kept gelatinous and the crust is kept petrified. In fact, the stronger the *intensifier*, the more gelatinous is the jelly and the more solid the crust.

The *liquifiers* are three modes of action of the *liquifier*. They can be thought of as envy, jealousy, and greed, but their activity needs to be understood and their essential unity comprehended. There is a common denominator that unifies the goal of their activity. This seems the best place to elucidate these three modes of activity. We take it as unquestionable that *envy* is destructive to the personality. We need to examine what occurs between the subject who envies and the envied object to see how it is self-destructive. There is an exchange whereby the subject evacuates his good qualities upon the object and introjects the bad qualities.[1] This dual process, whose consequence is an inability to know good qualities in the self, is what we call "envy". This projection of the person's own capacities into the envied person prevents the emergence of confidence and the ability to create because this rests upon the good inside himself, which has been expelled outside. The second act of the drama is where hated parts of the self are then expelled into god, the idealized object.[2] This usually brings about retaliation and bitterness from the object.

The second facet of the *liquifier* corresponds to what is known as greed. In this case there is an exchange where good and bad are introjected and the good within is smothered. This introjection

---

[1] This process has been described by Fairbairn, but I believe he has misunderstood the motivating principle. It is part of the process of envy and not undertaken in order that the individual should have the comforting feeling that he is in a world ruled by god. What initiates this procedure is a trauma, usually an infantile one.

[2] This second act of the drama is what has been described by Melanie Klein.

occurs with such violence that the boundaries between the self and other are disrupted. In the case of both envy and greed it is the totality of the operation that constitutes its self-destructive quality. So, for instance, the "good" is only so to the extent to which it serves to enhance the individual's own psychological being. What is good for one is not so for another. The result of this exchange ruled by greed is that the individual's own good is crushed under the weight of what has been imploded into the personality. We see then that truly the good and bad are defined not according to some preconceived static quality, but, rather, by the intensity of the projective and introjective processes.

The third facet of the *liquifier* corresponds to jealousy. In the formulation of envy and greed it is supposed that there are just two poles—the subject and the object—but in fact there is always a "third". Jealousy simply obliterates the third term. This obliteration of the third term operates in concert with the greed and envy. The processes of the latter two would not reach their intensity unless, as it were, they had the collaboration of their partner, jealousy, and this also would not be such a total obliteration if it were not working in concert with greed and envy. The jealousy acting in concert with the other two serves to keep out the third term, to prevent space of any kind.

It is the intensity of these three processes—introjection, projection, and obliteration—that liquifies the inner faculties and makes the inner personality into a jelly.

In Chapter 14 I describe how I think these *liquifiers* have come to be present in the personality. When I say that the inner personality is liquified, this means that the *liquifiers* dissolve all emotions into the gelatinous substance. So, the sadness and disappointment that constitutes the soul of the traumatic happening become spread through the jelly and have there a form that may be described as *depression, passivity,* or *melancholia.* The presence of these conditions tells the clinical observer that there has been a traumatic disappointment in childhood.

This gelatinous substance at the centre of the personality is an invariable constituent of the narcissistic personality. However, it cannot be considered on its own. It is one part of the structure of narcissism. It is surrounded by a rigid outer shell and this is partly fashioned by god, which we consider in Chapter 9.

I have referred earlier to the image of the personality being broken into bits. A patient said to me in the consultation:

"I am just a lot of bits inside."

I have also used the image of a gelatinous mass. It is possible to combine these two images by thinking of a jelly that holds small bits and fragments in suspension. It is these bits that are the source of action. It is a mistake to think that because there is a jelly inside, the individual is inactive. These bits in suspension or the crust, in whichever way it is conceptualized, are the agents of an intense activity. They stir an outer figure into rousing the individual into action. These agents in the jelly lead others to advise, bully, or exploit the individual. It often stimulates the clinician into "encouraging" the patient rather than elucidating the process. As has been said, the individual who is himself in a similar condition is thereby susceptible to the activity of these "bits in suspension".

A way of conceptualizing the state of the self when subjected to the corrosive action of the *liquifiers* is simply to say that it is dead. The incorrect aspect of this is that it is capable of coming to life. The creative self is crushed under the weight of god's power. Better than dead is the image of a dry seed awaiting fertilization.

As has been referred to in Chapter 5, the jelly is always accompanied by *uncreated projective action*, the source of which lies in ego fragments distributed through the jelly and the channel through which the projective action takes place being especially the eyes and, in a subsidiary way, through gesture, gait, tone of voice, and words used as objects.

I said at the beginning that the jelly-like state could be conceptualized as a gelatinous state held together by a surrounding line like a membrane. However, this is not correct, because the boundary between the self and the other is like a fence dividing sheep from cattle that has been blown down in a storm, and the two groups are all mixed up. The storm is the violent projections and introjections that totally disrupt the dividing membrane between self and other. Parts of the self are out in other people, and parts of other people are sitting in the self like alien bodies. Therefore the whole entity is membrane-less. So, although in one way the sense of a very rigid individual is one with a harsh membrane, yet his membrane is in a disintegrated state.

# CHAPTER NINE

# God

> We know existence by participating in it. This participation is
> action. When we expend energy to realize an intention we meet
> a resistance which both supports and limits us, and know that
> we exist and that the Other exists, and that our existence
> depends upon the existence of the Other. Existence then is the
> primary datum. But this existence is not my own existence as an
> isolated self. If it were, then the existence of any Other would
> have to be proved, and it could not be proved. What is given is
> the existence of a world in which we participate—which
> sustains and in sustaining limits our wills.
>
> John Macmurray, *Persons in Relation* (1961, p. 17)

God is part of the narcissistic personality. One manifestation of this is very familiar. We all know of this kind of
remark:

"Trouble with Jim is he thinks the sun shines out of his arse."

This is the case where the individual has, by thrusting his spirit
into god, become god, and although it is written in neon lights in

all his or her behaviour and is talked about by others, yet the person is unaware of it. Those who are intimate with such a person are very fearful of criticizing anything that issues forth from his or her mouth: it is the mouth of a vengeful god. Such a person exercises a tyranny on those around him or her. There are numerous variations of character that can be associated with this. The person may be aggressive and uncouth or be someone with the greatest charm, but whichever it is, these characteristics are put to the service of god. A man was humorous and good Company, but an observer noticed that his wife agreed with all his views even when they were detrimental to women, his four children were all very demure, and a colleague at work said that his work-mates were all frightened of him.

There is another type of narcissistic person who is also ruled by god, but she or he does not appear in that light. It is the person who is shy and inhibited and shows no signs of being godlike. In this case, the god within has been expelled into figures outside, who reign supreme on a pedestal. The inhibited individual then defers to god reigning on his throne *in* another.

These two different ways of dealing with god lead to very different character types, viewed externally, but internally there is a central characteristic that is the same: it is that with both types it is god who rules and determines not only the behaviour of the individual but also the theories this person espouses and his or her attitudes to religion, politics, science, or art. Those who live at close quarters with the shy and inhibited person experience him or her as just as tyrannical as the one who has placed himself in god. In each case, the outer clothing is very different, but the inner motivating principle is the same. Because the shy and inhibited type tends to run him or herself down, some analysts have named their condition "negative narcissism" or "anti-narcissism" (Bollas, 1989, pp. 159ff), but this designation is not a good one because it implies that true narcissism only exists in the type of person who has identified with god and that the inhibited person is the opposite. This is not so, for negativity is a component of both types. The difference, then, is between a god who reigns and has taken possession within and a god who reigns without, but even here, as suggested above, it is only a matter of superficial appearances. The person who "thinks the sun shines out of his arse" is also ruled and possessed, but from without. Very often, for instance, the bombastic pleased with self—man or woman—has a timid spouse, and outsiders wonder at such a marriage; in fact, the bombastic one is ruled secretly by the timid one. So therefore this distinction is one based on superficial observation. However, as it is a distinction canonized by language—for example, bombastic/timid; arrogant/shy, and so on—I suggest that we designate the two types with the common words "shy" and "arrogant". So we have arrogant narcissists and shy narcissists, both of whom are ruled by god. In both cases the godhead is concealed from the possessor's awareness, but in the arrogant one it is clearly seen by those outside, whereas in the shy one it is not seen, but the two are usually attached to each other.

What is it that determines whether the god is expelled or identified with? I think one has to posit that hatred is the motivating principle behind both acts. The person who identifies with god has done so on the basis of what Freud called "hostile identification". Because the identifying act is driven by hatred, the whole person is ruled by god. There is knowledge but, as long as the rule by god is total, there is no awareness. In the "shy" narcissist, god is expelled and the sane self is subservient to it; in the "arrogant" narcissist, the sane self is also subservient to god, but the god reigns within the personality and his domain extends outside it. In the latter, the creative self is crushed from inside; in the former, it is crushed from outside. Hatred is one motivating principle; the other is concealing god from oneself. In fact, hatred and concealing are one, because the hating act does conceal. The overall motive, then, is concealing godhead from oneself. But why are there these two different paths?—It is the fashioning of two sexes that are attracted to one another. It is that a fashioning has to occur such that you have two different psychic narcissistic "sexes" that are attracted to one another. A marriage of this sort is destructive. It produces shit rather than babies. Such marriages can be either actual sexual marriages between man and woman—or man and man or woman and woman—or between a dictator and his mob. Erich Fromm, in *Fear of Freedom* (1960), describes the way Hitler held sway over a youthful group suffering from *anomie*. This was such a marriage. Such a marriage also existed between Mao Zedong and his slave population, and between the Ayatollah Khomeini and the Iranian masses.

There is a division of narcissism into these two types, in order that these social marriages can take place. These marriages are extremely destructive to the human race. I do not know the reason why one individual chooses the "shy" path and another the "arrogant" one. We could speculate that it is probably determined by triggers that occur in early stages of life, but what there are is unclear. Probably when the inner decision to take the narcissistic option is made then at the same time the person opts for one of these two and remains fixed in that role. What is certain is that any coming together on that basis is destructive and produces shit rather than babies. The only way it alters is if narcissism is reversed.

God never exists as a detached mental reality; god is always *embodied* in a figure, in figures, or in institutions. In the arrogant narcissist god is embodied in the person himself, whereas in shy narcissism god is embodied in outer figures. This embodiment is always in a corporate personality. If it is embodied in an individual, then that individual is perceived as merged with the categories to which she or he belongs—whether it be lawyer, Frenchman, man, woman, politician, or artist. The narcissistic person perceives the individual not as a person but as a category entity. So the god in the personality coalesces individuals into group entities. Men are coalesced into one reality; a doctor is coalesced into all other doctors, so that one is not differentiated from another; academics are all coalesced; and so on. This psychological function is articulated in Durkheim's view that the social group is symbolized and embodied in "god". The more deeply the person is embedded in narcissistic currents, the more fundamental the coalescence. Slight narcissism will coalesce all doctors, medium narcissism will coalesce all men, severe narcissism will coalesce all living things. The objects in which God is embodied can be thought of as "narcissistic objects" (see chapter 21).

Through the narcissistic currents a person is merged with god. The subjective experience is that the person is swelled up by the god, and he or she derives his or her sense of self-esteem through being thus merged, but it is a precarious state of affairs and the individual frequently complains of feeling phoney. The god is often located in a status position. It may be in *being* a doctor, a lawyer, a member of parliament, a psychoanalyst, or an architect.

However, it is also frequently located in any identity type—a homosexual, a criminal, a husband, a wife, a father or mother—or in a group identity such as a Catholic, a Jew, an Englishman, working-class, and so on. A sense of pride derives from the state of being thus merged with god located in any of these identities. Analysing such a character type invariably reveals a depleted inner world. Being merged with god is a palliative for the inner destitution. This merging of the narcissistic individual with the group is the link between individual and group psychology, but it is social coherence bought at a heavy price. A society based on such psychological principles is an unhealthy one.

Loyalty is the individual's emotional obedience to the embodied god and always demands self-sacrifice. One of the greatest moral dilemmas is the point at which such self-sacrifice so damages the individual as to be contraindicated. The general social welfare is enhanced by the presence of a fulfilled personality within it. The answer must lie in this: that if the sacrifice is to god, then it crushes the person; if it is a giving to a person or persons, then it is mutually enhancing.

It is necessary to realize that there is a difference between practical perception and emotional perception. Someone with a god within such as I have described will from a practical point of view perceive that Dr Johnson is a different person from Dr Garibaldi, but emotionally they are coalesced under the category "doctor". "Doctors" are one homogenized group emotionally, but they are recognized as individuals practically. An understanding of these two forms of perception is crucial if the communications of those in whom narcissistic processes are operating are to be correctly interpreted. I differentiate here between "individual" and "person": the former is a figure whose personhood is buried in god, and the latter is one who is the creative author of his own enterprises.

The common denominator is that the person is obliterated both in the narcissistic individual and in those whom she or he perceives. This is because the other is always perceived as equivalent to the self when the "narcissistic constellation" holds sway.

In each of these cases the creative or sane self has been crushed by an inner act. In each case it has been an act of submission to god. In the arrogant one we called this act "identification", and in the "shy" one we called it "expulsion". This aspect determines where the god is placed, but the crucial act in both cases is the "submission" of the creative self. This is the self that is able to initiate action, that is able to be "subject of his own powers", to borrow a phrase of Erich Fromm; it is the self that is able sanely to assess the situation. This is crushed.

You will begin to see a connection here between the *liquifiers* and this act of submission. In Chapter 8 we saw that the whole inner personality was ruled by the poisonous activity of the *liquifiers*. So there seems to be some parity between the act of submission to the god and the passive renunciation to the poisonous three of the sane person. We can make some sense of this if the "*principle of inclusion*" is taken into account. In other words, there is an identification between god and the "poisonous three". God is envious, god is jealous, and god is greedy. Let us look to see how this manifests itself.

*God is envious.* A man was teaching his student philosophy. The pupil had just reached a stage where he grasped Husserl's theory of "categorical intuition", which was bringing a flood of understanding, and at that moment he insulted his teacher and said that he had deliberately not taught him this theory of Husserl because he wanted to keep him in an inferior position. The teacher became furious and said that he would not teach his pupil any more. The pupil then got into a sour rage and gave up studying philosophy altogether. The creative seed that was just beginning to bloom was irrevocably crushed. This was envy in action. I have said elsewhere (Symington, 1986, pp. 108–109) that it can be extremely difficult to become aware of a transference but particularly of one that is as violent and powerful as this. To realize that a patient experiences me as a cruel and powerful god filled with vitriolic envy is not comforting. A patient hid all her past creative achievements from me. It was because she knew with a dogmatic faith that I would savagely wreak retribution upon her. Her fear of me paralysed her entirely. That I was god I was able to deduce from various clues. She frequently reported being exploited by others. I inferred that this was because she was in obediential surrender to them. I knew then that this was god embodied in them and in me. She also was inhibited in relation to me. She could not ask me for a change of time, she paid me before receiving my bill, she quickly agreed with all that I said, and so on. I inferred that I was god filled with envy, jealousy, and greed. When it emerged that she had written a book but had concealed the fact from me, I said:

"I have written books. I am the best writer in the Southern Hemisphere. This book you have written is utter rubbish. Don't let me ever hear you boasting about it again."

There was a substantial pause, and then she said:

"When you were talking I was terrified. That is exactly my belief. I now realize that you were making an interpretation. I begin to think I may be able to talk to you for the first time."

*God is jealous.* The mother of a young woman had three sisters. The mother kept ordering her to go and visit this sister, to write a letter to another sister, to ring up a third, and so on. The young woman felt in rebellion against her mother's imperious orders. Because she so hated her mother, she would do the opposite of what her mother demanded. The result was that she was cut off entirely from her three aunts. So in truth the god is jealous and keeps the young woman clasped to himself. Or is it herself? Here god is feminine. The situation here is that the powerful goddess within is hated and expelled into her mother.

*God is greedy.* I said in my previous book on narcissism (Symington, 1993, e.g., pp. 34–36) that the essence of narcissism lies in a refusal of the *life-giver*. So also the destructiveness of the *liquifiers* lies in passionate refusal. In the case of greed, it lies in a refusal of love to the self. The sign that this love is being refused is that there is an intense appetite for tangible goods: food, money, prestige, and power. So a man who had a passion for power was the same man who refused to receive interpretations from a psychoanalyst whom he was seeing for treatment of depression.

There is another version of this greed. It is the individual who is extremely ascetic in her eating and drinking habits, and so, she says to herself, she is definitely not greedy and in fact hates greed, but she is enormously greedy for "spiritual" goods. She cannot miss out on any conference, she cannot refuse any offer to give a lecture, every new book that is mentioned has to be read. . . .

Another common symptom of this greed is seen when an institution puts on some event that is very successful, and immediately, rather than savouring the experience, another similar event is planned. Greed is not discriminating. A woman decided to have an analysis. She wanted to read everything the analyst had written, go to every possible lecture that he gave, and attend all the workshops that he conducted. After some of this she came to the realization that there was just one thing that she wanted: his understanding of her inner emotional state. When she came to realize this, she no longer wanted all the other things. Many people with great potential are destroyed through spreading themselves "too thin".

You can see here the point referred to in Chapter 8: the interpenetration of these different elements. So the refusal of interpretations might be read as envy but if seen as coupled with passion for power as a compensation, then these two interpenetrate, and in fact we can see that the "poisonous trio" are one reality.

Because of the *"principle of inclusion"* we find that people in submission to god are also subject to the "poisonous trio". This accounts for the way in which an individual is ruled or driven by one of the "poisonous trio". A telltale sign of this submission are remarks such as these:

"I just did what I was told."

This was a common line of defence by the Nazis responsible for the management of the concentration camps. But the same sentiment is frequently expressed by "shy narcissists":

"I thought it was better not to argue with him and just do what he wanted."

It is very common for someone to speak in this way when he or she has gone along with destructive or self-destructive behaviour. It is a safe principle that the adoption of a passive attitude is indicative of guilt. When someone is guided by the outer figure to whom they are in submission, their conscience is obliterated.

God is the expeller in the personality. God is the perpetrator of magic. A very common scene is one where a patient has been struggling with jealousy, and he gets some evidence of improvement and then tells himself

"Oh, good, I've got rid of it now. . ."

Through this magic incantation he gets rid of it—or so he believes. He gets rid of it into jealous behaviour around, and the projection has the effect of magnifying so that the outer person is jealous to the core. The effect on his own personality is to make him more jelly-like inside and stiffer and more rigid on the outside. There are many other ways in which god, as agent, manages situations. By being ritually punctual, someone believes he magically controls what occurs and protects himself from feeling the impact of events upon him. God is the agent through which psychic realities are magically swept away. As has been said, they are not truly swept away but continue to exist in a different form, but they do not exist as a feeling. So, for instance, a woman whose husband died when she was in her forties did not weep at the funeral but became a recluse. God magically prevented her from feeling but trans-formed the grief into a form whose language was withdrawal from social contact. When a storm got up on the Sea of Galilee, Jesus rose up, spoke a word of command, and the storm subsided. God in the personality acts like this. He magically gets rid of pain, of jealousy, of anger within and expels them into the embodied god in relation to which the person lives in a stifled paralysis.

The *narcissistic pattern* has the effect of dispersing good objects within the personality so that they are impotent or ineffective. We have seen how the *liquifiers* disperse all the emotions into the gelatinous substance; at the same time god is the agent whose hatred of the *liquifiers* expels them into outer figures or into the body. A man criticized his analyst, and a moment later he had a searing headache: a punishment that his god/analyst visited upon him. When the analyst explained why he believed this had just occurred, the headache subsided.

The nature of god needs some exploration. God can be male; god can be female; god is single, yet god is many. However, the most important thing is to distinguish between god as revealed in Judaism, Christianity, and Islam and the god that is arrived at through rational reflection, as was achieved by the seers of the Upanishads in the East and by Spinoza in the West.

I think it is necessary to delineate further the difference be-tween the god revealed through the Judeo–Christian tradition and the god or Absolute arrived at through contemplative reflection. The Judeo–Christian god is an externalization of one component of the narcissistic structure. This is a god that gets in the way of two people coming to know each other; a god who interferes with my thinking; a god who demands that I follow his instructions; a god who punishes me if I think for myself, who sanctions my sadism, encourages my masochism, hates my greed, my envy, and my jealousy, and so expels them into figures in the environment. It is a god who possesses me but despises me; a god who solves problems by obliterating them.

This portrait of god can be culled from the Bible, the Torah, or the Koran. Embodied in these ancient texts are aspects of this god that I have been trying to describe. There are also aspects that characterize the god of Spinoza, but these are embedded in the protoplasm of a narcissistic god. This cultural expression is manifest in the psychology of the individual. I can find in myself and in my patients traces of this god. This god is a narcissistic object seen from one particular angle. The narcissistic object is many-faceted, and it is a part of the self that has been expelled and embodied in a figure or figures outside. The outer figure is then enveloped by this part of the self. Bion describes how small particles that penetrate and encyst the object are expelled:

> Each particle is felt to consist of a real object which is encapsulated in a piece of personality that has engulfed it. [Bion, 1967b, pp. 47–48]

The first thing we infer is that this god is present in the personality as a potential for embodiment. This god never exists as a spiritual reality but always as a god incarnate in a particular person or institution. The prophets whose sayings are recorded in the Old Testament continually chided Israel for chasing after false gods:

> Every goldsmith is put to shame by his idols;
> For his images are false, and there is no breath in them.
> They are worthless, a work of delusion. [Jeremiah, 10:14–15]

False gods were gods embodied in statues, trees, rocks, or rivers: a type of religious belief known as *animism*. The prophets attacked this form of worship unmercifully. The ferocity of their attack is a hint that Yahweh himself also has elements of this embodiment. So the god, as part of the narcissistic structure, is always an embodied god. But how does the embodiment take place? The answer is that the figure or institution has to be a willing host for such an embodiment. The host, then, has to demonstrate one of the elements of the narcissistic structure. Going back to Bion, it is that something is projected, and the object—in this case the person—swells up, becoming an embodied god. The object that swells up in this way has some characteristics that pertain to that which is projected. I am going now to sketch just one correlate of the god. God and this correlate are just two elements of the narcissistic structure, though under the "principle of inclusion"[1] they are one reality with two manifestations.

The first of these is that the god figure within is hurt by the slightest criticism or neglect. It is typified when I am deeply wounded by the smallest slight and nurse this injury down the years. A man met a friend who said to him:

"Good Lord, John, you are looking well today. When I saw you last week, I thought you were a bit off-colour . . ."

He was deeply offended that his friend should have said that he had been off-colour. "Me . . . off colour" . . . what an insult! He was so insulted by it that it entirely wiped out the encouraging statement that he was looking well on this particular day.

I remember an occasion when a friend of mine asked a Spaniard to carry a letter for him from England to a friend in Spain, whither the Spaniard was travelling. It used to be a gentlemanly custom in Spain that if you asked someone to deliver a letter by hand, it was bad manners to seal the envelope. My English friend, not well up on this piece of Iberian etiquette, sealed the envelope. The Spaniard was deeply insulted and would not talk to my English friend again.

The other aspect, already adumbrated, is that the wound is tended and nursed as though it were the greatest treasure. A psychoanalyst, Mr A, said to Analyst, Mr B:

"Oh, you were analysed by Hanns Sachs, were you . . ."

and then, looking down his nose, said:

"You know I was analysed by Freud."

---

[1]The "principle of inclusion" states that two psychic elements are one and the same but with two manifestations, or it can be conceptualized that one is contained in the other.

Analyst B was still offended thirty years later and took revenge on Analyst A quite regularly year after year.

The hurt only makes sense if you put in the idea of a godlike ego:

> "Do you not realize that you are insulting a royal personage? Did you not know that you are insulting the King Himself?"

So the extreme sensitivity to self-hurt and godhead are included in one another and are therefore an instance of the "principle of inclusion". Such a person lives in a very restricted world. Because of the "principle of reciprocity", he believes that others are equally hurt and offended with the result that he cannot say what he thinks and feels, can never "let his hair down", and has to live in his own infertile world.

I think that what I have been describing would be formulated by a psychoanalyst as a split-off part of the self taking possession of the whole personality. It occurs because in the narcissistic part of the personality a wound has been incurred and the god arises because, having sustained an infinite insult, it thereby takes over the personality. The rest of the personality is utterly crushed by this overpowering god, who is antipathetic to thought. An example comes to mind from an incident that a colleague described:

> The analyst had a moment of deep empathic understanding of this woman's deprived childhood. She conveyed this to the patient, and there were a few moments of emotional "togetherness" of a deep kind. Then the cruel event occurred: the session, like an insensate executioner, came to an abrupt end. The woman was hurt to the quick. The next day she would not come into the consulting-room; she declared with emphatic certainty that there were hidden microphones in the room, and no rational argument could dissuade her from her conviction. An irrational god had taken over.

The god I have been trying to describe I call a "false god" in that it deceives the believer into trusting his dictates. He believes passionately in what the god directs. As I have tried to illustrate, this passionate belief cannot be shaken with reason, but it is more than that. The presence of this god precludes the possibility of thought.

It is intrinsically antagonistic to thought. The inner correlate of the god is the gelatinous psyche with no source of action within and therefore submissive to the god. There is no option other than to capitulate in total submission. The god and the gelatinous substance are two parts of an interlocking system. So the action and speech of a person dominated by such a system is false in another sense: that what is said does not represent the thought of a person. It is a pretend person standing in for a person who could be there but isn't. This is the false god that exists in individuals governed by narcissism; it is also the god that rules all religious observances of a primitive or superstitious kind.

The situation can be either polytheistic or monotheistic. Sometimes there are many bits in the personality exerting an influence, but at certain moments they coalesce, and then we have monotheism.

Now to consider again the true god. This is a god who is grasped through a supreme effort of thought—a god who is a triumph of the thinking process. Traces of this god can be found in Judaism, in Christianity, and in Islam, but it is largely overshadowed by the false god. The true god is reached through a deep and sustained reflection on the nature of reality. In our Western tradition the philosopher who best represents this endeavour has been Spinoza. It can also be found in Kierkegaard, but it needs to be separated out in him from the false god, which is disseminated through much of his writing. In the East the seers who are responsible for the school of thinking that produced the Upanishads showed the first and deepest understanding of what I refer to as the True God.[2] God is not a term that is ever used by these seers— they use terms like the THAT, the Absolute, the Truth, or just Reality. Wilfred Bion called this same Reality O. Through contemplative thought these seers came to understand the absolute character of existence. They also understood that reality is contingent. How these two can coexist is baffling to the mind because they are mutually contradictory. Parmenides ran into this problem when he said that all change is illusion. If reality is absolute, then how

---

[2]The True God is also found in the writings of the mystics in all the traditional religions.

can there be change? Parmenides, determined that the human mind should not be declared inadequate to any reasoning task, declared that because reality is absolute and because change is incompatible with absoluteness then change must be an illusion. Yet common sense declares that change does occur in our world. Aristotle believed that he had solved this problem by saying that reality existed in two modes: pure act and potency. By pure act Aristotle meant what the Seers of the Upanishads meant by the THAT or the Absolute. Potency meant a state of being capable of coming to Absoluteness. However, although Aristotle believed that he had solved this problem, yet he had not. He had given an account of the two horns of the dilemma and refused to deny either aspect, but he had not solved the problem.

We are confronted with the problem that our minds are not capable of grasping this conceptually. Kant emphasized the limitations of our minds. We do not have the categories necessary to be able to grasp the problem. The progress of evolution may enable our progeny millions of years hence to be able to solve this problem. What we need to acknowledge is that the human mind meets here a limitation rather than trying to deny either the absoluteness or the contingency or changeability of reality.

This absoluteness is arrived at through rational reflection and requires mental discipline and virtue to achieve it. When I say virtue, it implies that a moral dimension is necessary to achieve it. The moral and emotional are inseparable entities, and this domain is necessary to arrive at understanding. It is entirely different from the revelation of the Judeo–Christian–Islamic god, which is through an ecstatic experience directly or by faith and tradition. The Absoluteness of Being is grasped through a personal act of insight. It means that there is a grasp of the Absolute that is in stark contrast to the god who reveals himself through ecstatic communication. In the latter the god shall not be known—you shall not even pronounce his name. Although concentrated mental attention and emotional purification are necessary to achieve comprehension of the Absolute, there is no experience here of a being outside myself calling me to obedience, submission, or discipleship, because I am the Absolute.

You may ask whether this has any relevance to clinical work. I believe it does. I approach it in this way. The seers of the

Upanishads realized the Absoluteness of Being, *and* they partici-
pated in it. Their realization that they were part of it—or, rather,
they were IT—turned it from being a philosophical truth into a
religious one. It becomes religious at the point at which my own
being is challenged to act according to the understanding. In other
words, it rendered a piece of knowledge about their own selves,
which invited the self to action. Realization about the Absoluteness
of the self *necessarily* has a consequence. I say "necessarily" because the necessary is the essential attribute of the Absolute. This
realization led the Buddha, who traced the emotional consequences of this realization, to stress that attachment to what is
contingent, to what is passing, is to ignore the central character of
our being. It is worth noting, however, that the Buddha also recognized that to ignore or despise the contingent nature of our being
was to enact in the religious–moral domain what Parmenides conceptualized philosophically. The famous "middle way" of the Buddha is notoriously difficult to achieve. It requires us both to realize
the limitations of our minds and at the same time as to think
continually.

So the Absoluteness of Being is a truth arrived at through reflection. It is the product of thought. The thinking process has
produced an intuition that penetrates through into the nature of
Being. It is an insight that is grounded in rational processes. I call
the Absolute the true god; I call the god revealed in the religions of
Judaism, Christianity, and Islam a false god or, rather, a god who
is a mixture of the true and the false. Within this religious tradition
it has been the role of mystics to purify the revealed god of its
anthropomorphic accretions. Due to the fact that they bear a loyalty to their religious cult, they only achieve it on the basis of a
split.

\* \* \*

The false god is part of the narcissistic system. Other elements in
that system are a denigrated object, a state of being merged with
the embodied god, a paranoia towards the embodied god, the
psyche in a jelly-like state, and an absence of creative capacity. As
Bion (1967a) says in his paper, "On Arrogance", this set-up is the
living remains of a primitive catastrophe.

I referred to the effect of this godly activity within the personality at the beginning. The concept of *embodiment* is central to understanding the effects. There is no thinking process within the personality but only the appearance of such. There is substituted for it the embodiment of the thoughts of the god. The god is embodied within, and his or her thoughts are incorporated in the act of embodiment. The embodied god is frequently a person, though it can also be an institution. Due to *coalescence*, person and institution are also frequently fused. The individual in whom this narcissistic structure is operating is, then, in submissive identification with the god. Through this identification the thoughts and thinking processes of the god are understood, and yet there is always distortion. However, the most important aspect is that the creative capacity in the individual is crushed through this embodiment. It follows then that as all personal thinking is a creative activity, it is also crushed.

*   *   *

The realization of the true god in the personality is the product of an inner creative act. This is in contrast to the presence of the false god, which is through an act of submission in which the individual psyche is crushed. The realization of the true god lays a foundation in the personality for respect for the self.

I want to look at just two aspects of the true god: conscience and symbolism. Both of these are extremely relevant to clinical work. Let us take conscience first. Conscience is the subjective evidence of the Absolute aspect of our being. We feel conscience to be us yet not us. We experience it as inviting us. To follow conscience is a free act, not an obligation. Associated with the false god are words such as "driven", "obligated", or "compelled", whereas conscience is an invitation within the personality, and following conscience is a free act. The ontological truth that the Absolute is in the contingent finds its subjective realization in the free acceptance of the invitations of conscience. As the following of conscience is respecting the Absolute in which analyst and patient share, if I follow the promptings of conscience then it has to benefit both parties.

The Absolute is also relevant to the symbolical. I will start this topic thus:

A patient is covertly attacking the analyst, and the analyst points this out. He has made a transference interpretation. The question is, "Why?" Is the patient not free verbally to attack the analyst? What is the particular significance that makes the analyst decide to point this out to the patient?

We can find the answer to this question if we go back to our fundamental premise about the true god: I am IT, or THAT thou art. When the patient is subtly attacking the analyst, he is subtly attacking himself. In other words, what he is doing to the analyst is a symbol of what he is doing to himself. The purpose, then, of pointing out to him that he is subtly attacking the analyst is to bring him to an awareness of the way he is attacking himself. The other way of reaching this is to realize that his paranoia directed towards the analyst is a primitive hatred against his own submissive activity; it is the embodying activity, the making of a false god that is attacking himself. Then as one looks more closely at the self-damaging activity, it is possible to see the subtle ways in which he attacks his own thinking processes. In fact, it is mentality itself that has been severely damaged—to the extent to which the person is deprived of mentality. It has become so confused and embodied that it is difficult to see that there is a mentality there at all.

Symbolism is the name we give to that process whereby we recognize that an activity that is interpersonal, that is outer, represents what is inner. An ontological understanding of the Absolute tells us why this should be so. The true god then becomes not only the rational basis of symbolism, but also its creator. The false god, on the other hand, is the destroyer of symbolism, the destroyer of the inner, the destroyer of mind. Its subjective experience is of being under obedience to an embodied lawgiver.

Therefore it is the false god that is a component part of the narcissistic personality; the true god is the foundation of the healthy personality. An identifying feature of the false god is its sensory nature and that it can be represented in a sensible way. (We shall note again this sensory quality when considering the "flight of ideas" in Chapter 15.)

* * *

What are the elements that leads someone to generate this god? We may get a clue if we realize that god tells me what to do; god has no truck with thinking; god is impatient. One of the key elements here is *immediacy*. I want an answer straight away. I cannot tolerate any delay. Thinking, research, curiosity of mind are all very well, but I want to know *now*. So I fashion god. God will deliver straight away.

When I say "fashion god", I mean it. As we have seen, god is always embodied, but for that to happen the figure has to act according to the fashioning. A woman had her breast removed because of a cancerous tumour. She was terrified of dying. The oncologist told her that the chances of secondaries was no greater than for any other member of the population. Secondaries developed six months later, and two years after that she died. The oncologist's statement had lulled her into a state of false security. Why did he make such an ill-advised statement? The pressure put upon him to reassure her was enormous, and he succumbed. He would not have been aware of this. It may be a fact that once the primary has been removed, the chances of secondaries in that patient are as great as in any other person, though I doubt that very much.

So I want an immediate answer to my question because I am quaking with fear.

"Tell me quickly. I cannot bear the suspense . . ."

A woman said:

"I need you to be god because then you can give me an immediate answer."

So God is born in the personality out of intolerance of frustration, but this statement needs to be linked in the mind with the effects of trauma. These two, I believe, interpenetrate.

# CHAPTER TEN

# Acts of God

> I had simply acquired a new ability to perceive that my own self
> was merely a small part of one creation. And I no longer felt that
> whatever blame I bore was of enough importance to bring the
> concentrated forces of the universe to bear exclusively against
> me.
>
> Christopher Burney, *Solitary Confinement* (1952, p. 82)

God is present in the personality to the exact extent to which a natural self is absent. As has been said already, the god can only exist in an embodied form. The god's job, therefore, is to fashion such a body. It is like an army commander with no soldiers; to have power, he has to recruit an army; his power is only consolidated when he has achieved this recruitment. This analogy is not perfect. A better analogy might be this: a theory as to how the planets of the solar system formed is that swirling bits of matter accreted until a planet was fashioned. Only when considerable accretion has occurred is there a planet. Similarly, there is only a god when an embodiment has taken place. The start is in a godlike potential that is able to accrete to itself an embodiment of disciples. Therefore there has to be a god-forming activity. This begins in the evasion of pain, a surrender to instinct (instinct for survival), and in it is the need to persuade the external one into submission to its own nature; this is not a once-and-for-all happening. There is constant danger of the godhead collapsing, so recruitment has to go on all the time. It is like a dictator who has constantly to put out propaganda in praise of his regime, for he knows that if he doesn't, it will fall into disarray.

So the acts of god are all designed for maintaining the power of the godhead. This is their purpose, and therefore they are always consistent with a self-serving aim. As the acts are necessary to the existence of the godhead, there is always a desperateness about them and an urgency. The godhead's illusion is that if its power is not maintained, it will collapse in disarray. It is true that only by maintaining the illusion of power through reinforcement does the godhead stay in being.

This brings out an unexpected antinomy in the godhead. On the one side it is extremely powerful, on the other it is planted on foundations that are constantly disintegrating. It is like a crumbling building that needs buttresses from the outside to support it. So the god in the personality has to persuade both itself and others to adopt his propaganda and accept his view of matters.

The question here, though, is this: of what essentially does the god have to persuade both his subject and others?—that his activities are not self-destructive; that the best way of solving a problem is to obliterate reality; that short-term solutions are a must; that the surface and the sensual is reality in its entirety. In other words, it has to persuade the subject and others that he is not mad.

There is this special feature about madness: awareness of madness can be avoided as long as I can persuade another to my point of view.

### Activities are self-destructive

As I have said elsewhere (Symington, 1994), I follow the Socratic principle that it is not possible for a human being to do something self-destructive and know it at the same time. Therefore in order to do something self-destructive, it is necessary to destroy awareness of the act. A man had a great talent for graphic design and was awarded a scholarship that would have given him the opportunity to do post-graduate study and in all probability would have given him the chance to be employed with reasonable pay at a high level in a field that he found fulfilling. He refused it. However, if it had been as lucidly clear as that, then he would not have done so, because the refusal was a self-destructive act. So how did he obfuscate the issue? At the time he was approached by a head-hunting firm and asked to go on the board of a new computer firm that wanted some expertise in graphic design. So he passed up the scholarship and took the post on the board. He was young, and it gave him kudos, but it did not further his knowledge, which later he needed very much. Whereupon he recognized that this had been folly—that he had been acting for short-term aims.

A man thrust himself into the power of a woman who destroyed his career in the diplomatic service through making terrible *faux pas*. This was easy to see, but he was blinded to it by his sexual passion for her, which was overwhelmingly powerful.

A woman would attach herself to men who had some fatal flaw and become utterly beholden to them. She therefore suffered the effect on her of his flaw. She hid this from herself by believing on each occasion that she was devoting herself to the man out of love.

Another woman allowed all her creative qualities to be crushed by her dominant husband. She blinded herself to this by listening to friends' praises of him.

All these people who were engaged in self-destructive activities were blinded to them by the god in the personality. In this last case the woman would not have been blinded by friends praising her husband were it not for the god in her. The god feeds off these praises. As wife she feels they belong to her vicariously, and the god in her needs them. The jelly cannot exist without god. The woman who attached herself to men with some fatal flaw hid this from herself by believing she was a Florence Nightingale—this was the god that hid from her what she was doing emotionally to herself. In the case of the man in the diplomatic corps you might say that there is no evidence of a god in him but just sexual passion. It was the god in him that demanded and enflamed this passion. As it turned out in clinical research, he was naturally not very sexual at all. The man who passed up the scholarship was flattered by the offer to go on a board because of the god in him that needed such acclamation. The jelly that is god's underbelly has to have external flattery to survive by. Also, in all these cases god is in the service of immediacy. Immediate frustration is assuaged, but at the cost of long-term good for the personality.

## Reality is obliterated

The god persuades the personality to see things as they are wished to be. The god in a woman persuaded her that her mother was controlling and dominating and that she herself was tolerant and liberal. The reality was that she was herself extremely controlling, and her mother was much more tolerant than she was. To be successful in persuasion, the god acts in this way: it starts by expelling the controllingness into the mother's action pattern. This is shorthand for a more complex process that is worth describing. The god can only expel into an equivalent action pattern. The expulsion takes place at the moment when this woman's mother demonstrates controlling behaviour. The piece of reality that is present gives the woman conviction. The god obliterates the woman's inner reality and transfers it onto the person of the mother. Two pieces of reality are distorted: the woman's own inner reality is "cleansed" of controllingness, and the outer reality becomes the dustbin for the inner rubbish and is distorted thereby.

## Short-term solutions are a must

The god blinds the personality to the long term. It concentrates all attention on the present, to the exclusion both of the past and the long-term future. In a burst of sexual passion a diplomat gave up his career and his finer sensibilities for an exotic courtesan whom he encountered on a brief visit to Brazil. Shortly after he had resigned from the diplomatic service, his flame left him for another man. A woman excited by a lecture on aromatherapy bought a big chest of scents and potions in health stores and body shops, intending to set up an aromatherapy practice. She advertised for customers, read books and articles on it, but within three months all her interest in the project had faded.

If one thinks of time as a series of concentric circles going out-wards—to the north = future and to the south = past—god blots out all circles except the small one at the centre on which the subject is standing.


## Sensual and surface are the whole of reality

Also, it only brings sensual objects to the attention of the subject, cancelling out meaning and understanding. This is why words are experienced "concretely"—in other words, just the sounds, with-out the meaning behind them, so words become things. Distance in time, in depth, in meaning are all wiped out. One might postulate that empiricism and linguistic philosophy are the outcome of this godly activity.

# CHAPTER ELEVEN

# The quality of attachment

A characteristic of the narcissistic structure is its embodiment in outer objects. So, for instance, god is always an embodied god. The individual is stuck to this god with superglue. There is, then, a not-god part of the personality. It is not easy to see the not-god because it is submerged in god. However, it is important to realize that the not-god is the healthy part of the personality. It is not part of the narcissistic structure; rather, it is the healthy core of the personality being smothered by narcissism. The not-god is the Absolute in the personality. This may seem a paradoxical statement, but if viewed in the light of what was said in Chapter 1, it can be seen to make sense.[1]

This glue-like attachment is such that the outer figure becomes installed in the individual in such a way that the term "identification" becomes justified and is correct. The jelly takes on the im-

---

[1] It is important to note that this not-god, this Absolute in the personality, is not to be identified with what Winnicott designated the True Self. He derives the latter from Freud's id, and so it is something sensuous and true to the romantic tradition and therefore is itself part of the narcissistic structure.

print of the figure to whom the attachment takes place, but it is important to realize that, even in mimesis (see below), when someone has taken in the characteristics of another, it is not the imprint of a person. A person cannot be imprinted in this way; it can only occur through free choice (Chapter 3). The imprinted characteristics are either manifestations of an aspect of a person or are themselves the mimesis of an earlier figure. The glue-like attachment is to the characteristics as entities, and it is these that become imprinted upon the jelly.

We have to posit that the not-god is made up of particles of potential. The potential becomes actualized as the particles come together into a coherent pattern.

The attachment has the quality of being stuck. The sign that there is such an attachment is that the object to which the person is so attached is god. He enjoys supreme power. Someone's self-esteem and power derives from the god to whom he is bonded. However, it is a mistake to think that the attachment is to an individual person. God is embodied in a corporate entity in which individuals are coalesced. So, for instance, a man was attached to his analyst, his wife, his mother, and a close friend. In the absence of one, his attachment increased in relation to another, but the figure to whom he was attached was not differentiated from others in his mind. It was not attachment to a person but to an amorphous entity in whom god was embodied (Chapter 3). Although the attachment is to the corporate entity, the intensity increases or decreases in relation to one part rather than another according to where the persecuting stimulus is located. If I feel criticized by Point A of the corporate system, then I shall experience hatred and seek comfort in Point C of the system, and so on. The inner state that drives such an attachment is panic, though the person is not aware of the panic. Attachment of this sort is analogous to blindness. The object to which someone is attached is the figure leading the blind person. To be empty, fragmented, and with no autonomous centre generates panic. However, the prime factor that generates the panic is the presence within of the *intensifiers* that break up the mind in a continual series of attacks. These *petrify* and *liquify*. The panic is due to the knowledge of the presence of these *intensifiers* within. The terror is so great that it is not bearable.

Awareness of the panic arises only when the person is no longer terrorized by it. Panic is not conscious to the subject. Once it becomes conscious, it is no longer invested with the same terror. When it is conscious to the subject, it may not be apprehended by an observer—not even by an intimate. Panic, then, is the description of a state. Awareness of the panic indicates that the person is no longer in the grip of it. A woman described it thus:

> I was like someone on the running-board of a fast-moving train—just holding on with the fingers of one hand; terrified that I would be thrown off to my death at any moment."

When she described this state, it was already a past state of affairs. Wilfred Bion (1970, p. 19) describes the way someone can have pain but not suffer it. Yet it does exist prior to being experienced. Part of the drive to be *in* god, to be thus embodied, is to assuage pain, to assuage panic.

A woman's attachment to her analyst was intense and became buried *in* him. Her profession, her sexual partner, and her place of work and home all bore resemblances to her analyst. I referred to this phenomenon as *mimesis* (Symington, 1996), and it is characteristic of the narcissistic state. In this state of intense attachment the *intensifiers* are represented by figures outside the bonded couple (in this case of analyst and patient). In another female patient jealousy and envy were installed in her husband who raged at her in furious tirades. These tirades were generated by her treatment of him as a pitiful child. He became a jealous child and an envious one also. Another patient, a man, also became attached in this way. Others noticed that he even spoke like his analyst, and in this case also the jealousy, envy, and greed were installed in the wife. I think we can safely say, on the "principle of inclusion", that when one *intensifier* is present, then so also are the other two, although one may be more prominent. His wife, then, also got into rages, which again were promoted by a derivative of his intense attachment to his analyst, but it needs to be realized from what I have said above that this is because he has attached not from one person to another but rather from one part of a corporate entity to another, so that neither his wife nor his analyst are persons. Relation to a person requires a free creative act.

In fact, the personal centre is buried not directly in the other but in the god who is embodied in the analyst (or another figure). It is a feature of god/goddess that she or he dispels the *intensifiers* into outer figures. So another patient saw the analyst as a monster who was intensely possessive (jealous) and greedy and was therefore terrified of him. The deity is that part of the narcissistic structure responsible for the expulsion.

Clinical descriptions within psychoanalysis often refer to this glue-like attachment as "infantile dependence" or as the "infantile transference" or as simply as "the child". However, this is not adequate for what is meant here. The picture of the mother with the child at the breast does not convey the merged state of the emotional centre of the personality. A better image is of the little roo, an inch long, in the pouch of its mother. It is imprisoned in the pouch and would die if it were to fall out. The emotional centre of the personality is in a state like this. This image only covers one aspect of the set-up. It does not convey the human roo's hatred of the mother/analyst. The hatred is because the pouch is seen to inhibit its freedom. This, though, is not the reason. What imprisons the roo is the glue-like attachment. It is this attachment that prevents freedom; it is this that is hated but is hypostasized into the figure of the mother or analyst or some other figure. However, the person in this state believes that the freedom can only be bought by killing the analyst or the mother. In a marital relation it is often dealt with by divorce, usually following an affair by one or both partners.

Whenever there is a part of the self like the inch-long roo in the pouch, it is accompanied by a savage condemner. He is despised and sneered at. Very often the person acts in such a way as to invite scorn and hatred. Why the roo-in-the-pouch is always accompanied by such savage condemnation is mysterious. I think, however, that if we come back to our principle that everything that inhibits freedom is hated, then it makes sense because this tiny roo is attached to the pouch and is unable to get out. The pouch, then, is hated in the way that a prisoner hates the walls of the gaol that imprison him. The rationale of the condemner is like this:

"You filthy little parasite. If it wasn't for you clinging to the pouch, we could be free instead of being at the behest of a bloody pouch day-in and day-out . . ."

A psychoanalyst, psychotherapist, or psychiatrist is frequently the pouch and is hated, and the roo is condemned for its glue-like attachment. And the tiny roo admires the large encompassing pouch but also hates it because of its imprisoning grip.

* * *

All that has been said about the *intensifiers* and later about the Oedipus complex can be considered under this dimension of attachment. Greed is a clinging attachment to the material products of the maternal body; envy is hatred of the maternal body because it entraps; jealousy prevents a third dimension from releasing the self from this stuck/attached situation. Greed, envy and jealousy together make the maternal body into god. The reason for the fashioning of the god can be considered from the angle of greed and envy, acting in concert and from the perspective of jealousy. Envy endows the maternal body with its own good qualities, and greed supports this view, making what it wants into a good. Jealousy prevents the entry of the third dimension, which is the Absolute. The Absolute puts the subject, the object, and their relation into perspective. The Absolute is reached through an act of understanding.

This glue-like attachment prevents the maternal body from being seen in perspective—so it is just a breast to be exploited. There is no human face, because the person is seen as part of the breast. The subject is also just an "external" with no interior processes— also just a breast.

The emotional perception of self and other is that the other is god and the self is a worm. However, sometimes that perception is reversed, because in this dimension there is no separation between self and other.

## Images of attachment

I have already given the image of the roo in the pouch. An alternative image would be the foetus implanted upon the wall of the womb. This image or the roo in the pouch are much more apt than the baby at the breast. The latter image does not convey the stuck attachment. I believe that the image of the baby at the breast has misdirected clinicians towards a false set of interpretations.

Another image that derives from the implanted foetus is the baby in a bath of deep water, with its eyes glued onto mother's eyes as she prevents it from sinking. This image conveys the terror, and eyes glued to eyes is reminiscent of the foetus stuck to the wall of the womb. This can also be seen in many patients who fasten their eyes upon the analyst and, should the analyst look away or should his attention wander, immediately collapse. This phenomenon is interesting because the analyst's attention wanders because the patient's communications are dissociated from his emotional self. After this had been interpreted many times, a patient himself felt a force come and cut him off. In this particular case the overwhelming emotion was one of utter hopelessness, which was so unbearable that a force arose to cut him off from it. This utter hopelessness parallels the water that the baby is terrified of falling into. Amorphous hopelessness is one of the causes of panic. This emotional hopelessness can be thought of as the subjective experience of what I have called the jelly.

There is another perspective on this. Say a patient is seeing a psychoanalyst, psychotherapist, or psychiatrist, and she is distressed because he looks out of the window. It is a fine summer day, and the patient believes that he wants to be outside on the beach, having a swim. Let us further say that he has had just such a thought. We have, then, here a professional at work, but at the same time there is in him someone who would like to be on the beach. Here is someone in a state of conflict. The god in his personality would obliterate the someone who wants to be on the beach having a swim. But having two conflicting desires present in him is a state that typifies his personhood. If I were the patient, I would rather want to be with the professional who desires to go to the beach, who is a person, than with the one who is not. But why?— Because contact with a person is healing. Such a contact dispels the power of god, dissolves the glue; a responsible person takes over the management of the personality.

## Paranoia

This glue-like attachment is accompanied by an intense hatred that is felt to be towards the imprisoning object, whereas in fact it is towards the glue-like attachment, because it is this that imprisons the individual and prevents the enjoyment of freedom. But it is a principle that hatred is always displaced from the agent's activity onto an object (see "the principle of hypostasization", Chapter 18 and Appendix). Paranoia is, in fact, the psychiatric word whose translation into layman's language would be "primitive or intense hatred". The idea of the foetus that attaches itself with vampire-like aggression to the wall of the womb has been convincingly developed by Ployé (1986).

It is, I believe, this violent hatred towards the glue-like attachment that prevents integration. It is necessary to realize that, according to the "principle of inclusion", the *intensifiers* are components of the glue-like attachment and therefore also are hated and expelled into the object. This expulsion further entraps the individual because she is tied to parts outside the self that belong to it. There is magnetic attraction towards parts of one's own self. The expulsion fashions the glue-like attachment, and the latter generates the former.

## The eternal present

Another feature of this form of attachment in the present is the only emotional reality available. What occurs in the here and now totally overwhelms the individual. With a suction tentacle glued to the object, there is no space for the past or the present. It can be a shock to realize that what was said two minutes ago is no longer present and there is no memory of it. There is also no future. So, at the level of practical awareness, a child at school knows that he will see his mother when he gets home in the afternoon, but emotionally she has disappeared for ever. The sign of this disaster is that he is unable to concentrate and does very badly in his studies. In his school reports he keeps getting statements like: "does not concentrate", "daydreams", and so on. He is given the label ADD (Attention Deficit Disorder). The disaster that has occurred emotionally is that he has, like the baby roo, been ripped out of the pouch.

This glue-like attachment is always present and is part of the constellation that goes to make up the inner pattern of madness.

# CHAPTER TWELVE

# The worm

When one is oppressed it is a mark of chivalry to hurt oneself in order to hurt the oppressor.

G. K. Chesterton, *George Bernard Shaw* (1910, p. 27)

There had clung to me a feeling that I had been looked upon always as an evil, an encumbrance, a useless thing—a creature of whom those connected with him had to be ashamed. . .

Anthony Trollope, *An Autobiography* (1996), p. 43)

What I have said about the jelly implies that the person does not have within any capacity for self-generated decision-making. There is no integrated endowment of the self or objects. The person's inner substance is jelly-like, has submitted to god, and is devoid of inner decisions. Consequently there is an inner belief that he or she is a worm. He or she is full of the negativity that characterizes patients with schizophrenia or "illnesses" of a psychotic nature. In his *Textbook of Psychiatry*, Bleuler said long ago:

> The apparent counterpart of automatic obedience is *negativism*, which, however, frequently appears with symptoms of automatic obedience. [Bleuler, 1924, p. 154]

Bleuler judiciously uses the word "apparent" because it *looks* as though negativism is the counterpart of automatic obedience, but if we keep in mind that freedom is the central human desire, then an inner despair at being in a state of submission to god is entirely consistent with the situation in which the patient finds him- or herself. When a person is crushed by god she or he is full of negativism. Bleuler does uses the word "apparent" not because of this formulation, but because he saw from his daily clinical observation that automatic obedience and negativism go together. What I am saying is that his clinical observations fit with the schema that I am proposing for the *narcissistic pattern*.

There is a powerful voice inside the mind of the person afflicted with narcissism declaring that he or she is worthless. In extreme cases the person will actually hear voices telling him that he is worthless. A man who was depressed and morose at home went to a party where he cracked jokes and was the life and soul of the party. When he returned home, the voice said to him:

> "You see, you are just a phoney. You did all that to cover up. . . . You are totally worthless. All the time at the party you were over the top. You were laughing too loudly, and all that you did was too exaggerated. You're nothing but a phoney."

The telltale word here is "just". It was true that this behaviour was partly to hide depression, and the judgement that he acted in an excited way is true, but the conclusion that he is *just* a phoney and *totally worthless* is a cruel addendum aimed to justify his total obliteration. The voice's judgements denude the person of dignity. There is nothing good in the person, nothing worthy of respect. Very often, of course, the sentiments of that voice are mouthed by a family member—a parent or a spouse. But the voice is not felt to issue from another human being of equal stature but, rather, from someone who is invested with godly authority. In fact, the case of the person hearing a disembodied voice is the exception. The common rule is that the voice is embodied in a human being who becomes transformed psychologically into god. A man complained bitterly that his wife was always putting him down and castigating him, but the analyst noticed that the wife's condemnatory voice was also inside him. Often when he described an accomplishment, he would add, as in an aside:

"Oh, but it wasn't much good, really . . ."

In fact, the inner voice was more powerful than the one of his wife, and he stirred it up in her.

On another occasion a man said that his rheumatism was getting worse, and the analyst said to him:

". . .because of the impending separation"

and the patient said he knew that he was absolutely worthless and he thought he would kill himself. In this case the voice was now incarnate in his psychoanalyst, and he wanted to kill himself because the implication was that he was useless, that if he were a human being worthy of respect, he would not be affected by the impending separation. Suicide itself is the epitome of this process of disdainful obliteration.

I have referred to this "voice" that castigates the person within. It is in this voice that all the hatred of the inner *intensifiers* is embodied. The voice itself is so savage that the individual frequently vents its fury upon another person—most frequently a spouse, child, or parent. Clinicians in the school of British Object Relations refer to such an inner set-up as a bad inner object. However, this is a lopsided description, because it is a little personality within the personality, and this little personality is made up of a subject and object: a castigating subject and a despairing object. It cannot be over-emphasized how actively powerful this little personality is.[1] It is so fiercesome that it cannot be borne within the individual, so it is immediately expelled into an outer person. The host for this is usually a family member, but it can also be a racial group, an institution, an organization. The savagery of the Nazis gives one some idea of the violence and viciousness of such an inner set-up.

In Chapter 9, I emphasized that the godhead is embodied in personality characteristics—man, woman, doctor, husband, wife,

---

[1]Jung used the term "complex".

father, mother, lawyer, Australian, and so on—but the worm is also embodied in others. The worm is projected into worm-like imagos and worm-like imagos, are introjected into the worm. So there is an embodied wormhood. This wormhood is loved in one place but hated in another. So, for instance, a woman projected her wormhood into some poor Aboriginal children upon whom she doted. She also projected wormhood into her husband and hated it there with fierce contempt. However, if one looks at it more carefully, it is not difficult to see that the Aboriginal children are hated too, because when one of them grew up, flourished, and was successful she resented her. The doting love was hatred in disguise, because love fosters development and freedom, whereas hatred paralyses it. (Doting love or sentimental love is hatred in disguise.) Hatred of the worm is what leads to its expulsion out of the personality and into someone else.

The worm is associated very closely with a glue-dependent child.

The voice that tells me that I am worthless is in symphony with a passion to damage one's own self, and it is a passion that is effective. This is the kernel of madness. When someone commits suicide, it is common to hear "the expert" say:

"He was depressed."

This implies that he committed suicide because he was depressed, but the case is the opposite: he is depressed because of the suicidal tendency. This passion to hurt oneself is the primary desire; depression, psychosomatic symptoms, conduct disorder, and so on are the manifestations of this ultimate perversity. Freud started by thinking that sadism was primary and that masochism was inverted sadism. He later changed his mind and believed that masochism was primary (Freud, 1924c, pp. 159–170).

This passion to damage one's own self is one of the most mysterious realities in the human condition. The quote from Chesterton at the beginning of this chapter is only correct up to the point where he says that it is a mark of chivalry to hurt oneself. When he says that it is in order to hurt the oppressor, I think he is wrong: this is a consequence of the perverse passion, not its cause. Also, when he says that this passion occurs when someone is oppressed, it suggests that this is the reason for it. Again, I think he is wrong.

I am tempted just to leave the matter and say that it is part of the human condition and that it is utterly mysterious. However, I think it is possible to get an understanding of it if one takes into account the fact that chance events are interpreted by human beings in an animistic way. I elaborate this further in Chapter 22, where I try to show that an animistic mythology is frequently attributed to the chance event and relate this to the trauma that the individual has suffered through no fault of his own.

What I have said above is part of a perverse refusal to bend my will to the dictates of another:

"Me a victim of pure chance—Oh no, I am far more important than that."

I think Chesterton has sniffed out the reason when he says that it is a "mark of chivalry". It is the freedom of the grandiose aristocrat—the aristocrat within. It is therefore the activity that proceeds from the "narcissistic constellation" in the personality. The belief that I am worthless is the sane judgement not upon myself but upon this perverse mental savagery in which I am engaged.

Narcissism always has this characteristic: it looks like freedom, but it is not. I believe it is a free act, but it is in fact the opposite. I am impelled to do it. It is a refusal to bear something, a refusal to think, a refusal to create. A patient felt that his analyst was grandiose and arrogant, and he could not bear it and turned his back on treatment. An analyst could not bear the narcissism of his patient, got angry, and the patient left. On a similar occasion the analyst stopped the treatment. These look like free acts, but they are not, because they are not consequent on an act of the whole personality. They proceed from a personality that has expelled arrogance, grandiosity, or narcissism. It looks like freedom but is only a mimic.

This condition is dysfunctional because it paralyses the victim and prevents him from making a decision that will solve the problem. A woman who was an actuary was not functioning well at work. She calculated some figures incorrectly, forgot to forward some documents to an insurance Company, and missed her mother's birthday. So something was not right, but the situation was aggravated enormously by a figure that punished her with savagery:

"See how hopeless you are . . ."

"Your mother will hate you now and you deserve it . . ."

This has a paralysing effect, so that when she had calculated the figures wrongly, the voice told her that she was hopeless and what did she think she was doing pretending to be an actuary—so she couldn't do anything to remedy the situation. The voice prevents practical action. It is a sort of perverse indulgence that makes actions geared to solution impossible. One realizes that this type of state prevents decision-making.

When it is realized that god is usually situated in another person, it becomes clear what a widespread phenomenon we are talking about. The number of people who are paralysed in the presence of another are numerous. A man was tyrannized by his wife. She had affairs, mocked him in front of others, and alienated him from his children, but he was powerless in her hands. She was a goddess, and he was attached to her with glue-like intensity and could do nothing to free himself from her grip. When she chided him, he became like a dog with its tail between its legs and believed that all was his fault. He was bad, he was a worm, and he deserved all he got.

It is impossible to overemphasize the violent emotions that are encapsulated within this worm-like complex. When the complex is activated, it is like the trigger that sets off an atomic bomb.

# CHAPTER THIRTEEN

# Perversions

It may not be immediately obvious where sexual perversion fits into the schema that I have adopted for an understanding of madness—and first, of course, the tricky question of what is perverse and what is not. At one time, for instance, homosexuality was categorized as a perversion, but now this designation has been superseded in many Western cultures.

As, in fact, people who feel that their sexual activity is "abnormal" or reprehensible in some way often believe themselves to be abhorrent, then it seems, when we have considered "the worm", then this is the right place to think about perversions, especially as the belief in wormhood sometimes generates the perversion in order to legitimate the belief.

The question of what is perverse and what is not can, I believe, only be solved by scrutinizing the emotional activity of which the sexual activity is a sign. Normality and perversity in sexual mores cannot be determined by the outer activity alone. Sexual intercourse between a man and a woman cannot be called normal just on the basis of the physical sexual act. If it is done with emotional tenderness, it is different from when it is done out of hostile vengeance. When we look at it in this way, the very words "normal" and "perverse" seem to come out of the wrong mindset. Our categories of "sane" and "mad" seem to be more appropriate.

It is said that Hitler (Hughes, 1987) used to lie on the ground and invite a woman to piss on him. Whether this behaviour is perverse will now depend, according to our way of defining things, on what this represented emotionally. One could surmise here that he himself and the woman represented himself split in two, where one part was pissing on the other. It is not difficult to imagine his desecration of the Jews as being represented in this sexual drama. It is the emotional activity being represented by the sexual performance that determines what is sane and what is mad. If this is taken to heart, then only a detailed personality profile can determine what the sexual may represent. However, just as there are some archetypal symbols in dreams, so also one might posit that there are certain sexual behaviours that frequently represent a known emotional structure and activity.

Let us now suppose that a given piece of sexual behaviour has been analysed and categorized as perverse. How does it fit into our schema? I think a good starting point is to take Freud's point that masochism is the basic perversion. According to my schema, the underlying emotional situation is one where there is an absence of giving and this is replaced with a being-given-to at the surface level. In all perversion the need for the other to gratify dominates the sexual drama. The partner is being used as a masturbatory tool. Freud's point about foreplay is that in his judgement this is healthy if it is integrated within an orgasmic aim. Translating this into the emotional terms of this book, I would say that sexually gratifying activities are healthy if they are integrated within an interpersonal drama of mutual giving.

Now the *constellation of madness* that I have put forward strangles the capacity to give emotionally. This means that any sexual activity is perverse to the extent that it is not informed by emotional giving. This way of viewing sexual relations means that perversity cannot be defined by the outer sexual acts alone. Freud's idea that sexual activities are perverse if anything less than the genital orgasmic becomes the end-point of the activity has to be re-adapted in the schema I am putting forward here. For Freud, sexual activities are normal if they are coordinated under the hegemony of genital orgasm. In my schema the coordinating factor is not genital orgasm but emotional giving. This re-definition of perversion allows one to consider that "normal" heterosexual intercourse might be perverse and also that homosexual intercourse might be "normal".

Once this line of argument is adopted, then what about paedophilia? Incest?—and so on. There are two possible answers: either my line of argument can be extended into all these spheres of sexual activity or the argument I am putting forward is defective in some way. It is possible that some sexual activities that today people view with abhorrence may come to be considered "acceptable", just as homosexuality today has been legitimated in many Western cultures whereas thirty years ago it was still a criminal act. Then to consider whether my argument is defective, and I believe it is, for the following reason: "emotional giving" is a vague phrase, and the capacity of the individual to judge whether or not he is being "emotionally giving" is notoriously susceptible to self-deception. The stress in this book has been upon the "invisibility" of emotions but the body as an enveloping clothing for the emotions, has to be taken into account. Just as there are appropriate clothes for mountaineering and others for attending an important dinner, so also there are appropriate bodily configurations for different emotions, and there needs to be a "sexual clothing" appropriate to the inner emotional activity. Some sexual activities, such as pissing or shitting on each other, are difficult to think could ever enshrine emotional giving; they seem to symbolize the opposite, as in the case of Hitler.

I shall use Freud's "template" with the substitution of "emotional giving" for heterosexual orgasm as the basic schema that differentiates the perverse from the sane.

# CHAPTER FOURTEEN

# Trauma

The night is darkening round me
The wild winds coldly blow
But a tyrant spell has bound me
And I cannot cannot go
The giant trees are bending
Their bare boughs weighed with snow
And the storm is fast descending
And yet I cannot go
Clouds beyond clouds above me
Wastes beyond wastes below
But nothing drear can move me
I will not cannot go

Emily Brontë (1996)

S o far we have spoken of the *liquifiers* in the gelatinous substance, without any reference to the outer environment. Is there any reason for the presence of the liquifiers? My observation is that the *liquifiers* are always intensely active in people who have suffered severe traumata. Because the *liquifiers* are experienced outwardly as greed, envy, and jealousy, people are frequently unsympathetic to those who have suffered traumas in childhood. Their experience of the person is someone who is being hostile and resentful towards them. The extent to which people react to this hostility depends on the extent to which they are themselves under the sway of a "narcissistic constellation". As we saw in Chapter 9, these people continue to be punished by society throughout their lives. The punitive god is embodied in the society of people surrounding the traumatized individual. It is well known, for instance, that many criminals have had severely traumatized childhoods. A retributive theory of justice demands that revenge be taken against the criminal; a utilitarian theory of justice requires that society be protected against the dangers of criminal attack without demanding retribution. The latter theory and, indeed, policy of justice is in tune with our understanding of the origins of criminality.

The outer manifestations of a traumatized childhood can be described in external terms quite easily. A child may have lost one or both parents in infancy, may have lived the first few weeks in an incubator, may have been looked after by a cold and indifferent mother. There are also traumas that are much less obvious: for instance, a woman's parents did all in their power to protect her from painful experiences, with the result that she had not developed the resources to manage anything that caused her suffering.

What is most traumatizing to the child is parents who themselves are both extremely narcissistic. As mentioned in Part I, a core element in madness is the inability to give emotionally, so two parents who are very locked in this position are unable to give in this essential way to their children. Often this parental failure is not easily visible. It is common for someone to say of their mother or father that she or he was very much liked and respected by friends and the wider society but then to explain, usually in difficult-to-express idioms, the many ways in which they failed as parents. Very often what these accounts add up to is the parent's inability to give. A mother said to one woman: "Don't burden us with your problems"—meaning that she was unable to cope with them. She could not give herself to her child. Clinicians have to be cautious to differentiate between this and the child's envy but this being one of the *intensifiers* and the trauma transformed, the interplay between these two is frequently very intricate.

All these and also much more subtle traumata—like a mother and father who may show all the external signs of caring yet be emotionally negligent and indifferent—can be indicated through a description of the signs that point to the inner trauma; but even when all this has been said, it does not tell us what the core of the trauma is for the individual in his or her own inner subjective life. For a trauma to be a trauma, there has to be an *inner* catastrophe. There is a relation between the *inner* catastrophe and the outer manifestation, but the latter may have undergone all the transformations that Freud describes as happening between the latent and the manifest content of the dream. This differentiation that Freud made applies not only to dreams but to the disjunction that is present between inner and outer altogether. One might be tempted to use Kant's differentiation between *noumenon* and *phenomenon*, but this would not be right because Freud says that the latent (equivalent to *noumenon*) always represents a wish that the individual does not want to know about. In this way the philosopher who matches Freud's position best is Schopenhauer, who followed Kant's distinction between outer and inner but said, in contradistinction to Kant, that the thing-itself can be known, and it is the *will*—not *will* as popularly understood, but an idea that is closer to Freud's *wish* or Lacan's *desire*. To grasp the trauma, we have to understand what the *inner* catastrophe is: in other words, what has been the subjective response to the outer assault or what is the psychological structure indicative of catastrophe. Our thesis here is that the "narcissistic constellation" is the fossilized presence of the catastrophe. Darwin referred to the platypus as a living fossil—a living creature that is a leftover from a previous era. So also the "narcissistic constellation" is the living trauma of a past event or series of events. I believe that Bion was trying to describe this in his paper "On Arrogance" where, referring to the appearance of arrogance, curiosity, and stupidity he says, first:

> I shall suggest that their appearance should be taken by the analyst as evidence that he is dealing with a psychological disaster. [Bion, 1967a, p. 86]

And second:

> The analyst who is treating an apparently neurotic patient must regard a negative therapeutic response together with the appearance of scattered, unrelated references to curiosity, arrogance and stupidity as evidence that he is in the presence of a psychological catastrophe with which he will have to deal. [Bion, 1967a, p. 87]

The *inner* catastrophe occurs at the moment when the individual's spirit is broken. The saddest moment in the *Diary of Anne Frank* is a footnote added by an editor at the end of the book:

> In February, 1945, both the sisters caught typhus. One day Margot, who was lying in the bunk immediately above Anne's, seeking to rise, lost her hold and fell onto the floor. In her weakened state the shock killed her. Her sister's death did to Anne what all her previous sufferings had failed to do: *it broke her spirit*. A few days later, in early March, she died. [Frank, 1954, p. 224, italics added]

Trauma is the breaking of the spirit. In this case it seems clear that it was overwhelming grief that broke Anne Frank's spirit. Her spirit was broken in adulthood. Some equivalent occurrence in infancy constitutes childhood trauma. What event it is that finally breaks the spirit remains unknown, but I think it likely that it occurs quite suddenly, as it seems to have done with Anne Frank: there is a slow building-up of pain, which reaches a crescendo at a particular moment in time. This view is consistent with Freud's formulation of trauma as he puts it forward in *Beyond the Pleasure Principle* (1920g). His idea here is that there is a stimulus barrier that protects the personality from too great an onrush of painful stimuli. In trauma the stimulus barrier is broken.

When the spirit is broken, the emotional consequence is that sadness and disappointment are broken into bits, and these bits are what I have called the "crust in the personality". These are the bits that are responsible for projecting into the outer forum. Once sadness is in bits, its subjective structure is in the form of arrogance and pathos and is hated and projected into an outer object.

Our idea is that the rupture of the stimulus barrier is the template for the inner situation. In other words, there are no barriers within the psyche, so that envy, for instance, has no barrier around it; there are inner barriers that parallel the outer stimulus barrier. I refer to inner barriers as *psychic barriers*. The psychic barriers break down when the stimulus barrier collapses. The therapeutic task, which is considered in more detail in Chapter 21, is to re-establish psychic barriers.

What breaks the spirit of one child may not break the spirit of another, but we can posit that for every human being there is a breaking point. A moment comes when the child can bear it no longer and gives up. In my book on narcissism (Symington, 1993) I referred to this moment as a *decision*. I think this is a correct designation as long as it is not understood to mean anything like a conscious decision. When the spirit is broken, an emotional act on the part of the individual is an integral part of the event. Whether it could have been otherwise is a question that no one can answer. All we can say is that this is what happened to this individual and it was a personal act. When the editor says that Margot's death *broke Anne's spirit*, we could also say that her will to live was broken, that inwardly she gave up; that a decision was involved. We believe that this is paralleled in an infantile trauma.

Frances Tustin, in her book about the autistic boy, John (Tustin, 1972), calls his depression a "black hole" and associates it with the aftermath of an event causing unspeakable sadness—a sadness that was present in the personality in what might be called a *beta element* form. In other words, there is a transition from unbearable grief to acute depression. The agent of this transition is the *liquifier*. One might say that the therapeutic strategy of most Kleinians differs from that of Frances Tustin in that the former focused on envy and jealousy, whereas the latter paid attention to the trauma that these *liquifiers* had dispersed through the personality—that the *liquifiers* are evidence of a primitive catastrophe. The model for this catastrophe is something like this. When I was a child, I saw an elderly lady fall down a flight of stone steps and lie crumpled at the bottom. I and another rushed to give her assistance, but she put her hand out and yelled at us to keep away. The *liquifiers*, which often take the form of hostility, are equivalents of that old woman yelling at us to keep away. This way of conceptualizing it is consistent with the view that there may be a constitutional element that determines the quantum of aggression that endows the form of the *liquifiers* with their content, but the trauma determines the direction of its use. The physical strength of that old woman may have determined how loudly she could yell, but the use to which it was put was determined by the pain of the fall.

In this chapter I try to demonstrate that the two theoretical positions—those of Klein and Tustin—are manifestations of the one. In my book on narcissism (Symington, 1993) I had not fully grasped the unity of which these two theories were manifestations and therefore, although I had a chapter on trauma, I was biased towards an inner culpability on the part of the traumatized individual. As one person said to me:

"It is too voluntarist."

This breaking of the spirit, which enwraps personal activity in its embrace, has consequences, the prime one being a refusal of love to the self from outside. This is the inner state of the traumatized individual. The *liquifiers* insert themselves as compensatory ways of acting in the place of a spirit that should be there but is now broken. One can think of a bad spirit having taken the place of one in which there was hope and joy. The compensatory mode of action leads the individual to be a passive vessel for the guidance, manipulation, or exploitation by others. The person has no inner spirit to guide him or her because it has been broken, so she or he submits entirely to outer figures whom he or she employs to direct the inner life. These "outer figures" are god either concentrated in one figure or institution (monotheistic) or dispersed through an array of figures of institutions (polytheistic). This is just one aspect of it. What we are saying is that the *narcissistic system* replaces the inner spirit, which has been broken. The presence of the "narcissistic system" is a sign that there has been a catastrophe. It is frequently very difficult for those who bear the brunt of this hostility to recognize the inner disaster with which the person is trying to cope. In some cases bearing it requires nothing short of heroism.

The question is: has the spirit been broken entirely? This is a difficult question to answer in any general sense. Perhaps in many cases it has been broken completely, but in those narcissistic people who approach a professional for help we can say that a flickering spirit is still alive, though very submerged. Henri Rey said that many patients come to a psychoanalyst wanting help to bring a dead figure to life (Rey, 1994, pp. 229–248). I think this is a different way of saying the same thing. Bringing the flickering spirit back to life is, then, the task facing the clinician and patient together. It is a task that is fraught with pain and distress.

There is a more hopeful way of looking at this problem. The presence of narcissism is a signal that a disaster of spirit has occurred. What we know from clinical experience is that when narcissism is reversed, there is a slow and painful re-establishment of that original spirit of joy and hope. So one can look at it in this way: where narcissism is, there is the spirit of joy and hope. It is smothered by the "narcissistic system", which parallels and overshadows it. Narcissism is not a gravestone but a gardener's sign that below there is a seed waiting to be watered.

So to return to our point about the *liquifiers*. Where these are present, there is a refusal of love to the self. Many a therapist may come to realize this and try to remedy it by "loving" the patient, but this does not work because the *liquifiers* have to be robbed of their power—their power to contaminate the whole personality with an inner despair. When these *liquifiers* have been decontaminated, then the person begins to feel loved. The psychoanalyst or psychotherapist has the job of a bomb disposal unit.

As described in Chapter 8, these *liquifiers* also have the effect of spreading the sadness and disappointment throughout the gelatinous substance. We might perhaps take an example from a woman who had suffered sexual abuse in childhood. We discover that she seems dissociated from the event; she does not seem enraged or particularly upset about it. Let us posit that when it happened, she suffered a "shock of disappointment", and this "act" of hers was then *dispersed* through the jelly so that what is encountered is an hysterical dissociation. She remembers the event, but it does not seem particularly noteworthy; there is an "amused" relation to it. So she says:

> "But it does not really worry me, my dear; after all, if one hasn't been abused these days then you're not of interest to social workers and do-gooders, and I do *love* being the object of sympathy . . ."

Another case was of a man whose mother had died suddenly when he was five years old. When the psychoanalyst took the case history, it seemed likely that this had been an upsetting event, but the man gave no indication that this was so; rather, his whole manner, not only in relation to this event but to all the projects of his life, was one of disdain. This was not indicated in his words but in the listless tone in which all matters were discussed. It is possible to make sense of both these instances if one posits that the emotion of disappointment in the first case and sadness in the second were dispersed through the gelatinous substance through the *liquifiers*.

I think that one can further posit that the *liquifiers* come into being as a way of managing the emotional trauma. Seen in this light, the whole "narcissistic system" can be seen as a way of managing childhood traumata. There is an optimistic and a pessimistic way of looking at this. The pessimistic is to say that the trauma has been dispersed and has a permanently damaging effect on the personality structure; the optimistic is to say that the trauma is conserved in the gelatinous substance and is there to be exhumed into consciousness with the assistance of a mental health professional—a preconception awaiting a realization, to use Bion's formula (1963, p. 23). If we take it as a principle that wholeness of being requires that all the events of our life be integrated into the personality, then we can see that it is necessary that the traumatic event be conserved in this way. I shall call this drive to integrate the *integrity principle*.

This is the proper place to look at another aspect of the *liquifiers*: it is that they are always correlated with intense dependence. In Chapter 8 I referred to the way in which the narcissistic individual submits to the authority of others outside himself, and also in Chapter 9 it is clear that god directs and takes over and overshadows the possibility of personal thought. When I say that the narcissistic individual is intensely dependent, then this is another way of describing the same phenomenon. Envy and hatred go hand-in-hand with this intense dependence. I have had this realization with a patient: "My heavens, this person depends on me to think for him (or to feel for him or to decide for him)"—the realization being that this is such an intense dependence that it is no wonder that the person hates and envies me because I am felt to deprive him or her of their freedom. The *liquifiers*, then, are intricately related to a state of extreme dependence.

So we have a pattern of this kind. A severe trauma occurs in childhood. The narcissistic pattern is established. A part of this pattern is the glue-like dependence upon god. This is intense, and then the figure in whom the god is embodied is hated because she or he deprives the person of all freedom. What is referred to as oral rage (Kernberg, 1975, p. 228) in the literature is anger at being trapped in the way described.

Narcissism has had the function of keeping the organism alive. Its "philosophy" is "Survival is the first imperative", whereas the healthy personality has put emotional freedom as its top priority. When patients come for treatment, it is because they want more than survival. Narcissism has served them well, but now they want something more.

## Narcissism as frozen trauma

Narcissism freezes the emotions into fixed entities, so that they exist in the personality and are dealt with by being expelled either into the body or into a person in the outside world. The emotional entities are grief, sadness, guilt, and anger. What about joy? A person feels this when his her emotions create; in the absence of that capacity, joy is unable to flourish.

## Primary trauma and secondary consequences

I have suggested that the *breaking of the spirit* is the primary trauma. I would not want to pin down too minutely when this occurs in childhood. Otto Rank believed that the prime trauma occurred at the time of birth. Frances Tustin believed that it was a premature rupture from the mother, and Pierce Clarke (1933) believed that it was some adverse happening at the foetal stage of development. What is common to all these views is that a disaster occurred at a very early stage in the individual's development, and this left the individual in a state of vulnerability that is synonymous with saying that she is enwrapped in the "narcissistic constellation". This, then, is THE trauma—in fact, properly speaking, the only trauma. The events that are described as traumatic in a typical case history are secondary: so, for instance, a mother dying when the child is young, a sister whom the mother favoured, parents divorcing, a drunken father, and so on are secondary. Their significance lies in the fact that the already traumatized child, and therefore in a jelly-like state, becomes subsumed into the imago of the damaging event or figure. When Freud says in *Mourning and Melancholia* (1917e [1915]) that the shadow of the lost object falls upon the ego, this is only able to occur because the individual is already in a narcissistic condition. The same principle applies to other such events. I shall give here just one example.

A baby was adopted at six weeks. Her adoptive mother spoilt her, whereas her father was authoritarian and depriving. In adulthood her personality was split. There was a strong, firm, and resolved personality that came into prominence at one time, and a weak sentimental one at others. These two sides reflected the disparate characters of her two adoptive parents. The disconnection between the two was also reflected in her personality. Using Freud's metaphor, one could say that the shadow of the parental relationship fell upon her ego. However, one might surmise that the trauma that *broke her spirit* and made her susceptible to that incorporative imprinting was being expelled from her natural mother at the age of six weeks.

I believe that the realization that envy, greed, jealousy, and grandiosity *are* the trauma existing here and now alters the clinician's perspective. He will be firm but empathic. He will not be persecuting. In the last chapter I will also put forward a theory as to how the traumatic event gets transmuted into a masochistic pattern.

# CHAPTER FIFTEEN

# Psychiatric diseases

In this matter of transformation I suggest that, as a model, you might see photographs of what appeared to be two entirely different mountains which were, in fact, the same mountain; one from the southern vertex and the other from the northern vertex. Indeed, one could multiply those by all points of the compass.

Wilfred Bion, *Brazilian Lectures 1* (1974, p. 96)

The purpose of this chapter is to look at the classic pathologies of the psychiatric textbook in the light of the internal constellation that I have been proposing here and see if they can be understood according to it. There is a note of irony in the title of this chapter in that particular mental conditions are only diseases by analogy, but, as Thomas Szasz (1988) has emphasized, many practitioners have forgotten that it is a metaphor. It is my view that the classic psychiatric categories are particular manifestations of the "narcissistic constellation", and if they are subjected to such a scrutiny, they become understandable in an illuminating way.

141

## Schizophrenia

I take the identifying elements of schizophrenia to be:

1. flight of ideas
2. ideas of reference
3. hearing voices
4. concrete thinking
5. broadcasting

## Flight of ideas

Eugen Bleuler identified "distractibility" as being the core of this phenomenon. In other words, a person is distracted by the introduction of a fact that is incidental to the train of the thinking process. Bleuler gives this example:

> Thus a patient wishes to tell about a trip to the Righi Mountains and he suddenly thinks of the donkeys which were used there before the construction of the railroad, then of salami sausage supposed to be made of donkey meat and then of Italy where these sausages come from. [Bleuler, 1924, p. 71]

It is therefore the surface sensory impression that leads off in the new direction, impeding thereby the directing function of internal thought. Bleuler says:

> It shows a preponderance of external and word association at the expense of inner associations. . . . In place of inner associations there may be accidental connections . . . [Bleuler, 1924, p. 72]

It is clear from this quote that Bleuler was heavily influenced by the associationist psychology of his day. He sees the difference between thinking and flight of ideas as a difference between two processes that are essentially similar. What I am proposing in this book is that thinking is a personal creative activity and entirely different from an unguided associative process. What is known as *dereistic thinking* is as it is because the central governing processes that are productive of thought are absent. In Wilfred Bion's terms, there is an absence of *alpha function*.

The mental fixing on the passing sensory impression is a mani-festation of the glue-like attachment. This is an aspect of the attach-ment to the embodied god. God is sensory in nature and therefore an idol that enjoys this captivating quality (Chapter 9). The indi-vidual attaches to the next passing image, and then onto the next, and so on. There is in fact an absence of a thinking process.

What is central is that the individual takes flight from the inner mental creative activity. The reason for this is, I believe, that con-tact with this creative activity produces awareness.

The flight of ideas is particularly noticeable in schizophrenia, but observe the conversation at any dinner party and the rarity with which a central scheme of thinking will be followed and developed leads me to believe that this form of schizophrenic be-haviour is universal.

## Ideas of reference

Someone who believes that all ideas and everyone's talk refers to himself is diagnosed as having "ideas of reference". This occurs when god is installed in the subject.

## Hearing voices

Auditory hallucinations always come from a powerful figure. Here god is installed outside the individual and speaks to him or her. It is a case of the shy narcissist. The worm also comes in here because usually these voices castigate the individual, telling him what a worthless wretch he is.

## Concrete thinking

Concrete thinking is a diagnostic sign of mental disturbance and again one of the "notes" of schizophrenia. "Concrete thinking" is a misleading term because it is not thinking at all: it is aborted think-ing. Whereas thinking is an inner creative act that is the produc-tion of the psyche alone, what is known as a "concrete thought" is a declaratory statement that is sitting in the personality like an unproduced lump. It is unprocessed.

The relation of this sort of thinking to god is clear. God declares it, and therefore it is: "Let there be light, and there was light. . . ." God is always embodied either in a person or an institution (Chapter 9) and then the pronouncement that is made by that embodied god becomes a fact just because it has been spoken by god. It has now become a fact as solid as the firmament and the stars, and it is not possible to think with these. To think it is necessary to have "pliable objects". Thinking changes the pattern of experience and requires "pliability of substance" for this to be possible.

An example of "concrete thinking" is given in a passage from a book by Joanna Field:

> I seemed very liable to assume that because something was said it must be true. I would listen to one person's story of a quarrel and believe it as absolute fact, never remembering that thought is relative. . . . I would read a book review, accepting the judgement given as the final truth. . . . The same thing happened when I read the newspapers. I would believe implicitly whatever I read in any paper about political affairs . . . [Field, 1986, p. 117]

Those things that were said became facts within her. They are indistinguishable from tables or elephants or carpet-sweepers. This is because the focus of attention is upon god and the delusion that whatever god says "is". The reality of things is not according to the creative perception of humans but according to the dictates of God. So tables, elephants, carpet-sweepers, Father Christmas, "there are still dinosaurs in South America", and flying saucers are equally real because god has pronounced them to be so. The pronouncement of god makes them "concrete". The ramifications of this need to be considered. If the godhead is embodied in the analyst, then what he says become facts. His statements are not interpretations but "facts". I believe that this kind of perversion is very widespread and accounts for the reason why dogmatism reigns supreme in so many social, religious, and political organizations.

If we take what has been said about fear of freedom (Chapter 2) seriously, then we can expect to find that patients will do all in their power to avoid having to exercise it. The incentive, then, to make the analyst into god and to follow his dictates is enormous. The temptation in the analyst to enact the role is also enormous, and certain patients put huge pressure upon the analyst to do so. What an analyst experiences is a sample of a widespread phenomenon—where individuals pressure others to be their gods.

A patient focused in this way is crippled by this concreteness. A mentally retarded man was in the street with his mates, and a police car drove past with its siren going. The mates turned jokingly and said to him:

"They are coming to get you, Terry, and put you in prison."

For this man it was a fact, and he went into a panic. It means that his mates were invested with god-like qualities. In a moment of anger, a woman said to her husband:

"You are a deceitful liar; just a rat".

And he then was that. His wife was a goddess to him. This conversation took place between an ex-prisoner and a social worker:

"I became an alcoholic on the 18th of June 1961."

"How can you be so precise about the date?"

"It was on that day that I went to the Alcoholics Recovery Programme, and Jim Cooler told me I was an alcoholic."

He was told he was an alcoholic, so he was one. That was his identity.

A doctor said to a patient on September 16:

"You have got cancer and will die in three months."

She died on exactly the 16th of December.

This is why the psychoanalyst Wilfred Bion would say:

"I think it was a patient, and I think I am a psychoanalyst."

In other words, there has been no godly pronouncement. He concludes that he is an analyst following a rational inquiry.

Once this is realized, it becomes understandable why psychotic patients can get into such states of panic. When these statements are facts and someone says to you that the police are coming to pick you up and put you in prison, it is terrifying.

It also makes confusion understandable. When Marion Milner read one report in a newspaper, she believed that as a fact; when she read a contrary report, she believed that too; so she had inside her two contradictory facts, and this led to confusion.

This kind of concrete thinking also leads to violent projection. An analyst said to his patient:

"You are extremely intrusive."

The patient believed then that that is what she was. Just as someone might say "Mrs Smith is an American" or "John Faulkner is a solicitor" or "Mrs Simmonds is an Intrusive". When I hear the words, "I am an intrusive", it is such a torture that I push it away vehemently. Then, as I am that, then I will be that, and I will ring up the analyst in the middle of the night, stalk him when he goes out to the harbour to sail at weekends, and so on. There is no option but to be that. I am that, so I am compelled to be so, but I am then sour and bitter within. I am bitter because I am a prisoner and not free. Negativity is another angle on this sourness. Moaning is a manifestation of this same condition. The sourness, the negativity, the moaning are the emotional concomitants of being imprisoned for life by an inner gaoler: the sense of hopelessness of never being free. Therefore when the negativity, sourness, or moaning are perceived, it is a sign that god is present and that the individual is filled up with concrete objects that block his capacity to choose.

When the analyst says to this patient,

"You are extremely intrusive",

there is an unspoken but added statement in it. The patient hears the analyst saying:

"... and that's all you are ... you are nothing but a rotten worm ..."

It needs to be remembered that it is god speaking.

This leads us to another quality associated with concrete thinking. There is docile submission to god, and there is violent attacking rage against him. Why? The "docile" submission is because the patient is intensely dependent upon the psychiatrist, psychotherapist, or psychoanalyst; the violent attacking rage is because she was a prisoner due to the dependent attachment. However, as she cannot look in because it is so appalling to see, she believes it is the clinician who is her gaoler. (In fact, the dependent attachment is her gaoler.) This means that the concrete objects within are yet outside because there is no inside.

Another variant of this is the clinician who says to his patient strongly:

"You are promiscuous."

She then has an affair that is public and infamous, and the community in which she lives wag their tongues about the psychotherapist's or psychoanalyst's incompetence. Again, it is all "out there"; there is no inner life. Attachment is so glue-like that inner objects are all concrete outer figures.

It is clear to see that "concrete thinking" is the outcome of god and the worm. I have given examples taken from encounters between a psychoanalyst and his patient, but these same principles apply in many different settings. Children frequently feel similarly in relation to their parents. Governments trade on this propensity in people and make declarations and promises that are believed by many.

Concrete thinking can also be thought about from another angle: that it is a flight from intentional thinking. With intentional thinking comes pain—particularly the pain of guilt. Such is the panic that the sufferer takes flight into the arms of god who declares to him what to do.

## Broadcasting

This occurs when thoughts are spoken and not contained. In severe cases the individual shouts out the thoughts so everyone within a wide circumference hears the person. In milder cases they are immediately spoken so they are heard by those close at hand. This is either a reaction to the voices that are so persecutory or because the concrete nature of the thoughts is such a torture that they have to be immediately expelled.

These are the main diagnostic criteria for schizophrenia, and I believe that all of them are easily understood according to the schema that I have put forward. In fact, this schema makes sense of them. The psychiatric textbook has given us the phenomenology without the inner understanding that I believe I have provided.

## Manic-depressive psychosis

This condition is classified as an affective disorder in the psychiatric textbooks. Let me say at the outset that such a classification is based upon the presupposition that the affective and the cognitive exist in two separate departments of the personality. I take the view that there is one entity and this is viewed from two perspectives, because of the mind's limited ability to grasp the two as a unity. If we substitute the word "emotional" for "affective", it can easily be seen that the syndrome that is referred to as schizophrenia has a strong emotional element as well as a cognitive one in its circumference. Separating manic-depressive psychosis from schizophrenia on the basis of the first being an emotional disorder and the second a cognitive one can be seen to be a differentiation of emphasis rather than one that is qualitative. The same *flight of ideas* that characterizes schizophrenia also characterizes the manic phase in manic-depressive psychosis.

Put at its most simple: when the patient is manic, he has become god; when he is depressed, he has become the worm. When someone is diagnosed as manic-depressive, it is because he fluctuates between feeling he is god and feeling he is a worm. In this "illness" there is inherent recognition that the two are present in the personality but only one is manifest at any one moment in time. The duration in one mode or the other can be as little as a minute (or even a second) or as long as a month or a year. What determines the length of these periods is uncertain.

Another way of looking at this is to hypothesize that there is an ecstatic state, and subsequently the individual is depressed about it. The assumption here is that there is a knowledge of the pathological nature of the ecstatic state.

## Psychopathy

This designation typifies the person whose conscience about how he treats other people is obliterated by greed for personal gain.

Though what strikes the observer is the psychopath's callousness towards others, it is also the case that he does not care for his own self. The image of the psychopath driven by ambition with no space for leisure or fulfilling activities is a stereotype.

A conceptualization of this, according to my schema, is as follows: there is a jelly inside, and the crust is manifest in the outer drivenness; there has been a traumatic event in infancy: usually an overwhelming sadness that has broken up the personality into a jelly-like interior, and any relation with a person threatens to bring that sadness to consciousness. The greedy drivenness is to prevent the personality being overwhelmed by that devastating sadness.

## Conclusion

I have taken in this chapter just three disorders from the psychiatric textbook. I have left out those that are derived from these, such as alcoholism and drug addiction, which are invariably a way of soothing the paranoia and escaping from knowledge of the jelly and glue-like attachment. Addiction is itself a manifestation of this glue-like attachment. I have also left out those disorders that have their origin in organic dysfunction in the brain, like senile dementia, mental handicap, and epilepsy.

How the subjective experiencing person is related to that neurological tangle known as the brain has been grasped by no one. However, whether what has triggered the "mad state" is childhood trauma or brain dysfunction, the principles that I have been enunciating here are relevant to understanding the resulting state.

# CHAPTER SIXTEEN

# Psychoanalytic schema of narcissism derived from psychiatry

A diagnosis like "psychotic" or "borderline psychotic" does not allow room for elaboration, speculation, conjecture; it limits the possibilities of expansion.

Wilfred Bion, *Bion in New York and Sao Paulo* (1980, p. 24)

Otto Kernberg gives a very comprehensive description of the way narcissism manifests itself, and I have taken his book, *Borderline Conditions and Pathological Narcissism* (Kernberg, 1975) as a template of contemporary psychoanalytic understanding of narcissism and borderline conditions. His book, apart from being rooted in rich clinical experience of these conditions, also summarizes the views of most streams of analytic thinking on the subject. What is commended and what is criticized refers then not only to the thinking in his book but in current psychoanalytic understanding more generally.

Kernberg outlines 19 characteristics of the narcissistic condition, of which five are:

1.  an unusual degree of self-reference in their interactions with other people

2. an inflated self-concept

3. extreme self-centredness

4. idealization of people from whom they expect narcissistic supplies

5. arrogance, being a defence against paranoid traits

All of these are manifestations of god. In three cases god is installed in the subject, and in the fourth it is installed in others. In the case of arrogance, it is also god installed in the subject. I would not put it that it is a defence against paranoid traits but that what is called "paranoia" is a primitive hatred of those elements in the personality that inhibit freedom. At one point Kernberg says:

> ... the remnants of unacceptable self-images are repressed and projected onto external objects ... [Kernberg, 1975, p. 231]

I prefer to conceptualize this as the person's hatred of elements in the self, particularly the intensifiers. In other words, I would want to substitute the verb "are hated" for "are repressed". One of the projects of this book is to emphasize the emotional activities of the psyche. The fundamental emotion here is one of hatred. Words like "repressed" and "denial" are anodyne language.

6. a shallow emotional life

7. little enjoyment from life itself

8. boredom and restlessness

9. "emptiness behind the glitter"

10. little empathy for the feelings of others

11. control of others

12. very dependent on others for tribute and praise but unable really to depend on anyone because of a deep distrust

These seven can be thought of as manifestations of the jelly. It may not be immediately obvious why these are all manifestations of the jelly. The jelly implies that there is no creative centre, and it is this that enables someone to have empathy for the feelings of others. It is this that leads someone to control others so that they should function within the orbit of their own jelly-like state, and to depend truly upon someone requires an act of trust, which again is a creative act that is not possible to someone in a jelly-like state.

13. strong conscious feelings of inferiority and insecurity
14. a great *need* [italics added] to be loved by others
15. coldness and ruthlessness behind the charm

These three I place as manifestations of the worm. It may not be immediately obvious why the third comes under that designation. It is because the self-preoccupation associated with the degraded self-image leads the individual to keep others at a safe distance.

16. envy of others

This is one of the *intensifiers*.

17. on the surface: "no object relations but in fact their interactions reflect very primitive and intense object relationships of a frightening kind"

Kernberg makes the point that these patients appear to demonstrate a lack of object relationships, but at a deeper level it can be seen that they suffer from very intense, primitive object relationships of a frightening kind (Kernberg, 1975, p. 228). The objects become distorted through the activity of the *intensifiers* (Chapter 19). Once it is firmly grasped that such people have a glue-like attachment to god, then it follows that this god is not only powerful but also invested with the *intensifiers*, in a variety of manifestations, all of which are terrifying. They become fiercesome figures entrapping the person and therefore extremely frightening. There is also no good object within. In our terms, the good object is the Absolute, which becomes a good object in the personality through being chosen.

18. relations with people are exploitative and parasitic

This relates to the dimension of glue-like attachment, which necessarily is exploitative and parasitic. As soon as a figure is invested with elements of the "narcissistic constellation", he or she necessarily becomes an object or a puppet to be used. Sometimes people believe that a person is enhanced when idealized, but in fact this is not so. As soon as god is projected into the outer figure(s), its only status is then as an object.

19. extreme contradictions: inferiority versus omnipotence are a diagnostic sign of narcissism

This is an instance of the *coexistence of opposites*. It is on the basis of this principle that I would want to predict that in all the cases that I attribute to god there is also the worm, and vice versa. The external manifestation is always of one of the elements of the "narcissistic constellation", but the opposite, although not immediately obvious, is always there.

So the "principle of inclusion" is relevant. Where there is envy, there are the other two *intensifiers* also. I think the only one that needs further elucidation is No. 17. What I have referred to above is related to the hatred. The hatred of the inner elements can be so intense that it becomes a "killer" in that not just the particular element itself is hated but the whole personality that enshrines it. The problem becomes acute when that particular element puffs up and engulfs the whole person at one particular moment. It is at such a time that suicide occurs. The whole personality is enveloped in the "bad" element.

People suffering from pathological narcissism function socially in a smooth and often charming manner, and in this way they differ from borderline conditions, where the disturbed elements are clearer to see:

> What distinguishes many of the patients with narcissistic personalities from the usual borderline patient is their relatively good social functioning, their better impulse control . . .
> [Kernberg, 1975, p. 229]

I would maintain that the same "narcissistic constellation" reigns in each, but in the "narcissistic patient" god is installed in the subject whereas in the borderline patient it is installed in the others around him. My thesis is that the psychiatric categories are not different entities but, rather, diverse manifestations of the central "narcissistic constellation".

Kernberg differentiates between "normal narcissism" and pathological narcissism and believes that the former has arisen as a natural phase of infantile development, which is then worked through, whereas the latter is a defence against violent oral rage. Kernberg believes that there is no necessity for the concept of primary narcissism (Kernberg, 1975, p. 325), which I also maintain, but once this is accepted, then "normal narcissism" is also a concept that needs to be ditched. "Normal narcissism" is supposed to arise out of a fixation at the stage of development where primary narcissism held sway during infancy. Therefore once this latter is abandoned, then "normal narcissism" needs to go also. Infant research also supports the view that babies are object-oriented from the beginning of post-natal life. Rage against being trapped is part of the "narcissistic constellation" and not a unique aetiological factor.

I want here to differentiate between Kernberg's phenomenological description of narcissistic and borderline patients and his explanation of the schema. The phenomenological description is accurate and comes from a wealth of clinical experience, but what is being argued throughout this book is that the aetiological explanation, based upon the psycho-sexual stages, does not satisfactorily make sense of what has been observed. As was said at the beginning of this chapter, Kernberg's book has been taken as representative of contemporary psychoanalytical thinking. If, however, we knock out primary narcissism and its progeny, "normal narcissism", then we must look for the aetiology of narcissism elsewhere. I would wish to locate the origin of narcissism in childhood trauma and to look for the differential of severity also in that trauma. The nature of the trauma I have indicated elsewhere (Chapter 14). I would also want to restrict the term "narcissism" or "narcissistic" to a constellation in the personality that is pathological because it inhibits freedom and creativity. What is called "normal narcissism" needs to be thought of either as the equivalent for "self-confidence" or as a narcissism that, while less severe, is nevertheless still pathological. Into which of these two would one place the following?

> Such a "toned down", less grandiose, and more attainable ego ideal permits one the normal narcissistic gratification of living up to the internalized ideal parental images, and this gratification in turn reinforces self-esteem, one's confidence in one's own goodness and one's trust in gratifying object relationships. [Kernberg, 1975, p. 240]

I would want to argue that when something is done that flows from the personal essential being and accrues to its benefit, then this is self-confidence. If it is clear from what has been said (Chapter 1) that an action that, if it is done for the profit of the absoluteness of being existing in the self and others, is healthy and of benefit in the micro- and macro-social environment, whereas if it is gratifying to the sensual self, then it is narcissistic. "Living up to the internalized ideal parental images" might be either narcissistic or loving and creative. It would depend upon the nature of these ideal parental images themselves and also upon whether, if they are creative, the ego has personally assimilated them or submitted to them against the personally creative. In other words, the criterion that distinguishes what is narcissistic from what is emotionally healthy is whether or not the actions of the psyche proceed from what is absolute and outside the immediate or the temporary and sensual. A man lived in "time-segments" so that when he was in one he was totally in it, whereas when he was in another he was totally in that, and there was no connection to the previous one. Then an emotional change occurred where he had a perspective upon these different time-segments indicating that he was on an observation platform. This platform is part of what I refer to as the Absolute, the place outside each "time-segment" from which he can see them.

If contentment and satisfaction come from an inner creative act of love, then the emotional state is a healthy one; if they come from flattery and outer stroking, they are narcissistic. This criterion, which is the Absolute or contingent in action, is what tells us whether sanity or madness rules in the human household. When the centre of self-esteem comes from the outer stroking, then the individual is also within one "time-segment"—stuck glue-like to that stroking.

* * *

Kernberg distinguishes between borderline and narcissistic patients in this way. In borderline patients the disturbance, and in particular the clinging dependence, is more manifest, whereas narcissistic patients function much more smoothly and, on the surface, display what appears to be a confident management of life. I give just three quotes from Kernberg that emphasize this point:

> On the surface, these patients may not present seriously disturbed behaviour; some of them may function socially very well . . . [Kernberg, 1975, p. 227]

What distinguishes many of the patients with narcissistic
personalities from the usual borderline patient is their rela-
tively good social functioning, their better impulse control...
[p. 229]

the surface functioning of the narcissistic personality is much
better than that of the average borderline patient... [p. 230]

I believe that these two are different manifestations of the same
fundamental pattern, which I have outlined in this book. To put it
simply: in the borderline patient god is installed in the analyst,[1]
whereas in the narcissistic patient it is installed in the subject.
Kernberg notes the fact that narcissistic patients devalue the analyst. In other words god is installed in the patient, and the worm in
the analyst.[2] With the borderline patient it is the other way around:
god is installed in the analyst, and the patient is the worm clinging
desperately to him and manifesting his disturbance openly.

Kernberg notes, I am sure correctly, that narcissistic patients
adapt themselves to the moral demands of their environment out
of fear of attack (Kernberg, 1975, p. 232). The paranoia then is more
hidden. This has sometimes been referred to as "veiled paranoia",
which is frequently much greater than a paranoia that is more
obvious. The smooth surface, then, is to prevent attack. However,
no one can keep the smooth surface in operation on all fronts, so a
choice is made. One can only presume that this surface is presented where it seems to be most necessary. So, for instance, within
a family the paranoia may be well known but hidden from outsiders.

Kernberg attributes paranoia to the projection of oral rage. This
is the classical position, but I am doubtful about it, just as I am
doubtful about the idea that the death instinct can be projected.
The central matter is that paranoia is a persecuted attitude towards
something outside that originates from an entity inside that is

---

[1]Or in a figure or institution for the borderline patient who is not in analysis. For instance, Horst Richter gives the example of a superbly self-assured
social hostess who is nevertheless dependent upon her unassuming husband.
The god is installed in her and the worm in the husband, but in fact the
dependency is intense but not obvious (Richter, 1974).

[2]This is why Kernberg sees grandiosity as the core manifestation of narcissistic patients—p. 280.

hated and projected. But what is that entity? It can be either one of the *intensifiers* or any of the elements of the "narcissistic constellation", be it god, the worm, or the jelly. Any or all of these elements are hated because they prevent freedom. The usual situation is that one element is projected, and the individual structures his character around one of the remaining elements, thus creating a pseudo-identity. It gives the appearance to others and to himself that he is a free individual, but it is not so. In my description of envy I outline what I call its "first stage", which is where someone projects into another his own good qualities. Paranoia is then the suspicious hatred and sense of betrayal of another who is felt to have stolen a treasure from the subject (Chapter 8).

Kernberg attributes the origin of pathological narcissism to the projection of oral rage. I see its origin, as has already been stated (Chapter 14), in a trauma, and the "narcissistic constellation" is the trauma in a transformed state. However, Kernberg also has a view that is closer to what I am putting forward here when he talks of the external object being in

> . . . the image of a hungry, enraged, empty self, full of impotent anger at being frustrated, and fearful of a world which seems as hateful and revengeful as the patient himself. [Kernberg, 1975, p. 233]

Here is the notion of someone frustrated by the state of his inner world and a hatred of it because, according to my view, it prevents his freedom. It seems clear to me that when Kernberg sticks to the phenomenological description, he comes closer also to the aetiology. I think that narcissism finds its origin not in oral aggression but, rather, in the frustration arising from the fact that the self has been smothered because traumatic circumstances have forced the infant to adopt the "narcissistic constellation" as a way of coping. What I believe needs to be cleared away is the explanations that base themselves on the fixation and the projection of instincts. This is part of a mechanistic psychology whose inadequacy has been elaborated in Chapters 2 and 8. I think that a schema that explains in terms of the obstacles to freedom makes for a meaningful human psychology. Seeing the "narcissistic constellation" as trauma transformed also generates a more humane attitude to it, and also hope that it can be repaired.

The question arises as to why god is installed in the subject in what are termed narcissistic patients but in the object in borderline patients. I suspect that the key must lie in the fact that the difference lies in the appearance to the observer. What appears narcissistic to a psychoanalyst, for instance, may appear borderline to an outsider, and what appears borderline to a clinician appears narcissistic to the outsider. These two scenarios are common: the first where the patient seems to be functioning very assuredly in the consulting-room but is behaving in the most disturbed way with his family and people at work and, second, where the patient seems to be functioning extremely competently with family and at work but behaves in an extremely disturbed way in the consulting-room. There are other dualities also, the most common of which is where one form of behaviour is being displayed at work and another at home. The diagnosis of borderline or narcissistic is according to which observer one consults. The transition from pathology to health occurs when the splitting that is responsible for this separation of parts of the self is no longer total at any one point in time. At the point when the individual is able to encompass in one moment of time both the worm and god, he is "normal"; when one totally smothers the other, he is in a pathological state.

I think therefore that psychoanalytic research in particular and psychological research more generally needs to generate the psychiatric categories and not the other way around. Psychoanalytic understanding forces us to re-evaluate the present psychiatric categories. Seeing how they are generated from a basic inner pattern also leads us to alter the category boundaries.

# PART III

# THE SUBJECTIVE EXPERIENCE

We have considered the foundations necessary for an elaboration of sanity and then an interlocking pattern for an understanding of madness and its ramifications. We now need to consider the subjective experience of sanity and madness. It is my belief that the structure that has been put forward can clarify the subjective experience in an illuminating way.

It is my experience that there is usually a disjunction between theory and practice, and the whole purpose of this book has been to try to elaborate a theory that fits the human experience more closely. The test of this will be to examine human madness as we find it and see whether the theory put forward does anything to enlighten it.

Although the theory reaches the most extreme abstraction possible, yet it is capable of illuminating human problems if it is the outcome of accurate thinking.

# CHAPTER SEVENTEEN

# Human dilemmas

In this consists the excellence and nobleness of *faith*; this is the very reason why *faith* is singled out from other graces, and honoured as the especial means of our justification, because its presence implies that we have the heart to make a venture.

Cardinal John Henry Newman, *Parochial and Plain Sermons*
(1875, p. 276)

I have traced out in this chapter some of the psychological dilemmas that one frequently encounters and which, I believe, can be better understood in the light of the theory and models I am putting forward in this book.

## The sense of being a fraud

I shall start with a very common experience. A man says he feels phoney—a fraud. He is a successful lawyer, but he feels that he has his job under false pretences. He studied law at university and then went on to qualify as a solicitor and is now the senior partner in a medium-sized firm. Now the question is: why does he feel a fraud? I approach the question in this way. I have never been to Turkey and I know next to nothing of its history, but I go to an informative lecture about the country and then I meet some friends and I give them a potted history of modern Turkey. These friends are rather impressed, but I feel a fraud. Why? It is because the information that I have given my friends is a regurgitation of the lecture that I have just heard. I have learned it parrot-wise and repeated it. I have ingested the information while in a passive, unquestioning state. There is no judgement or act of understanding. A friend told me that prior to his psychology exams at university he learned a series of experimental studies by heart and that he had forgotten them two days later, and he felt a cheat. It was a short-term ingestion. Again, there had been no act of understanding.

According to my schema there can be no act of understanding when the centre of the personality is a jelly because it is a creative act that requires an inner cohesion of elements. When material has been assimilated according to the photographic mode, the person feels a fraud (Chapter 6). The only way of assimilating in the presence of the "narcissistic constellation" is through the photographic mode, and therefore the person feels a fraud, a cheat, or phoney. In contrast, the individual who has internalized through an act of understanding feels genuine and is a person because he or she has made a free response.

## Depersonalization

A person feels that he is blown by the winds of chance. One person suggests a holiday in Turkey, and he is all full of it and wanting to go there, but two days later someone else says that is over-rated and thinks a holiday in Armenia would be much more interesting, and then he is full of enthusiasm for that project. What this means is that such a person is very susceptible to being projected into . . .

The effect of the "narcissistic constellation" is to crush personal life. Personal life is the bridegroom of freedom because discernment, choice, and desire are elemental to it. It could be defined as life lived when emotional activities originate from within the boundaries of the self. When this source is crushed or imprisoned, the individual functions like a machine. This can take many forms, but what is common to all is that the individual acts under instruction from without. The outer figure, group, or institution is invested with godly power.

She does what she is told to do. But by whom? Some individual, institution, or cultural icon is invested by her with godly power. The question is, why is one figure selected rather than another? The answer to this question is not as simple as it first seems, because the figure selected is never an actual person as he exists but, rather, a selective schema from the manifestations of that person. So, for instance, the authoritarian traits in that person will be selected, and she will bow in submissive obedience to this "authority figure". This figure will not conform to the actual way in which that person exists and functions. Therefore what is divinized is a personality trait.

A further factor very frequently comes into this picture: the individual provokes the figure into exaggerating his authoritarian traits. Jamie makes a terrible mess in his father's office, thereby stimulating an authoritarian outburst. In this way the particular trait comes to dominate Jamie's picture of his father. Nevertheless, this is not a true representation of the father's personhood and this for two interconnected reasons: the first is that the father's personhood lies in the centre, which integrates the different traits into a unity, and the second is that the outburst is an effusion of the non-personal. In his outburst the father has not made a decision; he is in reactive mode, which, by our definition, is non-personal.

To be in machine-like mode always means that the individual is in relation to a divinized trait. There are certain mechanisms by which this mode is cemented. The individual is always *fascinated* by the character to whom he is held in thrall. This *fascination* is for a particular trait, and when the individual is held fixedly to the *lumen fascinans*, discordant elements are discharged both in the outer figure and in the self. However, the binding feature is an undigested passion shared in common. This passion is the *liquifiers*, which hold the two together like a clockwork toy because the liquifiers keep the centre of the personality gelatinous within a hard exterior. It is these two exteriors that couple in machine-like duality.

Phenomenologically, the emotionally controlling element is the hypnotic factor. The hypnotizer is the outer/inner god whom the other obeys in machine-like mode. Hypnotism is not a discrete phenomenon but a very widespread one, of which the therapeutic hypnotic procedure is a specialized instance. The general phenomenon differs from the specialized in that in the former each partner in the couple entraps the other in machine-like mode. The coupling takes place in this way: the jelly in one surrenders to the god in the other and vice versa. What is sacrificed in each is the free emotional act.

In its specialized form the hypnotist encourages the client to focus on an object while at the same time relaxing his self-will, thereby giving over his being to the instructions of the other. The focus is upon god, and the renunciation of self-will is a legitimation of the gelatinous state. The specialized form therefore encapsulates the situation and emphasizes the robot-like behaviour of the parties concerned.

What is the energy used to invest the outer figure with this power? The quick answer to this is that it is the erotic element that hypostasizes the activity in the outer figure. It is probably the erotic that "fixes" objects as "static" in the outer world. It might be argued that this could be so of the human world but not of the non-human world. It is our view that the non-human world is seen through the emotional categories proper to the human world. It is the erotic, then, that fixes objects as "static" in the world. This is a particular application of the *principle of anthropomorphic perception*. It is through an intensification of the erotic that objects become endowed with godly status.

The result of this investment of the figure with godly power is that the personhood of the individual is crushed, and the person then acts under direction from god and is a machine.

I cannot help reflecting on the fact that the machine-like view of human beings is inherent in the determinism that governs so much thinking about human beings within the social sciences, and I wonder whether such a view finds its emotional origin in the "narcissistic constellation" that I am trying to describe.

## Isolation

A woman was a competent public relations executive. She managed conferences and symposia for clients excellently. She was well able to perform in the public arena, but she had no friends at all, and at weekends was very lonely. When she acted in her professional role, she was "under instructions". She was obeying a set of self-imposed regulations. She had no personal life at all. On Saturdays she wandered around the city window-shopping and would sit in cafes sipping coffee, enviously eyeing groups of people enjoying themselves.

She did not know why she had no friends. She just had a vague feeling that there was something wrong with her. It was clear that she was very frightened of people. On the surface this was surprising because she coped so well when in her official role.

I believe that the schema I have put forward goes some way to explaining this conundrum. The "narcissistic constellation" is easily manifest. When she is in role, she has god embodied in her, and people carry out her orders and her projects and are frightened of her and her efficiency is admired. However, when she is out of role and mixing socially, god is embodied in others, and she is then fearful of approaching them. Other aspects of the "narcissistic constellation" are also in evidence. Because there is a jelly inside, she is unable to make the creative move necessary to make a bridge between herself and another person. The *worm* is also in evidence and leads her to feel that even if she does make an approach to anyone, they will feel that she is uninteresting and boring.

She is hostile towards those people whom she sees with friends. It is their suave confidence that she hates. But why? It is their godhood that she hates. But why? This is a godhood that she has disowned into them, but then why the hatred? They are hated because the godhood within stifles freedom.

One can see here that the origin of the pathological cycle is the intense hatred of the godhood. When it was accepted, then she no longer expelled it. Even more basic than this is the intolerance of frustration. Toleration of unfreedom rather than hatred of it leads to freedom, whereas hatred of it leads to further imprisonment. This is because the hated elements are expelled into surrounding figures, which then become prison walls.

## The moaner

This man complained that he could not implement his innovative ideas for a new housing complex because of a rigid and conservative group on the Housing Development Committee.

> "But did you disagree when they proposed making it on the same model as the last housing scheme?"

> "No, I didn't. Well, it just wasn't worth it. Then they said that they would appoint the architect who had built the last project so successfully."

> "But did you challenge it?"

> "Well, no I didn't . . ."

> "Why?"

> "Well I am not sure, really. I just didn't think it would do anything. You have no idea what the atmosphere is like with those conservative committee members. Their minds are closed. You just can't do anything."

> "You mean *you* can't."

> "Well, I don't think anyone could. . ."

This man was impotent in the face of these conservative members of the committee and continually moaned about their depressing attitudes, but he could do nothing to change them and so he moaned on and on. This is seen from outside but what he feels himself is that these committee members are all powerful; he is up against a legal system that cannot be contravened. "I can do nothing", he says to himself and believes it. What has happened here is that there is an all-powerful godhood installed in these committee members. The godhood is embodied in these committee members, but also in him. The sign that it is also in him is that he said that one of these committee members had criticized one of his directives—*his* directives, indicating that a royal personage had been insulted. His own sense of powerlessness can be seen as manifestations of the jelly and the worm—probably a combination of both. The "principle of inclusion" is operative here.

## Obsessional indecision

We are all familiar with the person who cannot decide. This in-decision lies at the heart of an obsessional neurosis. Joseph could not decide whether or not to propose marriage to Louisa. When he got close to her, he feared being engulfed by her and when they were apart, he felt isolated. He was also still attached to Gillian and to two previous girl-friends also. He could not decide because he was attached in such a way that he was unable to see Louisa as a person. He was, as it were, stuck to her skin. He was a roo in her pouch. Also, he could not move away. When she threatened to leave, he became desperately upset. She would then feel sorry for him and come back to him, and so the cycle went on. He would collapse inside because the glue-like attachment held him together. It fashioned a wall around the jelly but not a very secure one.

This is not exactly how he felt, however. He felt that Louisa needed him, and he felt compassionate towards her. He felt terri-bly upset when she got angry with him. He also felt confused because these two feelings seemed incompatible with each other. If Louisa needed him, then he must be the strong one, so why does he get so upset when she gets angry? So there are these three feelings: pity, upset, and confusion. When he realizes that he is very needy, he castigates himself. He despises the fact that he is a roo in the pouch.

## Manic denial

With god installed in the subject the individual can get rid of obstacles and exaggerate the belief in his capacities. Every time he gets rid of a problem in this way it intensifies his belief that he can do everything. An England county cricket team won 11 matches in succession but then deteriorated dramatically. A nascent analyst investigated the reason for the decline and discovered that the team members had come to believe in their invincibility. Because they believed they were invincible, they stopped practising in the nets, drank late into the night before a match, and so on. Cricketers need to practise, but this had become an unnecessary inconven-ience. All those life-burdens which are necessary for any accomplishment were swept away. Those life-burdens are necessary to human beings, but not to god. God sweeps them away.

God exaggerates the individual's capacities and diminishes the obstacles. A woman went swimming in a cold sea, but so certain was she that coldness was not something that troubled her that when she came out of the water half an hour later, she was suffering from hypothermia.

A man had a religious conversion and now believed that he did not need sex. He then abolished entirely all feelings of sexual attraction. He became a new age ascetic, went to India, and preached against the evils of fornication, adultery, and homosexuality. However, a newspaper reporter published his finding that he regularly visited prostitutes. This indicates that god does not get rid of the sexual in him but that the man believes this to be so. In all probability this man would convince himself that he was helping the prostitutes, giving them the care that they did not receive from other clients. Yet the other side is that sex is abolished because it is dirty and bad.

## Hypochondria

A woman worried incessantly that she had a fatal disease; nothing seemed to diminish her worry. Then one day she had an insight: that her fear of bodily disease was a displacement of a diseased state of mind—one of passive submission, of going off into red-herring tracks, being pressured by my god presence into talking not for communicating but for discharging. So we see here her submission to god—god in me and also in her and one of the predictable results of god's activity: the discharge of the "problem" into some location. In this case it is into her body. This was such an important insight for her that she was intent on holding on to it.

Next session: she had not spoken to others, fearing that she would lose it if she did. She had held it within herself. She noticed that there was no derogatory voice after going for a job interview. She felt OK about it. She felt entitled to the knowledge inside her. Why? It was due to her belief in a capacity to hold rather than expel. In other words she had *done* something—that is, held rather than expel—and this action strengthened her ego. Also in the session she had pointed out that I was being negative, which was true. She felt entitled to the knowledge because it was not only I who had given in the session, but she had given actively as well. She was therefore entitled to the knowledge that had been acquired through the interaction. It was more than just entitlement: she achieved knowledge because she had done something. This is an illustration of the effects of positive emotional action.

If she talks to unburden herself of "stuff", she feels guilty. If she talks to communicate, to give, then she is entitled. In passive mode in relation to me she feels she has acquired knowledge through robbery, and she is therefore not entitled to it. Robbery is to take without giving and is obviously closely associated with greed.

When she pointed out that I was being negative, she took a risk. She did not know how I would reply to her statement. This risk, the step of faith, released her from the grip of the "diseased communication". The importance of this risk, this venture, this act of faith cannot be over-emphasized. It is why I have put that quote from Cardinal Newman at the head of this chapter.

This diseased communication is symbolized by the spider of which she is terrified.


## How about Oedipus?

In all that has been said there has been no mention of Oedipus, and yet Freud referred to this as the "core neurosis" (Freud, 1916–17, p. 337). Has it disappeared with the schema I am presenting here? I will address the question by first giving a clinical vignette.

This man glued himself to me like a clam to a rock. He ingested my attitudes, or what he believed to be my attitudes. He warily watched for my intent behind interpretations while not listening to the interpretations themselves. He was focused like an expert marksman onto any signs of my self-interest, on my narcissism. He believed dogmatically that the intention of interpretations must be care of myself, my own *amour-propre*. He ingested and merged with these narcissistic emotions and rejected interpretations made to him. This was the oedipal set-up: sleeping with mother and slaying father. Sleeping with mother = merging with my own amour-propre; slaying father = rejecting the interpretations. All was quiet on the Western Front as long as I allowed this to continue. When I pointed out what was occurring, when I insisted on the interpretation, when I showed how the interpretation was used to solve some practical problem instead of its proper use (viz. for his emotional development), he became bitterly contemptuous and wanted to sleep with my wife. Uninterpreted, the crime of Oedipus was hidden; interpreted, it became revealed. What drives Oedipus are the *liquifiers* that can be clearly seen in each of the components.

When this secret crime is revealed, when it is interpreted, it provokes an outburst that is verbally violent. Whereas before the violence was enacted "in silence", now it is spoken in words. The analyst has become a hated enemy because he is the revealer of the criminal.

One can understand it by saying that the merging with the analyst's defects is generated by envy. Envy smashes the interpretations with contempt so truth is rejected, and he is left with dross. It is through jealousy that the analyst's interpretations are shut out while "sleeping with mother"—that is, narcissism merging with narcissism. "Sleeping with mother" is not a relationship to another or the other but a merging where the other is made to merge and be an extension of the self. When enlightenment occurs through the action of an interpretation, it is greedily devoured—that is, used in the service of some temporal practical issue that is pressing. The individual is in a "time-segment". When an interpretation is given and the patient's attempt to deflect it is also interpreted, he then violently attacks the analyst by withdrawing into silence, putting the analyst to sleep, missing a session, being violent towards his own wife, or abusing the analyst violently with words that are missiles rather than the carriers of thought. This is the slaying of Laius.

It means that true interpretations are the ambassadors from the inner court of the Absolute—they come from an observation platform outside the "time-segment". "Sleeping with mother" is the sensuous self-protection, time restricted, at the cost of the Absolute, which is shut out. Every time that a message from the Absolute is received, the self-protective, sensuous, and contingent reality becomes further incorporated into the Truth. Self-protection incorporated into the Truth becomes self-respect; with the Truth shut out, it becomes a godlike self-centredness. The Absolute is that which is most personal in the human being, as has been outlined in Chapter 1.

What needs to be noted in this merging is that the engine that drives the process is the narcissistic element in the personality. So, for instance, a patient noticed that her analyst was hyper-sensitive to criticism, and so her own hypersensitivity to criticism was the factor that drove the merging. Therefore elements from the *shadow side* (a term of Jung's) of her personality were merged with echoing ones in the other, which obliterates awareness.

What makes a habit of mind vicious is its repudiation of the Absolute. Once it is received within the orbit of the Absolute, it becomes a source of strength in the personality.


## Sense of inferiority

A person feels inferior because he is poorer than his neighbour, is less knowledgeable than his classmate, belongs to a despised racial group, is less well travelled than his contemporaries. . . . These are the reasons that he tells to himself. It is often also the reason that a psychotherapist or psychoanalyst will believe and put into words to her patient:

> "You feel inferior because your contemporaries are all richer than you . . ."

Or:

> "You feel that I know more than you about psychological matters, and this makes you feel inferior . . ."

Or:

> "Because you are short in height, it makes you feel inferior . . ."

These are reasons to which the individual attaches the inferiority, but they are rationalizations. The individual feels inferior because she does not give emotionally. As she began to give emotionally, so her feeling of inferiority diminished.

We have seen that inability to give emotionally is part of the "narcissistic constellation". It is this aspect of it that is responsible for what is referred to as an "inferiority complex".

This is a summary of some of the subjective experiences that can be better explained according to the schema I have suggested than via the classical explanation, which is, I believe, defective.

# CHAPTER EIGHTEEN

# Guilt

> Guilty man cannot face himself as he is. In spite of the fact that
> this is an age in which introspection has become almost a
> science, it is also an age in which few men dare face themselves
> and to see themselves as they are. Consequently nearly
> everyone has made a fictitious self, and in contemplating this,
> he is able to forget "what manner of man he is".
>
> Caryll Houselander, *Guilt* (1952, p. 49)

There is a relation between trauma and guilt. In Chapter 14, I said that the *liquifiers* disperse the emotion through the jelly. The other possibility is the containment of the emotion. Guilt lies in the refusal of this option. This is because the very refusal itself damages the psyche, and it is self-damaging acts that produce guilt. The human personality is not a given but, rather, a "possibility" that can become a personality through a creative act. Guilt occurs when that creative act is refused. Shame is the emotional consequence of this damaged state. In other words, guilt concerns the act itself, whereas shame refers to the consequences of the act. Shame may result from the act either of the self or of another, which reverberates upon the self. The *liquifiers* disperse the emotion through the jelly, whereas guilt is responsible for hypostasizing inner action onto an outer figure. Guilt is self-blame for the action that jellifies the core of the personality, which prevents the necessary from structuring the contingent. In the narcissistic state this guilt is not suffered. It exists as an entity and is responsible for the projection of inner activities from within to without.

To reverse narcissism means to become aware of what one has done to one's own being. Bearing this knowledge brings pain. Because many of us avoid it, we thereby fail to achieve mental growth.

Guilt is that emotion suffered on account of damage that I have done to my own selfhood through my own inner acts, consequent upon trauma. It becomes the instrumental agent responsible for projection onto others and attribution to others of self-damaging activities that belong to the self. It is very common, for instance, for someone to blame his mother or father for his current emotional difficulties, whereas the responsible agent has been and remains an inner act of submissive attachment. The parents' responsibility generates anger, not guilt. Our thesis is that in infancy submission may have been the only option open, but guilt accrues as opportunities to reverse this are rejected. Our human nature is not a given but a possibility.

All actions of the personality fashion entities. I have called this the "principle of sedimentation". Those actions that repudiate reality's absoluteness form an entity that we call guilt. The essential existence or its absoluteness is the creative centre. The activity of that creative centre recreates those disintegrated bits into wholes: for instance, the passivity or depression is re-fashioned into sadness. In the jelly are guilt particles that are responsible for the expulsion of hated elements into outer figures, where they become hypostasized. They are hated because they prevent freedom and because they produce guilt. When the hated element is propelled outside, it swells up and engulfs the whole person, making him or her into an object. Hatred coincides with intolerance of frustration and in fact is a synonym for it. The element cannot be tolerated, so is expelled. At the same time because this expulsion deprives the personality of an element needed to create a person, the individual is left with a quantum of guilt within. This is a guilt that is not experienced: it is there as an entity. As I said elsewhere (Chapter 14), the "narcissistic constellation" holds the entities in a paralysed state. As it is not felt, it is acted. For instance, on account of the guilt, the person punishes another, usually through projecting hated elements into that other.

Some readers will notice a similarity here between this form of projection and Bion's hypothesis of *beta elements* that are projected into the outer world. The difference between what is being said here and Bion's formulation is that I am positing that the process is the consequence of a trauma and a complex process of hypostasization. This does not contradict Bion, because he does not investigate the origin of *beta elements*. *Beta elements* exist in patterns of recognizable elements, and the reason for their being in beta mode is through trauma that has not been processed.[1] However, I am further saying that guilty refusals aggravate the effects of the original trauma. On this view Bion's *beta elements* are the effect of trauma and guilt. The trauma itself does not produce the guilt, but because trauma and guilt are so interwoven, some psychologists have been seduced into thinking that the outer event itself has produced guilt.

The typical form of this argument is as follows. A mother tells her little boy that it is dirty to touch his penis. This then produces guilt whenever he does so. It leaves out of account the psychological state of the individual concerned. In terms of my account I would say that the reason why the mother's words are so decisive for the child is that god is embodied in her, and the inner state of the child is jelly-like. When the inner emotional state is a jelly, then the outer attitudes of the mother become "imprinted" in a way that would be impossible if the inner state were not jelly-like. In other words, the "narcissistic constellation" is in place in him. The guilt, then, is for those acts of refusal. The theory that is produced to explain the guilt avoids the individual's own emotional acts and his or her inner emotional state.

---

[1] There is an unresolved conflict in Bion on this issue: sometimes he invokes the death instinct to explain the psychotic state, but at others he invokes trauma, to which he refers as a primitive catastrophe.

In Chapter 14 I suggest that the "narcissistic constellation" is the presence of the trauma in a preserved form, and the *intensifiers* can be thought of as a consequence of trauma or as the trauma in psychic form. If this is right, then the question arises as to why there is the presence of guilt. There are two ways of approaching this problem. One is to posit that there is more than one responsive form to the infantile trauma, and that guilt arises if the narcissistic alternative is opted for. This, however, suggests that the infant is able to opt one way or another. If one conceptualizes trauma as the rupture of the stimulus barrier, then it is difficult to see how guilt could find a place. If one thinks of Anne Frank (Chapter 14), it seems insulting to suggest that she could have opted for another direction when her sister died. So also it is not credible that the infant, experiencing a parallel trauma, could do otherwise than cope by adopting the protective clothing of the "narcissistic constellation". There is a true sense in which the creative self of the individual is crushed to death inside the "narcissistic constellation" (Chapter 8). How, then, is guilt possible if no alternative course of action was open to the individual? The other possible solution is to say that the "narcissistic constellation" was the only available solution at the time, but opportunities to alter this mode of acting and being are available at later stages of development— our natures are always in a state of possibility. In fact, many people who present themselves for psychoanalysis, for instance, do so because they are moved to try to replace the "narcissistic constellation" with a creative alternative. This is because although the "narcissistic constellation" has been functional for the individual and enabled him to survive, yet it has been at the cost of his own inner freedom and *personal* fulfilment. The suggestion I am making here is that every time such an inner beckoning to adopt a better alternative is rejected, guilt arises. If we say that the narcissistic state is ineradicably self-damaging, then every time we have an opportunity to oppose its mode of action but do not take it, we accumulate guilt. I believe that it is this refusal of inner possibility that is responsible for guilt. My observation tells me that the presence of guilt plays a very important part in maintaining the narcissistic state.

I believe that if guilt is conceptualized in this way, it helps us to understand why it is that people frequently feel guilty in situations for which they are in no way to blame. A woman whose elder sister had been born without an arm felt guilty at her own physical integrity. Many Jews who survived the Nazi terror felt guilty that they survived while other members of their families did not, even when they were in no way responsible for their deaths. I believe that these phenomena are explicable in terms of a displacement of guilt from the place where it truly belongs—to this inner refusal—onto a factor that is easily identifiable to the senses. If narcissism is either totally or partially transformed into creative love, then guilt gives way to sadness and the sense of tragic loss.

This clinical vignette I have already used (Chapter 17), but I shall use it again.

## A clinical illustration

This woman's insight was that her fear of bodily disease was a displacement of a diseased state of mind. This state of mind is one of passive submission, of going down false trails, being pressured by my "superego" presence into talking not for communicating but for discharging. These multifarious states of mind become displaced into the body, so it deflects her attention from where it needs to be. This was such an important insight for her that she was intent on holding on to it.

Next session: she had not spoken to others, fearing that she would lose it if she did. She had held it within herself. She noticed that there was no derogatory voice after going for a job interview. She felt OK about it. Felt entitled to the knowledge inside her. Why?

In the session she had pointed out that I was being negative, which was true. She felt entitled to the knowledge because it was not only I who had given in the session, but she had given actively as well. She was therefore entitled to the knowledge that had been acquired through the interaction.

If she talks to unburden herself of "stuff", she feels guilty. If she talks to communicate, to give, she is then entitled. In passive mode in relation to me she feels she has acquired knowledge through robbery and is therefore not entitled to it. Robbery is to take without giving and is obviously closely associated with greed.

When she pointed out that I was being negative, she took a risk. She did not know how I would reply to her statement. This risk, the step of faith, released her from the grip of the "diseased communication".

## Resume

There is, I think, a simple formula that encompasses all that has been said here. We have said that hatred is responsible for the expulsion of sedimented entities from the psyche either into the body or into figures or realities outside. What is within then exists outside, but what remains in the psyche is guilt. This is the deposit in the personality for the act committed. So the hated element is located outside, and guilt is the reality located inside. Guilt is then responsible, within the narcissistic structure, for further expulsions.

The greatest therapeutic problem is to help the person to experience those actions that have produced guilt. A hint of condemnation from god blocks such a possibility. What is it that enables the acceptance of one's own self-damaging behaviour? I think the inner desire for integrity must be one factor and the meeting of this with an outer container of tolerance must be another. (The reasons for this self-condemnation are considered in Chapter 22.)

Are we saying here that *beta elements* are guilt particles, and their acceptance is responsible for their conversion into *alpha elements*? I believe that this is so. I am putting forward here a development of Bion's theory: that the *beta elements* are the consequences of a primitive catastrophe (Bion, 1967a, pp. 86, 87), but the maintenance of this state of affairs is not necessary, so to the extent to which the *narcissistic state* remains in being, just to that extent does guilt in the form of *beta elements* remain untransformed. Guilt begins to accrue from the point when transformation of the narcissistic state becomes possible.

Another way of stating this dilemma is to say that there is in every human being a desire for freedom, and when that is sabotaged, guilt accumulates. The "narcissistic constellation" is what imprisons a person. Opportunities for freedom that are refused lay down a heavier burden of guilt in the personality.


## The violence of expulsion

The intensity of the guilt is in exact proportion to the violence of the expulsion, because the more violent the expulsion, the greater the damage that is done to the self. This damage occurs from two sources. On the one hand, the expulsion itself, being violent, rips the self into ribbons; on the other, the figure who is the recipient of this projection reacts violently towards the individual, which has a punishing effect, usually in terms of imprisonment through control.

It is necessary to bear in mind that the greater the guilt, the less is the individual able to see his own actions and the more therefore is everything attributed to the outer figure. This is one possibility. There is, however, another. It is where the individual beats his own breast and accuses himself, but it is an accusation levelled against the self not for the violent acts of expulsion but, rather, as a static object to protect the self from seeing its own violent acts of expulsion. In this latter case god is installed in the personality, and therefore I say to myself:

"All events must be due to me. . ."

just as all creation must be an effect of god. In this latter case it is noticeable that when creative activity begins to free itself from the prison of narcissism, the individual then sees others in their true colours. For instance, a woman who was married to a man who was extremely insensitive and exploitative only saw it clearly when she began to come out of this prison. While in the prison, she was preoccupied with her own self to such a degree[2] that it obscured her perception of her husband. In another case a woman tolerated her husband's infidelities for the same reason. It was only

---

[2]Even though this preoccupation is with her own unworthiness. It is just as narcissistic to be preoccupied with your own unworthiness as it is to be preoccupied with your own excellence.

when a person in her began to emerge that she began to think that her husband's infidelities were callous and not something she wished to countenance any longer. Also in such cases what is frequently not seen are the spouse's good qualities. So a man had not seen his wife's artistic sensibility until his own creative activities began to come into play.

### The plate-glass syndrome

A man said:

> "I am like someone looking out of the window at a crowd of people but not joining in."

Another man said:

> "When I am talking to someone it is always as though there is a sheet of plate glass between me and him or me and her."

In both these cases the men said they were guilty. I believe they were guilty for not throwing their psyche to the other. Had they done so, they would have enriched the other person, but their own souls would also have been enriched through interpersonal fertilization. The action of holding the psyche within an inner castle produced guilt.

Guilt, then, is the activity of those disintegrated particles. The re-integration of them endows the person with sadness and disappointment, and these become the person's own possession.

# CHAPTER NINETEEN

# Generation of perception and belief

> It is of the very nature of the imagination to change the order in
> which things have been impressed on the senses, and to
> connect the same properties with different objects, and different
> properties with the same objects; to combine our original
> impressions in all possible forms, and to modify these
> impressions themselves to a very great degree. Man without this
> would not be a rational agent; he would be below the dullest
> and most stupid brute.
>
> William Hazlitt, *Essays on the Principles of Human Action*
> (1990, p. 41)

## Generation of perception

In his paper "Differentiation of the Psychotic from the Non-Psychotic Personalities" Wilfred Bion (1967b, pp. 47–48) describes the way in which a part of the personality is projected out into an object that, having been engulfed, then swells up. Say, the object into which the projection takes place is a telephone, then it is believed to be listening to the person. The individual's perception is structured by this projection. When reading Bion's paper, one may think that the case he describes is both extreme and rare. A case such as he describes, where the projection is into an inanimate object, is rare, but projection into a human being is extremely common.[1] In fact, the projection is not into the person but, rather, into a hated element in the person. The projection goes into this element, which then swells up and engulfs the whole person. So, for instance, greed is detected in someone, and the greedy part is violently projected into what has been detected; then that part swells up and engulfs the whole person, so that nothing other than that one characteristic is perceived. Everything that person does is seen to be motivated by greed. In a full-blown paranoia, which is a psychiatric description for violent expulsive hatred combined with the first stage of envy, there is no room for any other motives. The hated part has been expelled and has totally engulfed the person into whom the projection has occurred.

This has to mean that perception is governed by such projections—that the emotional act is primary and governs perception. We see according to our inner emotional acts. The way we perceive is determined by them. This has to mean that we are perceiving not what is there but what the emotional activity directs us to perceive.

A judgement comes in here: that some perceptions are paranoid, and some are sane. We have suggested that the paranoid ones happen when a hated part is projected into an equivalent part in the other. What, then, constitutes a sane perception? What is the underlying emotional activity that governs it? The answer is at hand if we consider that the core of paranoia lies in a violent hatred of a part of the self. It is the violent hatred that is responsible for the expulsion. It is the desire to be free that initiates the process, but it is the inability to tolerate frustration that leads to violent hatred, which in turn is responsible for the expulsion. Associated with violent hatred is immediacy. The frustrating inner object must be discharged immediately. Toleration of the frustrat-

---

[1] In the case that Bion describes the projection occurs into an object rather than into himself because the patient believes that such a violent projection into the analyst will provoke a savage attack. So the projection is into an object to "protect" the analyst and himself.

ing object is the emotional activity that is at the heart of sanity. An object that is tolerated, loved even, is contained rather than expelled. And here lies the kernel of the matter: that the nature of the object is determined by the emotional activity in relation to it. So, for instance, the object hated might be greed, whereas the object tolerated might become generosity.[2] We are positing therefore that it is two opposite emotional activities that determine the way we perceive our objects. Hatred and expulsion lead to a perception of external actions that we call mad; toleration and containment of inner entities we call sane.

When someone believes that his next-door neighbour is a Martian come to spy on him and goes and kills him, we have little difficulty in calling him mad. However the inner act of emotional hatred and corresponding expulsion that is responsible for his perception can have other external outcomes that look entirely different but in fact have a similar internal structure. The external outcomes could be any of the following: a man discharges something that becomes envy into his son, who then smashes the windscreen of his father's car; a woman hates the ambition in her so violently that she goes to a plastic surgeon to have her nose straightened because having a different nose from that of her mother, whom she believed to be passionately over-ambitious, she would be free of the hated element within; a woman so hates an element in her that becomes greed that she lives in submission to her exploitative husband in whom the greed now lies expelled; and so on.

---

[2] This explains a stream in spiritual thinking where our vices are the key to our virtues, where great sinners became great saints, and where such dicta as "We fashion virtue on the anvil of our own sins" find their meaning. This same sentiment lies behind this verse of the *Exultet*:

*O certe necessarium Adae peccatum,*
*Quod Christi morte deletum est.*
*O felix culpa, quae talem ac tantum*
*meruit habere Redemptorem.*

[O truly necessary sin of Adam,
which the death of Christ has blotted out!
O happy fault, that merited such
and so great a Redeemer!]

When, however, one of these elements (frequently the *intensifiers*) is tolerated, accepted, loved because of its different relation to other aspects of the personality, then it is are transformed into creative potencies within.

## Generation of belief

Whereas perception is concerned with the shape, dimension, and colour of the object, belief is concerned with the emotional capacity of the subject, which is governed by whether the centre is active or passive. The presence of *intensifiers* determines the degree of this emotional capacity. In other words, when the centre is passive and jelly-like, the individual's emotional capacity is severely limited. His belief, which is used to apply to a whole spectrum of instances, is generated from his own inner emotional situation. His belief will usually be true of himself, but its generalization is false. I shall turn to an example to try to illustrate how this works.

A man believed that he was unable to communicate with his young daughter—that only his wife was able to do this. Everyone knows that mothers understand their baby daughters and fathers cannot. This was his belief, and he confirmed it with a series of examples from among his friends. He was declaring a limitation in his emotional capacity. This incapacity seemed to be verified by some consonant features. When his mother died suddenly, he displayed no grief, yet he developed pneumonia a few days later. He felt no distress when his analyst took a long holiday, but in the week beforehand he said that his daughter would not speak to him at all. These were signs that his emotional centre was unable to process these events. There was a clamour: death is a disaster I cannot manage; I have no spirit within enabling me to ride such a disaster; I am a jelly inside. It is not only death that I cannot manage; when someone criticizes me, I cannot manage it; when my daughter turns away from me, I get so hurt that I have to go out for a drive on my own. So his belief that fathers can never have a relationship with their daughters is generated by his jelly-like state. The truth is that he is unable to communicate with his daughter, that for him death is a disaster, that he cannot manage criticism. Yet in the jelly-like state there is no "he".

Now, as is clear to the reader, I have a theory about what it is that keeps the jelly-like state in being—that it remains so through the presence of the *liquifiers*. I concentrated my interpretations upon the activity of the *liquifiers*. This had the result that he felt distressed when a close friend died, he felt abandoned when his analyst went away, and he found, to his amazement, that he was able to communicate with his daughter. He now no longer subscribed to this belief that fathers cannot communicate with their baby daughters. The belief, which is couched as a generalized statement, is constructed out of his own inner emotional state.

What has happened here is that a someone who engages with his environment has appeared. The way the belief is formulated— viz. "everyone knows fathers cannot communicate with their daughters"—is a pronouncement from god. The more gelatinous the inner state, the more solid or petrified is the godlike pronouncement. Because it is a pronouncement from god, it is not susceptible to rational argument. The godly pronouncement correlates with the gelatinous state in which there is no "he". As has been fully explained (Chapter 9), god is embodied. In this case, the statement "Everyone knows fathers cannot communicate with their daughters" had been preached to him by a boon companion in whom god was embodied. It was not in his mind just embodied in the drinking pal, but also in the so-called practical (I should prefer to call it cynical) wisdom of the community.

What happens subsequent to his experience of being able to communicate with his daughter? Does one belief supplant another? This is not so. What he now says is: "Well, I know, *I* am able to communicate with my daughter." Knowledge has supplanted belief. The move within from passivity to activity is manifest at the surface level as a change from belief to knowledge. But the belief itself has also changed. The inner emotional situation structures the belief just as it also structures perception.

# CHAPTER TWENTY

# Self-knowledge
# versus self-consciousness

The monster is the "ego", the execrable "ego" of the thankless
and presumptuous egoist. It is this "ego" which renders us
insensible to sweetest strains and to most pathetic melodies. This
rampant being with its coarse and passionate uproar so silences
all celestial music that we pass by the claims of Nature and are
obsessed by material cares. Many imagine that it is sufficient to
be lulled by the murmurs of the forest. Not at all! It is still
necessary for Siegfried to exterminate the dragon Fafner. Thus
only do we divine a new language, a language marvellously
caressing and musical, a language lisped in a former existence,
in the far-off fairy days of this world: the language of birds and
beasts.

Constantin Photiades, *George Meredith:
His Life, Genius and Teaching* (1913, p. 213)

S elf-consciousness is often mistaken for self-knowledge; the
latter is the real thing, whereas the former is the mimic.
Narcissism always masquerades as something else, and
in no place is this more true than in the self-knowledge department.

Self-knowledge comes to someone as an unbidden insight. An uncomfortable image of oneself suddenly comes at an unexpected moment. An acquaintance told me this story: he was talking to a very self-centred man when he unexpectedly had an image of this man as a mirror reflecting himself. His realization that he himself was self-centred set off a train of exploration that led him in a quite new direction in his life.

Self-consciousness is an obsession with one's own character defects. It is a vanity in reverse. Instead of preening oneself with one's good qualities, it is a preoccupation with one's defects. A man refrained from making a decision because he kept asking himself: "Am I being arrogant?" A woman kept hesitating about a decision because she kept being worried by the question "Am I acting out of jealousy?"

This kind of self-consciousness is prevalent especially in psychoanalytic circles, but also in all those departments of mental health that have been influenced by psychoanalysis. "Have I become an analyst in order to see problems in others and avoid my own?" and so on. Me–me–me is at the centre of these preoccupations. It is a case of me-itis. There is not a real question here to which someone wants an answer. There is no movement of change. There is no engagement with the preoccupying question. It is quite different when someone wakes up in the night in a sweat realizing that that is why he became a psychoanalyst, and he is overcome with painful horror.

Self-knowledge is like knowledge of any reality in the world except that it is of the self. Self-knowledge requires detached observation of the self; what therefore is the position of the observer in relation to the self? Or where is the observer? It seems that when the actions of the self are accused, the observer plunges into the self. The same thing seems to happen when the self is praised: the observer buries himself in the inflated self. Both a praise and an accusation are in danger of inflating the self so that it envelopes the observer.

The observer is a scientist. It is the embodiment of the scientific mentality within the personality. Self-inflation distorts the scientist's perception. The errors in judgement in the course of life cannot be seen because an inflated self cannot make errors. All those activities undertaken to sustain the erotized self are not seen for what they are. The object-goals of these activities are misperceived. A man married a prostitute but believed that his newly wedded wife was a respectable member of society. A woman bought a house in a slum but believed that it was in the most exclusive area. Another man believed himself to be rich; he convinced himself of this by always having a lot of cash on his person. He would count out $1,000 in notes, and this was enough to convince him that he was rich. Another man, who was rich, believed he was poor; he would go to look up the balance in his current account and would see that he was down to his last $100. The fact that he had share certificates worth a $100 million did not dissolve the delusion.

The erotization can exaggerate either the richness or the impoverishment. I am god, or I am a worm. In either case the detached observer is smothered by the erotic self. The achievement of self-knowledge, which is the foundation-stone of mental health demands, a detachment from this erotized selfhood so that the scientist in the personality can have a view of things undistorted by inflation of the contingent in the personality.

# CHAPTER TWENTY-ONE

# Technique

WORST WORDS

The worst words, the words that hurt,
Are the words you don't use.
You are afraid to use them, because they hurt
And you know they will hurt.
So you go on using another set of words.
They are the words that please, or at least get by.
They make life easier, they grease the wheels,
And no one notices them as they go by.
Until there comes a moment when the worst words
Are the ones you need, the words to do the trick,
The worst trick, to tell the terrible truth.
But it is too late. You have lost the trick of those words.

Anthony Thwaite, *Times Literary Supplement* (27 November 1998)

Psychoanalysts, in their discussions about the pathology of their patients, differentiate between theory and practice.

"Now you've filled my head with all this theory, but how do I apply it in practice?"

asks the exasperated psychoanalyst? The disdainful answer might be:

> "If you've internalized all that has been said about narcissism in this book, then you will just naturally apply it in your dealings with your patients."

Let us say that this is true, but frequently a theory is understood only when its implications are seen "incarnate". Looked at in this light, we could say that the aim of this chapter is to give us another chance to *realize* the theory. Frequently I have had the experience, when I have studied a theory, that I have not understood it, and then a chance remark of the author elucidates the whole matter. The purpose of this chapter is the hope that it may contain that "chance remark" for the reader. An even more important reason might be that it may offer the author the chance to understand his own theory.

After my book on narcissism was published, I was contacted by several non-analysts asking for help with a narcissistic person. Sometimes this person was a member of the enquirer's family, but more often it turned out to be someone in their professional orbit. So the *cri de cœur* was:

> "I have this narcissistic person at work torturing me. Please, please—how do I deal with him?"

This problem, then, is not confined to psychoanalysts; it is a problem for all of us.

In Bourton-on-the-Water in Oxfordshire there is a model of the village and, as that occupies about an acre on the ground, it has a model of the model within it, and so on. This chapter on technique is like the model of the contents of the book. Just as in the book it would have been possible to start anywhere because all the elements discussed are transparencies of all the others, so also with technique. An understanding of narcissism shifts all the interactions between analyst and patient. But we have to start somewhere, so let us start with the embodied god.

## Need for a catholic approach

In Part II I set out the elements of the pattern that governs madness. A basic requirement for a psychodynamic therapist is that he
holds all the elements of the pattern in his mind. The knowledge
that one element implies the others is essential for the successful
treatment of patients.

If an analyst sets it in his mind that envy is the patient's root
problem and pursues it relentlessly, he will not succeed in allevi-
ating the problem. He will only aggravate it. Its more obvious
manifestations will be hidden, but it will remain active in the personality, and its damaging effects will be even greater. A motive
that leads an analyst to pursue just one element in a relentless
manner is frequently his own hatred of it in himself. The patient
then knows that he is copping what belongs to the analyst. Patients
frequently sense this over-determined interest on the analyst's part
and produce the hated element as a defence. Also, a relentless
pursuit of this nature is rarely endowed with understanding.
Meaning is the outcome of the relationship of one thing to others;
meaning is the subjective experience of the place in the system of a
psychological element.

It is very common for one element in the pattern to be manifest
on Monday and another on Tuesday, and so on. It is a mistake to
imagine that the disappearance of the Monday element on Tuesday is a defensive escape on the patient's part. It may be, but it
may also be a healthy movement to bring the whole interlocking
pattern into the analytical process.

## The embodied god

Primitive hatred gets rid of the hated inner object. The more violent the hatred, the more it is fragmented, and the more powerfully
is it expelled. The presence into which it is expelled becomes the
persecutory god. One might say that there are three responses a
clinician might make to this situation:

1.  to reassure and encourage the patient to believe that she or he
    is good and worthwhile

2.   to attack the patient for his/her ruthless self-centredness

3.   to interpret

### I. Reassurance and encouragement

The analyst is confronted with a patient who makes these sorts of remarks:

"I am not very good at my job, so I suppose I deserve all the criticism I get."

"I know I am probably boring you, so I won't go into it any further . . ."

"I know the talk I have to give tonight won't be as good as John Smith's."

"I've just had a thought, but I don't think it's worth telling because I know you will think it trivial"

and so on. The analyst is goaded into offering encouragement or reassurance along these lines:

"I wonder why you think you are no good at your job . . .?"

"I am not sure where you get the idea from that you are boring me . . .?"

"What makes you sure that your talk will be worse than John Smith's?"

"How do you know I will find your thought trivial . . .?"

The inference in all these cases is that the patient is reassured that the analyst has a more favourable opinion of him than he has of himself. What has occurred here is that the good opinion is in the outer person of the psychoanalyst and not in the patient himself. The inner denigration remains. The problem is that the *liquifiers* are still active in the personality. The psychoanalyst in these cases has tried to counteract the effects of their activity through outer pacification. It may be worth asking why the psychoanalyst does this? What are his inner reasons? I think it must be that he cannot bear this negativity pouring forth from the patient, and he tries to dam its flow. It is a safe principle that if you cannot bear something, if you hate it, it is because it is present in yourself. If the analyst has a *liquifier* inside that he hates, then he cannot bear signs of its activity in another. Another way of saying this is that if the analyst is narcissistic, then he will also have a *liquifier* within. Truly, then, the analyst is reassuring himself. The only solution to this problem is for the analyst to begin to tackle his own narcissism. One of my contentions is that *one* reason why analysts, despite having been analysed, are extremely narcissistic is that there has been no model, no theory, that has been capable of illuminating it. The contention of this book is that this condition is central and needs to become the focus of analytic work—that the purpose of an analysis is to transform the entities, entrapped in the "narcissistic constellation", so they can become vehicles of personal growth.

It needs to be noted that the attacking god remains in harness with all strength. The analyst's attempt to massage away the godly assaults have failed. The savage god remains within the patient, and the analyst is perceived and remembered as a benign soother. The patient will never be able to manage without such a soother—but what happens in an extreme situation, where no such soother is available?

The outcome of this situation is that the patient then embodies the savage god in another: perhaps in a boss at work, perhaps in a husband or in some figure representing a group. The hated figure that presides as head of a group or the embodiment of a society is frequently the place where the savage god resides. The only solution is for the analyst to interpret the god that exists in him and its relation to the worm, the jelly, and so on.

In the next scenario the analyst has himself become the chastising god instead of an interpreting analyst.


## II.  Persecuting the patient

The other mode is where the analyst chastises the patient because he is shocked by his self-centredness, which is felt to be ruthless. There are many different variations of this.

Here is one scenario. A woman had her session times in mid-morning, which was very inconvenient for her. She asked whether it was possible to have them during the lunch hour or in the evening. With some considerable trouble the analyst gave her lunch-time appointments, and, once they were all set up, she languidly dawdled into the consulting-room and said in an off-hand manner:

"I think I'll miss the sessions for the next three weeks, as I am rather busy. . ."

The analyst was furious and said that she was deliberately mocking him after he had taken all the trouble to give her sessions at a suitable time. She replied:

"I brought it up for discussion, to see what you thought, not as something definite . . ."

She was asking for an interpretation but was given instead an angry retort. The patient then became frightened of the analyst and remained so for several years. God was now firmly installed in the analyst. Her inner view of things was that god saw her as a contemptible worm. It is clear here that the analyst's own *amour propre* had been stung.

These problems will be avoided to the extent to which the analyst realizes that he is an embodied god for the patient. This realization led to a particular technical approach with one patient. There was abundant evidence that the patient saw the analyst as god himself. She said things such as this:

"When I told you I wanted to study psychology, my impression was that you thought, 'Who does she think she is . . .'"

"When you asked me how I managed my son's rages, I knew you thought I shouldn't be a mother at all. . ."

Then, after a break, she said:

"I found your absence very frustrating, and I know you are looking down on me for being so hopeless."

After another break she was depressed and bedraggled. I said this to her:

"In my absence I looked down on you with contempt and sneered you into the ground . . ."

"Well, you're powerful enough to do it to me . . ."

Communications of this sort were evidence that I was a god look-ing down on her with contempt. She was married, and she had an affair with a married man. Then his job moved him to the States, and the relationship came to and end. In the sessions she was bitter that he had a wife and new country to enjoy while she was left in solitary isolation. She wrote and told him how cruel he had been. I could have pointed out that her situation was somewhat parallel to his—he with his wife and new country, and she with her husband and a new job—but I did not do so because she would be crushed by god saying this; so I interpreted many other things, but not this. Then Annabelle, a close friend, said to her that she was ill-advised to write to him about his cruelty because she was in exactly the same situation as him. Because Annabelle was a friend and an "equal", she was able to accept it. I believe it was technically right to wait until this happened, as it was received as an interpretation rather than a condemnation from god. It is sometimes necessary to wait and allow the interpretation to come from someone else other than the psychoanalyst or clinician.

### III.  To interpret the liquifiers

From what has been said, especially in Chapter 8, it will be clear that what needs to be interpreted is the presence in the pa-tient of the *liquifiers*. Three distinct stages of approach are needed:

(a) *The analyst has a task: to contain his feelings.* He may feel like reassuring the patient, or he may feel like attacking the patient. In the first case he feels in sympathetic alliance with the patient against god. In the second he becomes god. Neither of these proce-dures does anything to reduce the power of god. His job is to contain and process. It is to notice in the first case his wish to reassure the patient and in the second his impulse to condemn the patient. Either set of feelings may be very strong and insistent, and the analyst's task is to process it.

It is a great mistake to think that the analyst's first task is to interpret. It is not. His first task is to contain the feelings that are being stirred in him by the *liquifiers*. His task is to strive to achieve awareness of these two states of arousal. He is aroused either to side with the patient against god or to become god. It is only when he has contained these stirred feelings that a suitable interpretation may present itself.

So the reply to the first of the statements made to the reassuring analyst might be:

> "Your statement implies that you receive a lot of criticism. I wonder why this keeps happening to you?"

This opens a path to explore the activity of the *liquifiers*, to identify and name them. However, I think even this last comment may be too persecuting. It may be necessary for a long time to stay with the observation that the patient receives a lot of criticisms and then to wait until some curiosity as to why arises in the patient.

In the case of the woman whom the analyst attacked for scorning his efforts to arrange suitable times for her, he might have said,

> "This is really the first moment that you have had the chance to be fully in the analysis without worrying whether you shouldn't be at work or what others will be thinking. It seems that this unencumbered encounter with me in the analysis fills you with panic . . ."

This again leads straight to what it is *in her* that stimulates such panic.

*(b) & (c) will be first the identification of the liquifier and then the hurt (c) and then the self-castigation (d).*

A central problem already alluded to in Chapter 2 is to bring about the transition from hatred of the *liquifiers* to acceptance of them. Hatred of the *liquifiers* is situated in god. The change from hatred to acceptance can be achieved if the distinction can be made clear between the scientist in the personality and the erotized self (Chapter 20).

## Restoration of psychic barriers

We have said that in the narcissistic structure the psyche is in a gelatinous state, and this is due to the fact that psychic barriers have been destroyed. The therapeutic task, then, is to restore these barriers. Let us say, for instance, that sadness is present in the personality as an entity with no permeable barrier around it. The personality is then flooded with sadness. The result is that the personality is weighed down and dejected. A psychiatrist might diagnose the patient as depressed. The task now is to establish a permeable barrier around the sadness, so that it becomes sadness and is no longer depression. The psychopath, for instance, makes the sadness exist outside. When treating the psychopath, the analyst's task is to locate the sadness within and to establish a *psychic barrier* around it. The problems in achieving this are considerable and can be considered in stages.

When psychopathic traits are noted, the analyst is in possession of some hypotheses:

a.  that there is within an excruciating sadness;

b.  that this sadness has not been experienced;

c.  that activity is geared to causing distress outwardly;

d.  that the *psychic barrier* is fragmented;

e.  that guilt is present in the personality.

The reason for this last hypothesis is that the activity of (c) to the extent that it has occurred leaves a deposit of guilt, according to the "principle of sedimentation". The importance technically of conceptualizing all these hypotheses is that in the treatment, whichever of these is to the forefront is the one that needs to be contained and interpreted. To focus on one to the exclusion of the others will consolidate the defensive process. Although these five hypotheses are set out separately, yet they are manifestations of one reality, which needs to be tackled as a whole. To tackle one aspect is to attack the symptom rather than the condition that generates it.

As mentioned in Chapter 9, there is a moment when the patient begins to feel free of his or her own submissive activity. At this point the person is in a state of fury towards the figure to whom he or she has been in submission. In extreme cases the person can even be in danger of physical attack, but in lesser cases the person might on impulse start an affair with someone else, and the situation may lead to divorce.

### Savage god and the nature of love

At one moment a person will be dominated by the presence of a savage god that is embodied in an intimate figure (as is usually the case). She will be tyrannized by it and will complain in a self-pitying manner of being put down and exploited. Sometimes she will hear a voice castigating her. Once this is established, it is always the case that her own love will be accompanied by sadism. What is done to her is in turn done by her to her love object. The more savage the god, the more severe is her sadism towards her love object. She will be aware of the former but not of the latter. This is a case of the *principle of self-ignorance of negative emotional acts*. There is always an interplay between being attacked by the savage tyrant and doing the attacking herself. Her emotional centre is either the object of attack or the subject of attack. In the latter case the savage god has taken possession of her emotional centre.

The realization of this polarity is extremely important technically. For example, a woman said to her analyst that he was no good and that she would be having a much better treatment if she were seeing so-and-so. It is a mistake for the analyst to fasten upon her denigration of him for several reasons, but the one I am concentrating upon here is that his mind-set needs to encompass the totality of her mental constellation. He needs to realize that this patient is in the possession of a savage god who is now in active mode. The realization of this will predispose the direction of his interpretation. It will probably direct the analyst towards describing the state of mind to the patient—it is a state of mind where she is in the grip of what seems like an alien force, which leaves her feeling hopeless: that her marriage is no good and that her analyst can no longer help her. From such a description the patient experiences the analyst as containing her anxiety. Interpretations based on the idea that the patient is denigrating the analyst are experienced as defensive—that the patient should not be treating the analyst in this way. It is the analyst's narcissism that steers the interpretations in such a direction.

## The patient who feels phoney or a fraud

It is common for someone to feel a fraud. The analyst may be puzzled as to why this is so. The key to understanding this is that someone feels a fraud if there is an absence of *realization*. If someone's own active self is passive or dead and he has ingested the living pattern of another through which he lives, then it is likely that he will feel phoney or a fraud. What he says and acts does not come from his own suppleness of self but, rather, from the ingested pattern. So this is the diagnosis, but what does the analyst do about it?

It will be clear from what has been said about the jelly and god that the diagnosis is consistent with the "narcissistic constellation" that has been outlined. There is no active self operating in the artistic creative mode, but, rather, what is being done is in the photographic mode (Chapter 6).

A clinical vignette may illustrate the matter.

> This successful accountant sat opposite me and had his attention focused upon me. He was engaged in telling me about a client at his work whom to he was able to speak firmly for the first time; then he carried on speaking, and my attention wandered, and his narrative instantly ceased. I pointed out that the moment my attention wandered, he collapsed. I subsequently pointed this out frequently. One day when it happened again his focus was not upon my wandering attention but on a "bolt from within" that overwhelmed him with a feeling of utter helplessness.

An intense focus on the other is nearly always due to a phobic flight from an active worm-like horror within. If a psychoanalyst, for instance, treasures this attention to himself and sees it as transference without realizing the phobic flight, then the inner horror remains in place.

## Interpretation of narcissistic objects

In Chapter 5 I tried to describe how an activity becomes hypostasized in a static figure. I will start with an example. A man was ruled by his wife, who was very demanding. In analysis he behaved like a craven soul in deferential submission to his analyst, but in his eyes there was hatred. As the submissive mode was interpreted, he became aware of his hatred, not only towards his analyst, but towards his wife also. In fact, analyst and wife coalesced into one entity. This entity can be thought of as the *narcissistic object* or as god embodied, but the true object of hatred is the submissive clinging inner emotional act. As this hatred comes to awareness, it presents the analyst with technical problems that require considerable courage and wisdom to manage.

When this object is secretly hated, there develops another, which is passionately loved. Whereas the hated object scorns and depreciates the person, the loved object consoles and builds him up. However, in relation to both he is a passive recipient. What is clear is that there is lacking any inner creative capacity. The person is dependent upon the "rewards" of the erotized figure for his own sense of self. One can get some purchase on this if one thinks of the *worm*, which gets confirmation from the hated object and disconfirmation from the loved object. The object is loved because it flatters: the object is hated because it derides. In each case it is uncreative love and uncreative hatred.

It might be profitable to see how these two processes are different from creative love and creative hatred. Hatred that is creative occurs when the object points out something—let us say, the person's grandiosity—and the person feels insulted, but the object is still there, and the person is not rejected. One might call this creative hatred because it is an active repudiation of the other, which is trying to make itself felt. It is the contingent, the narcissistic part of the personality resisting the impression of the other. Creative love occurs when the other finally breaks through, evoking love as it does so.

## Manifestations of the glue-like attachment

An analyst noticed that he frequently fell asleep during the Monday session of a particular patient. He made the following reconstruction: in the state of sleep he was dislocated, out of contact with the patient. He surmised that this symbolized the patient's own dislocation from himself. The pain of rupture from the analyst was so great that he broke into two. As the week progressed, he felt more together, but then on Friday the patient had a dream in which he was beating an old man to death. This was his rage at the analyst for leaving him. However, according to my schema, it was also a rage at being so attached to his analyst—a rage at being tied to someone in such a way that it had such a momentous effect on him, a rage at being imprisoned in this way. It was important that the analyst interpreted this in such a way as to indicate that it would be surprising if he did not experience this rage at being imprisoned. Therefore the interpretations were focused on the nature of the attachment and the hatred of it as it prevented him from being a free manager of his own life. This was the glue-like attachment aspect of the pattern, and it manifested itself regularly.

However, the other elements were present also. There was a bitter resentment towards the analyst for being so important. When he made a correct interpretation, the patient envied this so much that it prevented him from taking the interpretation in. The interpretation would have had a liberating effect had he been able to take it in, but instead he was further imprisoned. He was further imprisoned also because of guilt accruing from the refusal of the interpretation, and this was another element in the pattern.

He suffered intense inferiority, which he attributed to being born into the lower middle class. This was evidence of the worm. A further reason was that he was on his third marriage, which he attributed to his inability to hold a woman's emotional and sexual interest. However, the inferiority was partly due to the guilt just mentioned. It was also clear that when he did take an interpretation in, his sense of inferiority decreased. There was a dual attitude to many interpretations: a hatred combined with a feeling that the analyst was a sadist and being deliberately cruel and a knowledge that the interpretation was right. The procedure was usually that it was initially greeted with the hatred, and subsequently the knowledge of its correctness would emerge. When he gave in to the feeling that the analyst was deliberately cruel, his inferiority increased; when he assented to the knowledge of the interpretation's correctness, he became more confident of himself.

He hated the envy, jealousy, and greed within himself, and the elements had to be identified and also his hatred of them. He believed—in fact he was certain—that the analyst hated them also.

God was installed in the analyst and was one of the reasons why interpretations were experienced as declarations from on high. The analyst was not just god but a savage god and he a miserable worm.

He was also jelly-like in that he could not initiate his own communications, and very frequently in the early stages of the treatment the analyst had to initiate the conversations.

All these elements were present, but what first manifested itself to the analyst was the glue-like attachment.


### Attachment to words and formulae

Very often in psychotherapy we accept the reasons for a person's fear of taking a step, but the reality is that we do not know the reason beforehand, so the spoken reasons are spurious. I shall give an example.

A young woman managed her professional life extremely competently, and everyone thought her to be a mature, well-functioning human being. She "managed" the analysis in the same way for the first three years, and then a fear of needing me like a small baby filled her mind. She feared stepping any further in this direction because, she said,

"You might not give me what I want."

"You might become cruel towards me."

"I don't want to use you as an anti-depressant."

"I don't want to be a parasite."

Yet the real reason was that it was a step into the unknown. These were all reasons that she gave to herself . . . rationalizations, if you like.

## The analyst as agent of negativism

In Chapter 12, I pointed out how when the "narcissistic constella-tion" is in place, god tells her that she is useless, and all evidence is mustered in order to prove this. The analyst points out that the patient is grandiose, and the patient assumes that this god also believes her to be utterly worthless. It is more than that—it is that the god is declaring her to be useless.

Does this mean that the analyst cannot point out that she is grandiose? There are two answers to this. It depends on how this is pointed out, and it is well kept in mind that this is part of the "narcissistic constellation" that is the presence of trauma in the personality. If one keeps the principle in mind that our human nature is always one of possibility, then this can be pointed out when the ability to manage a changed mode of being becomes possible. Also, what follows in Chapter 22 needs to be kept in mind.

# CHAPTER TWENTY-TWO

# Reverse perspective

The greatest wisdoms are not those which are written down but those which are passed between human beings who understand each other.

Salley Vickers, *Miss Garnet's Angel* (2000, pp. 232–233)

I said at the beginning that it was necessary to read this book twice, but I am going to try to gather some of the key elements together into one.

The first thing that needs to be said is that the model I am proposing in this book is a myth. It is not a concrete thing. It is one way of organizing the internal determinants that go to make up the state that we call madness. It is a particular observational angle upon it, and in that statement is already the suggestion that other angles are left out. The question I want to address here is "How does the perspective that gives rise to madness become reversed so that we no longer have madness but sanity?" If we can answer this question, we shall have made a momentous contribution. The problem is that the answer is something that each individual clinician has to make, and what is more we are not talking of an intellectual answer alone but one that is intellectual and emotional. Therefore it requires not just an intellectual effort but an emotional transformation. What we are looking for, then, is a reversal of the perspective that generates madness.

An essential component of the pattern of madness that we have outlined is a primitive hatred. What I have called the *intensifiers* whose subordinate categories are *liquifiers* and *petrifiers* do their damage because of an intensity that is generated by hatred. This hatred is understandable because the individual knows (though he is not aware) that this pattern within him restricts his freedom very seriously, and an exasperated intolerance impels him to get rid of the irritant as quickly as possible. It is very often precisely as the frustrating inner constellation comes to awareness that the intolerance reaches its highest point. An example from current penal practice in Britain can serve as an illustrative example. A man has been in prison for eight years and is now due to be released in nine months' time. At this juncture he is given a week's "home leave"—in other words, he is allowed out of gaol for a week and goes home with the understanding that he returns at the end of the week. It happens quite frequently that the prisoner does not return, tries to avoid re-capture, and is then finally caught, and his sentence is extended for another few years. All logic would dictate that he should return to prison at the end of the week, see out the final nine months of his sentence, and then enjoy his legitimate freedom.

This situation is replicated in the inner forum of many patients who become aware of the restrictions being imposed upon them. One might suppose that the prisoner who jumps his parole had accustomed himself to the restrictions of prison life, had almost forgotten what free normal life, was like and then, on home leave, he suddenly realizes what he had been subjected to for the previous eight years and in a tantrum of annoyance "breaks free", as he believes, but in fact instead of "breaking free" he imprisons himself further. Something like this very often happens as an individual begins to realize the way he has been held captive, and so he breaks out in impulsive behaviour that brings disaster upon his head.

Such breaking out is initiated by the hatred of the imprisoning factors within. I want now to go through the imprisoning factors and see how any clinician treating such a person is required to address the matter. To start with the *intensifiers*: these are made up of envy, greed, and jealousy together with god. The three are acting in concert. The first stage of envy is where I see someone with undoubted abilities and then discharge my own good qualities into that person. The person now has more good in him than before. It is as if I perceived a rich man and gave him a large donation from my own dwindling funds. Someone has great imaginative capacities, and I endow him not only with his own but with mine also. I now see him as fantastically imaginative. This perception is right because I see the figure as I have now endowed him. Then I hate him for having robbed me and for having good things, whereas I have none. I have impoverished myself with the first action and then I am using up all my psychic energies in the second. This is envy.

With greed, I see a good quality that is on offer to me and rather than take as much of it as I need, I grab the whole lot. I do this with such force that it ruptures the boundaries of my psyche, so that now everything flows in and also everything flows out. One day I come across a new teaching that is very appealing. It may be Catholicism, Communism, Buddhism, psychoanalysis, or the teachings of Jung, of Freud, of Klein, of Bion, of Piaget, of Billy Graham, of Karl Marx, of Erich Fromm, of John Macmurray, of St. John of the Cross, of Tolstoy, or of Thomas Aquinas. The teaching or the figure floods me, and I become indistinguishable from the teaching, the outlook. It may well be my own psychoanalyst whose wisdom overwhelms me and whose devoted disciple I become. I am flooded by the *persona* of the other, and my own person disappears in a tidal wave.

It is the sanity of a third party that modifies the intensity of these processes. It is jealousy that shuts out this sane presence. This is why jealousy is an essential component of this baneful triumvirate.

We now come on to god. God has been given a bad name in this book so far. I have said it is the god in the personality that is responsible for obliterating pain, getting rid of emotion, blotting out memory, distorting perception. So when I am talking to a patient, I may refer to this god-like persona, and the patient will get the idea that it is a bad thing to have within. Other words and

phrases—like grandiosity, the royal self, and omnipotence—also
carry this pejorative sense. Also when someone blames himself
excessively this castigation is always felt to come from some superior being looking down—god looking down upon this miserable
worm.

A patient, called Nadie, had had a traumatic childhood. Her
mother died giving birth to her, and she was then brought up by
her father's sister, but as a young child she was told that this aunt
was her mother. Later, when she learned that the aunt was not her
mother, she referred to her as "Aunty–Mumma". Now she illus-
trated two aspects of this goddess in her. She would castigate
herself in the fiercest way, and she would tempt me, her therapist,
to do the same. Also, she had damaged herself very severely, both
financially and otherwise. She put all her inheritance into a most
farcical investment, and she had partnered up with men who were
extremely exploitative of her. The question is "Why?" It was also
clear that Nadie was broken up inside; she used to say: "I am all in
bits." When she was in an agitated state one day, she would not
remember anything about her agitation the following day. In a
session she would make an angry retort to an interpretation; when
I referred to this half a minute later, she would utterly deny the
retort. It took me time to realize that she had forgotten it—so she
was in bits, but also time was chopped up into bits, and one bit was
unconnected to another. So Nadie was truly in bits: yesterday had
no connection with today, and this morning had no connection
with this afternoon. It seemed that this broken-up state of her
psyche had a connection with this self-destructive behaviour and
self-castigation.

My proposition is that to have a god castigating her was preferable
to being the casualty of a traumatic accident.

The best way of approaching this question is to start by quoting
this passage from the Bible:

> And when they came to the threshing floor of Næcón, Uzzah
> put out his hand to the ark of God and took hold of it, for the
> oxen stumbled.

> And the anger of the Lord was kindled against Uzzah; and
> God smote him there because he put forth his hand to the ark;
> and he died there beside the ark of God. And David was angry

> because the Lord had broken forth upon Uzzah; and that place
> is called Pê'rêz-ùz'æh to this day. [2 Samuel, 6: 6–8]

Now the question is: "What has happened here?" This is the way I
interpret it. The ox-cart carrying the Ark of the Covenant was
coming down a rough mountain path, and one of the two oxen
stumbled; Uzzah rushed forward to try to steady it, but it fell and
crushed him to death. In modern journalistic reporting the incident might go like this:

> "At Nacon, twenty kilometres from Jerusalem, the oxen carry-
> ing the Ark of the Covenant to the Temple stumbled. A man
> rushed forward to steady the cart, but it toppled over and
> crushed him. He was rushed by ambulance to hospital but was
> dead on arrival. The man's name was Uzzah."

Or even perhaps:

> "At Nacon, twenty miles from Jerusalem, the truck carrying the
> Ark of the Covenant had a tyre burst, and it skidded and
> crashed into a bollard at the side of the road. The driver, Mr
> Uzzah, was killed. . ."

So why in the Bible is this incident attributed to God, to Yahweh?
I think it is significant that David was angry with Yahweh. I believe it was attributed to Yahweh because it is easier emotionally
to manage than to attribute it to sheer accident. Henri Bergson said
that if a rock rolled down a hill and hit a stone-age man and killed
him, he would attribute it to an evil spirit (Bergson, 1935,
pp. 119ff). Freud makes a similar point in *The Future of an Illusion*:

> There are elements, which seem to mock at all human control:
> the earth, which quakes and is torn apart and buries all human
> life and its works; water, which deluges and drowns every-
> thing in a turmoil; storms, which blow everything before them;
> there are diseases, which we have only recently recognized as
> attacks by other organisms; and finally there is the painful
> riddle of death, against which no medicine has yet been found,
> nor probably will be. With these forces nature rises up against
> us, majestic, cruel and inexorable; she brings to our mind once
> more our weakness and helplessness, which we thought to
> escape through the work of civilization. . .

Impersonal forces and destinies cannot be approached; they remain eternally remote. But if the elements have passions that rage as they do in our own souls, if death itself is not something spontaneous but the violent act of an evil Will, if everywhere in nature there are Beings around us of a kind that we know in our own society, then we can breathe freely, can feel at home in the uncanny and can deal by psychical means with our own senseless anxiety. We are still defenceless, perhaps, but we are no longer helplessly paralysed; we can at least react. Perhaps, indeed, we are not even defenceless. We can apply the same methods against these violent supermen outside that we employ in our own society; we can try to adjure them, to appease them, to bribe them, and, by so influencing them, we may rob them of a part of their power. [Freud, 1927c, pp. 15–17]

God is fashioned to protect us from the senselessness of an accident. A trauma is an accidental happening—something that the individual was incapable of avoiding or preventing. It may have been something that happened in childhood. Nadie's mother had died giving birth to her, and many unfortunate consequences followed from that. Neither the disaster of her mother's death nor the consequences could have been prevented by Nadie. And this trauma, as emphasized in Chapter 14, breaks the spirit. It breaks the human psyche into those bits that I have named the "narcissistic constellation", of which god is a part. It is an animistic way of talking to say that it is the god in the personality that obliterates pain and self-destructiveness or propels hated elements into the body or surrounding figures. That such obliteration and propulsion takes place is accurate, but to call god the agent is the same as the Biblical author saying that Yahweh struck down Uzzah. The agent of the obliteration and propulsion is the scattered "bits-in-the-jelly". We call it "god" because it looks to the observer like grandiosity or it feels to the subject like a godlike authority subjecting him or her to a fierce castigation. In other words, this definition arises from the subjective experience of the other, even if "the other" is the recipient in one's own self.

The conversion of "an accident" into godlike activity is the source of masochism. The authoritarian voice in the personality condemns and tells the individual that this is all his fault or that she is to blame. It is very common for a clinician to point out some limitation to a patient, and then the latter adds to what has been said:

> "Yes, I am always very bad at listening to people. Often I don't bother and frequently I just indulge my own thoughts . . ."

> "Yes, I know it is not only my brother I put down. When I am teaching, I often put down my pupils quite unnecessarily . . ."

> "I am just a rotten bastard. I don't deserve to be trusted in people's company at all. . ."

It is preferable to think in this way. There is some sense that this limitation is under control rather than uncontrolled activity flowing from "bits-in-the-jelly", from an accidental disaster.

Masochism or self-harm is the very soul of madness. It is self-destructive activities that we define as mad. Suicide is its prototype, but all the derivatives of these constitute those actions that we call mad. If I do something to hamper my development, then it is a madness. Now it is precisely the "narcissistic constellation" that interferes with creative development, and of this constellation it is god who condemns, who pronounces that the individual is a worm, worthless, unfit to live, that is responsible for the active diminishing of the person's talents and capabilities.

An understanding that even the most perverse, mad, or psychopathic behaviour is the existence of the trauma in transformed mode is the clinician's foundation stone. A patient comes to a clinician with the hope that he can get help for this state of affairs. If help is available, then it must lie in the communication between the clinician and the afflicted individual. How it is that communication is curative is what we must now try to understand.

What the science of mental health urgently requires is a theory of emotional communication. A patient comes to see a clinician in the expectation that the conversations that she has with him will help to resolve her problem. Recent research within psychoanalysis teaches that what is crucial in severe disturbance is the psychoanalyst's containment of the patient's anxieties. In terms of the schema that has been presented here, it means that the clinician is not disturbed by the "bits" that are being projected towards the figure of the clinician. If the patient's hatred hits, as it were, the "narcissistic constellation" of the clinician, then he will bounce back what has come at him. Hatred meeting hatred = expulsion meeting expulsion, so there is a reactive chain set up between the two individuals. However, if the expelled elements are received by the essential being of the clinician, then they are absorbed by him into a new organizational pattern, into a pattern of sanity.

One has to ask why this is of benefit to the patient. Here we come back to what was said about symbolism in Chapter 1: that the nature of one symbolizes the essential being of the other, and here a very important characteristic of symbolization comes into play. It is that the symbol affects that which it represents. It is because of the unity of being that what occurs in the clinician also occurs in the patient. The unity in contingent and essential being is symbolized and established rather than disrupted; in other words, the containment of hatred by essential being is something in which both participate. The consequence is that there is a transformation of the "narcissistic constellation" into a pattern of sanity.

There are certain implications in all of this. It is not the words in themselves that are effective in the clinical transaction but, rather, the mentality of which the words are the messengers. We cannot expect that the clinician be totally sane and with no traces of the "narcissistic constellation" within him. Therefore there has to be an aim that is the transformation of the "narcissistic constellation" wherever it may be most in evidence. Sometimes the evidence will be that it is manifesting itself in the patient: that is the place to which the clinician's psychic attention needs to be directed. Sometimes it will be manifesting itself in the clinician: that, then, is the place to which the clinician's psychic attention needs to be directed. The clinician's capacity to manage this will depend not on his skill but, rather, on the level of his self-awareness. What will be crucial here is the clinician's own level of emotional functioning and the degree to which he is aware of the "narcissistic constellation" within himself. There are no guarantees. After all, life is full of perils, and clinical engagement is one of the greatest.

# Principles of action

*Anthropomorphic perception.* The notion that our perception of the non-human world is structured according to the emotional principles upon which our perception of the human world is based.

*Coexistence of opposites.* It is the principle that any emotional state that is being described is always paired by its opposite.

*Communication thrust.* This is a basic communicative thrust that is capable of becoming either *projective identification* or *creative communication,* depending upon the response of the object.

*Creative communication.* It is the process whose source is in a pattern-of-fragments or alpha function and whose result is the creation of free desire. I think it is probably the same as what Bion described as a *commensal* relationship.

*Principle of conservation.* That a psychic quality cannot be annihilated but only turned into a different form.

*Principle of emotional action.* The presence of an emotional state is evidence that an emotional act has taken place.

*Principle of homogenization.* The process whereby distinct psychic

215

processes are coalesced into one category. This is a process characteristic of narcissism.

*Principle of hypostasization.*    Whereby the activity that is hated is displaced onto the figure who is the receptacle of the activity. This is different from "principle of sedimentation", where the psychic act fashions an element in the personality, whereas in hypostasization there is displacement from an act onto an object.

*Principle of inclusion.*    Whereby any one of the elements of the "narcissistic constellation" is contained in all the others.

*Principle of integrity.*    That there is a drive to integrate all parts of the personality into one whole. This means that when one part of the self has been expelled, the individual is attached to that part and is unable to separate him- or herself from it.

*Principle of ontological identity.*    Because the self and the other share the absoluteness of reality, what is being done to the other is also being done to the self.

*Principle of reciprocity.*    When acting under the influence of the "narcissistic constellation", the individual believes that what is true for him is also true for the other. So, for instance, he is extremely sensitive to criticism and therefore believes that the other is also. Or he is intensely jealous, so he believes that the other is also, and so on. It is necessary to realize that this is only so of elements in the personality that are disowned.

*Principle of sedimentation.*    Every psychic act leaves a residue, which then exists in the personality as an entity. Those psychic acts that block the integrity of the necessary crystallize into guilt; those psychic acts that channel the necessary crystallize into a centre of confidence.

*Projective identification.*    The process whereby hated or painful elements in the psyche are discharged into outer objects, which can be either the body or people in the close environment. The outer objects can also be non-human animate or inanimate objects.

*Psychic barriers.*    The *stimulus barrier* is what protects the personality from being flooded with damaging stimuli from outside. Freud postulates this mechanism in *Beyond the Pleasure Principle* (1920g). Trauma occurs when this barrier is broken and the personality is flooded with a quantum of stimuli with which it cannot cope. A *psychic barrier* is the inner correlate of the *stimulus barrier*; it protects the personality from being flooded not by an outer event but by an inner entity, such as envy, for instance. A *psychic barrier* is permeable. It prevents an entity not from affecting the personality, but from flooding it.

*Self-ignorance of negative emotional acts.*   People do not *feel* their own destructive emotional acts; they can come to *knowledge* of them through experience and logical thinking.

*Stimulus barrier.*   A structure that protects the personality from a quantity of stimuli that is too great for it to manage. Freud said in *Beyond the Pleasure Principle* (1920g) that rupture of the *stimulus barrier* is responsible for trauma.

*Two perceptual modes.*   There is practical perception and emotional perception; the former delineates according to linguistic usage, whereas the latter according to a set of emotional principles. One such principle is that of coalescence, where disparate entities are perceived as singular; another is where what is a unity is perceived as separate: a process known as splitting.

# REFERENCES

Aries, P. (1976). *Western Attitudes toward Death from the Middle Ages to the Present*. London: Marion Boyars.

Aries, P. (1981). *The Hour of Our Death*. Harmondsworth, Middlesex: Penguin.

Aries, P. (1986). *Western Sexuality*. Oxford: Basil Blackwell.

Aries, P. (1987). *A History of Private Life*. Cambridge, MA: Harvard University Press; London: Belknap Press.

Bennett, A. (1969). *Anna of the Five Towns*. Harmondsworth, Middlesex: Penguin.

Bergson, H. (1935). *The Two Sources of Morality and Religion*. London: MacMillan.

Berlin. I. (1976). *Vico and Herder*. London: Chatto & Windus.

Berlin. I. (1979). *Against the Current*. London: Hogarth Press.

Bion, W. R. (1962a). On hallucination. In: *Second Thoughts*. London: William Heinemann Medical [reprinted London: Karnac, 1993].

Bion, W. R. (1962b). *Learning from Experience*. London: William Heinemann Medical [reprinted London: Karnac, 1991].

Bion, W. R. (1963). *Elements of Psychoanalysis*. London: William Heinemann Medical [reprinted London: Karnac, 1989].

Bion, W. R. (1965). *Transformations*. London: William Heinemann Medical [reprinted London: Karnac, 1984].

Bion, W. R. (1967a). On arrogance. In: *Second Thoughts*. London: William Heinemann Medical [reprinted London: Karnac, 1993].

Bion, W. R. (1967b). Differentiation of the psychotic and non-psychotic personalities. In: *Second Thoughts*. London: William Heinemann Medical [reprinted London: Karnac, 1993].

Bion, W. R. (1970). *Attention and Interpretation*. London, Sydney, Toronto, Wellington: Tavistock Publications.

Bion, W. R. (1974). *Bion's Brazilian Lectures, Vol. 1*. Rio de Janeiro: Imago Editora.

Bion, W. R. (1980). *Bion in New York and Sao Paulo*. Perthshire: Clunie Press.

Bleuler, E. (1924). *Textbook of Psychiatry*. New York: Macmillan Company; Arno Press, 1976.

Bollas, C. (1989). *Forces of Destiny*. London: Free Association.

Bonhoeffer, D. (1970). *Ethics*. Collins: Fontana Library.

Brentano, F. (1973). *Psychology from an Empirical Standpoint*. London: Routledge & Kegan Paul.

Bridges, R. (1921). *The Spirit of Man*. London: Longmans, Trench.

Bronte, E. (1844/1990). To imagination. In: *Wuthering Heights, with Selected Poems*. London: J. M. Dent [Everyman's Library].

Brontë, E. (1996). *Poems*. London: Everyman's Library: Pocket Poets.

Burney, C. (1952). *Solitary Confinement*. London: Clerke and Cockeran.

Chesterton, G. K. (1910). *George Bernard Shaw*. London: John Lane, The Bodley Head; New York: John Lane Company.

Collingwood, R. G.(1969). *An Essay on Metaphysics*. Oxford: Clarendon Press.

Dostoyevsky, F. (1978). *Crime and Punishment*. Harmondworth, Middlesex: Penguin.

Durkheim, E. (1915). *The Elementary Forms of the Religious Life*. New York: Macmillan; London: Allen & Unwin.

Durkheim, E. (1952). *Suicide*. London: Routledge & Kegan Paul.

Eliot, G. (1989). *Middlemarch*. Harmondsworth, Middlesex: Penguin.

Ellenberger, H. (1970). *The Discovery of the Unconscious*. London: Allen Lane; Penguin Press.

Field, J. [Marion Milner] (1934). *A Life of One's Own*. London: Chatto & Windus. Reprinted London: Virago Press, 1986.

Forster, E. M. (1974). *A Passage to India*. Harmondsworth, Middlesex: Penguin.

Frank, A. (1954). *The Diary of Anne Frank*. London, Sydney: Pan.

Frankl, V. (1959). *Man's Search for Meaning*. London, Sydney, Auckland, Toronto: Hodder & Stoughton.

Freud, S. (1905d). *Three Essays on the Theory of Sexuality*. S.E. 7.

Freud, S. (1914c). On narcissism: An introduction. S.E. 14.

Freud, S. (1914d). *On the History of the Psycho-Analytic Movement*. S.E. 14.

Freud, S. (1916–17). Development of the libido. In: *Introductory Lectures on Psycho-Analysis*. S.E. 16.

Freud, S. (1917e [1915]). *Mourning and Melancholia*. S.E. 14.

Freud, S. (1920g). *Beyond the Pleasure Principle*. S.E. 18.

Freud, S. (1924c). The economic problem of masochism. S.E. 19.

Freud, S. (1927). *The Future of an Illusion*. S.E. 21.

Fromm, E. (1960). *The Fear of Freedom*. London, Henley: Routledge & Kegan Paul.

Fromm, E. (1972). *Psychoanalysis and Religion*. Toronto, New York, London: Bantam.

Greene, G. (1980). *Ways of Escape*. London: Bodley Head.

Hazlitt, W. (1990). *Essays on the Principles of Human Action*. Bristol: Thoemmes.

Hesse, H. (1972). *Steppenwolf*. Harmondsworth, Middlesex: Penguin.

Hoggart, R. (1961). Introduction to *Lady Chatterley's Lover* by D. H. Lawrence. Harmondsworth, Middlesex: Penguin.

Houselander, C. (1952). *Guilt*. London, New York: Sheed & Ward.

Hughes, J. G. (1987). *Getting Hitler into Heaven*. London: Corgi.

Huxley, A. (1980). *The Perennial Philosophy*. London: Chatto & Windus.

Jaques, E. (1982). *The Form of Time*. New York: Crane, Russak; London: Heinemann.

Jones, E. (1972). *Sigmund Freud: Life and Work, Vol. 1*. London: Hogarth Press.

Jung, C. G. (1983). *Memories, Dreams, Reflections*. London: Flamingo, Fontana Paperbacks.

Kazantzakis, N. (1972). *Zorba the Greek*. London: Faber & Faber.

Kernberg, O. (1975). *Borderline Conditions and Pathological Narcissism*. New York: Jason Aronson.

Koestler, A. (1975). *The Act of Creation*. London: Pan.

Lonergan, B. (1954). *Insight*. London, New York, Toronto: Longmans, Green.

Macintyre, A. (1967). *A Short History of Ethics*. London: Routledge, 1993.

Macmurray, J. (1932). *Freedom in the Modern World*. London: Faber & Faber.

Macmurray, J. (1936). *The Structure of Religious Experience*. New Haven, CT: Yale University Press.

Macmurray, J. (1949). *Conditions of Freedom*. Toronto, Canada: The Ryerson Press.

Macmurray, J. (1961). *Persons in Relation*. London: Faber & Faber. Reprinted Atlantic Highlands, NJ: Humanities Press International, 1991.

Milner, M. (1934/1987). *A Life of One's Own*. London: Chatto & Windus/Virago Press.

Newman, J. H. (1875). *Parochial and Plain Sermons, Vol. 4*. London, Oxford, Cambridge: Rivingtons.

Newman, J. H. (1888). *An Essay in the Aid of a Grammar of Assent*. London, New York: Longmans, Green.

Newman, J. H. (1927). *The Idea of a University* London & New York: Longmans, Green.

Petocz, A. (1999). *Freud, Psychoanalysis and Symbolism*. Cambridge: Cambridge University Press.

Photiades, C. (1913). *George Meredith: His Life, Genius and Teaching*. London: Constable.

Piaget, J. (1932). *The Moral Judgment of the Child*. London: Kegan Paul.

Pierce Clark, L. (1933). *The Nature and Treatment of Amentia*. Baltimore, MD: William Wood.

Ployé, P. (1986). *On Prenatal Levels of Transference*. Private circulation.

Rey, H. (1994). That which patients bring to analysis. In: *Universals of Psychoanalysis in the Treatment of Psychotic and Borderline States*. London: Free Association.

Richter, H. E. (1974). *The Family as Patient*. London: Souvenir Press, Condor Book.

Russell, B. (1946). *History of Western Philosophy*. London: Allen & Unwin, 1974.

Schafer, R. (1976). *A New Language for Psychoanalysis*. New Haven, CT, London: Yale University Press.

Scholem, G. (1995). *Major Trends in Jewish Mysticism*. New York: Schocken.

Schopenhauer, A. (1969). *The World as Will and Representation*. New York: Dover.

Solovyof, V. (1918). *The Justification of the Good*. London: Constable.

Symington, J., & Symington, N. (1996). *The Clinical Thinking of Wilfred Bion*. London, New York: Routledge.

Symington, N. (1986). *The Analytic Experience*. London: Free Association Press.

Symington, N. (1993). *Narcissism: A New Theory*. London: Karnac.

Symington, N. (1994). *Emotion and Spirit*. London: Cassell; New York: St. Martin's Press.

Symington, N. (1996). *The Making of a Psychotherapist*. London: Karnac; Madison, CT: International Universities Press.

Symington, N. (1996). The seductive therapist. In: *The Making of a Psychotherapist*. London: Karnac; Madison, CT: International Universities Press.

Szasz, T. (1988). *Schizophrenia*. Syracuse, NY: Syracuse University Press.

Tolstoy, L. N. (1986b). *War and Peace*. Harmondsworth, Middlesex: Penguin.

Toynbee, A. (1962). *A Study of History*, Vol. 4. London, New York, Toronto: Oxford University Press.

Trollope, A. (1996). *An Autobiography*. Harmondsworth, Middlesex: Penguin.

Tustin, F. (1972). *Autism and Childhood Psychosis*. London: Hogarth.

Vickers, S. (2000). *Miss Garnet's Angel*. London: HarperCollins.

Vygotsky, L. (1962). *Thought and Language*. Cambridge, MA: M.I.T. Press.

Weber, M. (1971). *The Protestant Ethic and the Spirit of Capitalism*. London: Unwin University Books.

Whitman, W. (1986). Song of myself. In: *The Complete Poems*. Harmondsworth, Middlesex: Penguin.

Winnicott, D. W. (1971). *Playing and Reality*. London: Tavistock Publications.

# INDEX

Absolute:
in act of understanding, 118
in constellation of sanity, 23, 114,
    155
as contemplative reflection, 99
of existence, 28–31, 61, 103–107
as personal, 36
in Spinoza, 32–33
acceptance, 18, 20–24, 40–41
*Act of Creation* (Arthur Koestler), 8
act of faith, 28, 32, 34
acts of understanding:
and Absolute, 118
and ontology, 34
and "other", 59
and Parmenides, 26
and perception, 28, 32
revealing inner processes, 9
Adam, 31
*Against the Current* (Isaiah Berlin), 10
alpha activity, 27
alpha elements, 61, 62, 180
alpha function:
absence of, 142
and conscience, 42

in personality, 27–28, 61–62
and thinking, 46
analysand, 8
animate:
governed by mechanical principles,
    31
and ontology, 15, 26, 29
and perception, 43
animism, 100, 126
*Anna of the Five Towns* (Arnold
    Bennett), 39
Anna Karenin, 5, 10
anti-vitalist, 31
Aquinas, St Thomas, 30, 31, 208
Aries, Philip, 10
Aristotle, 26, 74, 104
Ark of the Covenant, 210
"Arrogance, On" (Wilfred Bion), 106,
    133
attachment, 114, 119
attention deficit disorder, 121
Augustine, St, 30
autism, 2, 8, 12, 135
*Autobiography, An* (Anthony Trollope),
    122

Ayatollah Khomeini, 93

Balint, M., 8
behaviourism, 11
Bennett, Arnold, 39
Bentham, Jeremy, 51
Bergson, Henri, 66, 210
Berlin, Isaiah, 10, 30
beta activity, 27
beta elements, 61, 135, 177, 180
*Beyond the Pleasure Principle* (Sigmund
       Freud), 134
Bible, 100, 210
Bion, Wilfred:
    alpha and beta activity, 27
    alpha and beta elements, 61, 177,
       180
    alpha function, 42, 46
    as analyst, 145
    "On Arrogance", 105, 133–134
    *Bion in New York and Sao Paulo*,
       150
    *Brazilian Lectures*, 141
    "Differentiation of Psychotic
       from the Non-Psychotic
       Personalities", 183
    and envy, 63
    and god in personality, 100–101,
       144
    hallucinations, 64
    and jelly, 85
    and mother's reverie, 40
    and panic, 116
    principle of integrity, 62, 138
    and utilitarian view, 15
*Bion in New York and Sao Paulo*
       (Wilfred Bion), 150
Bleuler, Eugen, 8, 122, 123, 142
Blondel, Maurice, 9
Bollas, C., 50, 92
Bonhoeffer, D., 9
borderline pathology, 2, 150–154, 156,
       158
*Brazilian Lectures* (Wilfred Bion), 141
Brentano, F., 8
Bridges, Robert, 64
British Object Relations, 124
Brontë, Emily, 10, 37, 131
Brucke, Ernst, 32
Buddha, 29, 105
Buddhism, 9, 208

Burney, Christopher, 109

categorical imperative, 15, 30
Catholicism, 208
Chardin, Teilhard, De, 9
Chesterton, G. K., 122, 125–126
China, 10
Christendom, 43, 50
Christians, 31, 33, 36, 99, 103
Clarke, Pierce, 139
coexistence of opposites, 153
Collingwood, R., 9
communication:
    interpersonal, 27
    intrapersonal, 27
communism, 20, 208
comparative method, 11
condemnation, acts of, 20, 22–23
conscience:
    as creation of alpha function, 28
    and emotional action, 57, 59
    and emotional health, 42–44
    obliteration of, 98
    and psychopathy, 149
    as subjective experience of
       absolute, 106
conscious, 7, 71, 116
consciousness, 2–5
contingent:
    coexistent with necessary, 28, 30,
       31, 32, 36, 59
    and conscience, 42–43, 106
    divorced from Absolute, 61, 155,
       172
    divorced from necessary, 57, 176
    and freedom, 29
    as narcissistic, 26, 80, 202, 213
    self-knowledge, 190
    as sensual, 15
contract theory, 21
creative act:
    and conscience, 44
    and integrity of personality, 40–41,
       44–47, 69, 155, 164, 175
    and Real, 68
    in relation to others, 116
    structuring perception, 24
    as thinking, 143
    and trust, 151
*Crime and Punishment* (F. Dostoevsky),
       45

crust:
    in constellation of madness, 80
    fragments in jelly, 90
    as petrifier, 88
    and projection, 134
    and psychopathy, 149
culture, 3, 8, 9, 34

Darwin, Charles, 38, 50, 51, 54, 133
death instinct, 2, 54, 156, 177
decision-making theory, 8
delusion, 19, 21, 23, 68, 190
denial, 40, 151
depression:
    and autism, 135
    and narcissism, 41
    as sadness, 176
    and trauma, 89
dereistic thinking, 142
Descartes, R., 31, 67
determined:
    deterministic philosophy, 72–73
    vs. freedom of choice, 26–27
    and social sciences, 166
determinists, 18, 33
diagnosis, 7, 51, 158, 201
*Diary of Anne Frank* (Anne Frank), 134
"Differentiation of the Psychotic from
        the Non-Psychotic
        Personalities" (Wilfred Bion),
        183
disavowal, 47
displacement, 38, 179
dissociated, 11, 119
*Don Quixote*, 64
Dostoyevsky, F., 10, 45
dreams, 46, 129, 133
Du Bois, Reymond, 32
Durkheim, Emile, 10, 94

economics, 11, 34, 53
ego:
    fragmented, 69, 90
    internalization in, 66, 155
    necessary and contingent in, 43
    persecutory figures in, 20, 68
    principle of integrity, 62–63, 86,
        170
    and trauma, 140
    unconscious decisions in, 71
ego ideal, 51, 154

egoism, 2, 51, 56
Einstein, Albert, 38
*Elementary Forms of Religious Life*
        (Emile Durkheim), 10
Eliot, George, 5, 10
Ellenburger, H., 9
emotional action:
    as internalization, 66
    vs. motor action, 56–57
    and perception, 65
    response to conscience, 59
*Emotion and Spirit* (Neville
        Symington), 6
endometriosis, 1
Enlightenment, 43
envy:
    in constellation of madness, 79, 82,
        204
    and dependence, 138
    identification with god, 96–98, 100
    inherited, 63
    integrated, 40
    as intensifier, 152–153, 208
    and jelly, 68–89
    and maternal body, 118
    and Oedipus, 172
    and paranoia, 157, 184
    and principle of inclusion, 116
    and trauma, 132–135, 140
    unintegrated, 21
*Essays on the Principles of Human
        Action* (William Hazlitt), 183
ethics, 15, 33n
existence, 25, 26, 28, 29
*Exultet*, 185

Fairbairn, W. R. D., 8, 71, 88n
fantasy, 3, 15
*Fear of Freedom* (Erich Fromm), 93
Ferenczi, S., 8
Field, Joanna, 144
fixation point, 2, 154
formless infinite, 85, 86
Forster, E. M., 63
Foucault, Michel, 7
Frank, Anne, 178
Frankl, Victor, 15
freedom:
    as act of creation, 44–45, 53
    of choice, 26–30
    and dependence, 138

freedom (*continued*):
  vs. determinism, 33
  and guilt, 176, 178, 180–181
  and happiness, 38
  and intensifiers, 42, 58
  and Isaiah Berlin, 10
  and sanity, 23, 139
Freud, Sigmund:
  "Beyond the Pleasure Principle",
    134
  and conscience, 42
  and cure, 41
  death instinct, 54–55
  "The Future of an Illusion", 210
  hostile identification, 93
  latent and manifest, 133
  and masochism, 125, 129
  metapsychology, 30, 72
  mourning, 68–69
  *Mourning and Melancholia*, 140
  "On Narcissism", 56
  Oedipus, 171
  perversions, 130
  resistance, 58
  species survival, 51–52, 70
  unconscious processes, 60
  and utilitarian view, 19
Fromm, Erich, 8, 93, 96, 208
*Future of an Illusion, The* (Sigmund
    Freud), 210

Galileo, 74
*George Bernard Shaw* (G. K.
    Chesterton), 122
*George Meredith: His Life, Genius and
    Teaching* (Constantin
    Photiades), 188
gestalt, 61
glue-like attachment:
  and addiction, 149
  to embodied god, 80, 82, 143, 152
  and hatred, 120
  in impersonal action, 47
  in madness, 121, 155
  manifestations of, 203–204
  and narcissistic pattern, 139
  and obsessional neurosis, 169
God:
  creator, 25, 30–33, 36, 50, 63, 99–100,
    103–104, 210–211

  and denial, 169–170
  and ego, 20
  embodied, 44, 180, 106, 109, 143–
    144, 192
  and envy, 96–98
  and erotization, 190
  and hatred, 40–42, 204
  and intensifiers, 57, 59, 79, 152–153,
    208
  and jelly, 81–82, 87–89, 111–113, 166,
    187
  and mourning, 69
  and narcissism, 91, 93, 105, 139,
    157–158, 181, 201
  and negativism, 123, 205
  as omnipotent object, 6
  and persecution, 195–198
*Gorgias*, 61
*Grammar of Assent* (Cardinal John
    Henry Newman), 8
gravity, 37, 38
greed:
  and god, 96–99, 100, 204
  and intensifiers, 40, 47, 79, 116, 208
  and jelly, 82, 85–89
  and maternal body, 118
  and projection, 184–185
  and psychopathy, 149
  and robbery, 179
  and trauma, 132, 140
Greene, Graham, 64
guilt:
  awareness, 46
  and intensifiers, 41
  intentional thinking, 147
  interpretation of, 203
  and narcissistic constellation, 65
  and passivity, 98
  and principle of sedimentation, 199
  and trauma, 175–182
*Guilt* (Caryll Houselander), 175

Hazlitt, William, 183
Heathcliff, 10
Helmholtz, Hermann, 32
Herder, J. G., 10
Hesse, Herman, 52, 53
Hinduism, 9
history of mentalities, 10
Hitler, A., 93, 129, 130

Hoggart, Richard, 7
homosexuality, 128–130, 170
hostile identification, 93
Houselander, Caryll, 5, 175
Hughes, J. G., 129
Husserl, E. G. A., 96
Huxley, Aldous, 9
hypnotism, 166

id, 71, 114
*Idea of a University* (John Henry
    Newman), 9
idealization, 65, 88, 151
identification, 95, 114, 198
ideology, 2, 12, 20, 38, 73
illusion, 26, 27, 73, 103–104, 110
"Imagination, To" (Emily Brontë), 37
imago, 47, 140
inanimate world:
    emotional judgements of, 18, 22, 29
    mechanical principles in, 31–33
    ontology, 15, 26
    perception of, 43
    and science, 73
India, 10
inferiority complex, 174
inner act, 21, 22, 48, 75
instinct:
    biological survival, 26, 37, 54–55,
        110
    death instinct, 54–55
    as hateful act, 24
integrity principle, 39
intensifiers:
    in constellation of madness, 79
    and creative act, 24, 44, 186
    and emotional action, 57–60
    and envy, 152–153
    and hatred, 39–42, 45, 124, 207
    and jelly, 88
    and narcissism, 38
    and panic, 115–117
    and projection, 47, 120
    and trauma, 82, 133, 178
internalized object, 6, 67
internalizing act, 66, 69
interpretations:
    altering perception, 23
    false set of, 119
    and god, 196–197

of liquifiers, 187
and narcissism, 5, 171, 201
rejection of, 97–98, 171–172, 209
Schafer, Roy, on, 71, 73
and self-knowledge, 12, 204
introjection, 20, 68, 88–90
Islam, 36, 99, 103, 104–105
Israel, 100
Israelites, 36

Jaques, Elliot, 8, 59, 60
jealousy:
    and god, 79, 96–100
    and hatred, 44, 204
    and intensifiers, 40, 82, 116, 208
    and jelly, 86–89
    Klein on, 135
    and maternal body, 118
    and Oedipus, 172
    in self-consciousness, 189
jelly:
    in constellation of madness, 79–81
    vs. creative centre, 46, 122, 164,
        166–169
    and emotional action, 45
    and hysterical dissociation, 137
    and god, 111–112, 122, 195
    and guilt, 175–177
    and liquifiers, 186–187
    manifestations of, 151
    in narcissistic constellation, 48, 105,
        114, 157, 201
    and projective identification, 63–64,
        99
    in psychopathy, 149
    and sense of hopelessness, 119
Jesus, 47, 99
Jews, 31, 95, 129, 179
John of the Cross, 9, 208
Jones, Ernest, 8, 32
Judaism, 36, 99, 103
Judeo-Christian tradition:
    absoluteness of being in, 36
    and Freud, 63
    God in, 99, 104–105
    and narcissism, 7
    ontology in, 28, 30–31, 49
Jung, C. G., 8, 59, 173, 208
*Justification of the Good, The* (Vladimir
    Solovyof), 49

230   INDEX

Kant, Immanuel:
  categorical imperative in, 15, 30–31
  and mental limitations, 104
  noumenon in, 133
  and perception, 65
  phenomenon in, 133
  and psychology, 9
Kazantzakis, Nikos, 17
Keller, Helen, 28
Kernberg, Otto, 41, 51, 139, 150–107
Kierkegaard, S., 103
Klein, Melanie:
  depressive position, 41
  envy in, 63, 65
  influence on author, 8
  teachings of, 208
  and Tustin, 136
Koestler, Arthur, 8, 11
Koran, 36, 100
Kraepelin, E., 9

Lacan, J., 133
Lady Chatterley's Lover (D. H. Lawrence), 6
Lawrence, D. H., 6, 7
Lewis, C. S., 9
Life of One's Own (Marion Milner), 5n
liquifiers:
  and act of submission, 96
  destructiveness of, 97
  as elements of intensifiers, 79
  and guilt, 175–176
  and jelly, 99, 131, 165, 187
  as mode of action, 88–90
  and Oedipus, 172
  and trauma, 135–138
liquifying–petrifying, 57
literature, 10, 11, 53
logotherapy, 15
Lonergan, Bernard, 8
Ludwig, Emil, 32

MacIntyre, Alasdair, 61
MacMurray, John:
  and human freedom, 30, 46
  influence on author, 9
  and narcissism, 5
  "Persons in Relation", 91
madness:
  and act of acceptance, 24
  awareness of, 110
  constellation of, 79–82, 121, 129
  constitution of, 1–4, 206
  kernel of, 125
  and masochism, 212
  and narcissism, 155
  pattern of, 15–21, 193, 207
  and species survival, 50, 55
  understanding of, 10–12
manic-depressive psychosis, 2, 148
Mao Zedong, 93
masochism, 100, 125, 129, 140, 211–212
Metaphysics (R. G. Collingwood), 9
metapsychology, 30, 31, 70–72
Michelangelo, 38
Middle Ages, 43
Middlemarch (George Eliot), 5, 10
Milner, Marion, 5, 8, 146
Miss Garnet's Angel (Sally Vickers), 206
Moral Development of the Child (Jean Piaget), 8
mourning, 7, 68, 69
Mourning and Melancholia (Sigmund Freud), 140
Muhammad, 36
Muhammadans, 31
mystics, 5, 10, 105

narcissism:
  as core of madness, 57
  diagnostic signs of, 38
  differentiation of types, 50–51, 94
  and embodiment, 114
  essence of, 89
  and god, 101, 106, 117
  and interaction with patient, 192, 201
  introduction to, 1–5
  and jelly, 89
  Kernberg's characteristics of, 150
  in literature, 10
  narcissistic systems, 136–137
  and Oedipus, 171
  pattern of, 99, 123, 139
  preventing emotional action, 84
  and religion, 7
  vs. self-knowledge, 188
  structure of, 4
  as struggle for survival, 54
  transformation of, 179, 181

and trauma, 139
*Narcissism* (Neville Symington), 10
"Narcissism, On" (Sigmund Freud),
    56
narcissistic constellation:
    as core of madness, 80–81
    vs. creative act, 46–47, 65, 69, 126,
        164, 201
    elements of, 157
    and god, 152–153, 167, 205, 211–213
    and guilt, 177, 180
    and inferiority complex, 174
    and principle of reciprocity, 48, 95
    and psychiatric categories, 141
    transformation of, 195
    and trauma, 132–133, 139, 178
necessary:
    vs. contingent in reality, 26, 28, 42,
        57
    and ego, 43
    and jelly, 176
    in ontology, 30–32
    as personal, 36
negative narcissism, 92
negativity:
    to analyst, 194
    and god, 146
    and narcissism, 92
    in personality, 21–22
    and psychosis, 122
*New Language for Psychoanalysis, A*
    (Roy Schafer), 70
Newman, John Henry, Cardinal, 8, 9,
    163, 171
Newton, John, 38
Nightingale, Florence, 111

object relations, 51, 152
obsession, 2, 169, 189
Oedipus, 63, 118, 171
Old Testament, 100
ontology:
    and Absolute, 106–107
    as foundation of understanding, 15
    and personality composition, 25
    in philosophy, 30–35
    Schafer, Roy, on, 71
    and theology, 49
orgasm, 129–130
*Origin of the Species, On the* (Charles
    Darwin), 38

paranoia:
    and beta functioning, 27
    and god, 79–80, 105
    in Kernberg, 156–157
    as primitive hatred, 41, 107, 120,
        151, 184
Parmenides, 26, 27, 31, 103, 105
*Parochial and Plain Sermons* (Cardinal
    John Henry Newman), 163
*Passage to India* (E. M. Forster), 63
pathology:
    vs. health, 158
    history of, 9
    narcissism as, 1–2
    as social disease, 34
    and technique, 191
patients:
    attachment to analyst, 203
    borderline, 155–156
    communication with, 212–213
    decision-making in, 59
    and depression, 41
    and embodied god, 193–194
    jealousy in, 98
    and resistance, 3
    and social disease, 34
    suicide, 52
    transference, 96, 106–107
    trauma in, 209
    treatment of narcissistic patient,
        85
Paul, St , 42
perceptual process, 23
perceptual system, 21, 23
*Perennial Philosophy* (Aldous Huxley),
    10
persecutory figures, 20, 68, 193
personality:
    entities in, 27
    god in, 98–101, 106, 111, 208
    guilt in, 180–181, 199
    and intensifiers, 40, 42, 186
    and jelly, 84–87, 89–93, 164, 176
    and love, 69
    narcissism in, 3–5, 81, 202
    and ontology, 25
    and projection, 183
    scientific mentality in, 189
    splits in, 34, 140
*Persons in Relation* (John MacMurray),
    91

perversions, 128–130, 144
Petocz, A., 54
petrifiers, 79, 207
petrify, 40, 88, 115, 187
phenomenology, 2, 148
*Philosophiae Naturalis Principia mathematica* (J. H. Newton), 38
philosophy:
    determinism, 33
    and ethics, 15
    as godly activity, 113
    influences on author, 9–10
    and religion, 105
    of Schopenhauer, 133
phobic flight, 44, 201–202
Photiades, Constantin, 188
photographic, 20, 66, 164, 201
*Physicalische Gesellschaft*, 31
physical-mathematical method, 32
Piaget, J., 8, 208
Pietà (Michelangelo), 38
Plato, 64
pleasure principle, 51, 54
Ployé, P., 120
post-Enlightenment, 43
primary object, 57
principle:
    of coexistence of opposites, 63, 64
    of inclusion:
        applied to sanity, 18
        and intensifiers, 116, 120, 153
        in jelly, 87
        and submission to god, 98, 101–102, 168
    of integrity, 62
    of opposites, 80
    of plasticity, 54
    of reciprocity, 48, 102
    of sedimentation, 57, 176, 199
    of self-ignorance of negative emotional acts, 200
*Protestant Ethic and the Spirit of Capitalism, The* (Max Weber), 10
projection:
    and god, 99
    of good, 65
    and guilt, 176, 181
    into inanimate objects, 183–184

and Judeo-Christian symbols, 7
Kernberg on, 156–157
and liquifiers, 88–90
projective identification, 60, 61, 63
psyche:
    creative act in, 143
    and guilt, 175
    influence of mythology on, 63
    in jelly-like state, 105–106, 199, 209
    lack of barriers in, 134, 208
    and memory, 19
    and narcissistic constellation, 211
    splitting in, 48
psychiatrist, 118, 119, 146, 199
psychiatry:
    failure of, 51
    influence on author, 8–9
    pathologies in, 141–149, 158
psychoanalysis:
    and creative act, 44, 45
    and freedom, 38–40
    Freud's view of, 15
    glue-like attachment in, 117
    and healing, 12
    influences on author, 7–9
    and natural science, 72
    patient's anxieties in, 212
    and philosophy, 33–35
    pleasure principle in, 51
    reducing narcissism in, 3, 178
    transference in, 58
psychoanalyst:
    and attachment, 118–119
    author as, 5
    and narcissistic patient, 85, 102, 158
    and negativity, 194
    and phobic flight, 201–202
    and refusal of interpretations, 97, 197
    Rey, Henry, as, 136
    Schafer, Roy, as, 30, 70
    and sense of inferiority, 173
    and theory, 191–192
psychologist, 10, 30, 43, 50
psychology, 8, 11, 34, 71, 196
*Psychology from an Empirical Standpoint* (F. Brentano), 8
psychopathology, 3, 199

psychopathy, 10, 149
psychotherapist:
    and change in patient, 19
    dependence on, 146–147
    and glue-like attachment, 118–119
    and reduction of narcissism, 3, 85
    and sense of inferiority, 173
psychotherapy, 3, 15, 204
psychotic, 62, 122, 145, 150

quale, 62–63

Rank, Otto, 139
rationalization, 23, 173, 204
Read, Herbert, 64
real (the), 17, 18, 19, 20, 23, 69
Reality (O), 103
relativity, theory of, 38
religion, 49, 53, 63, 103, 105
reparation, 6
Republic (Plato), 64
resistance, 3, 48, 58
reverie, 40
Rey, Henri, 136
Richter, Horst, 156n
Russell, Bertrand, 43

Sachs, Hanns, 101
sadism, 100, 125, 200, 203
sanity:
    and acceptance, 20–21
    and creative acts, 24, 155
    as free act, 82
    and jealousy, 208
    pattern of, 213
    vs. pattern of madness, 17–18, 206
    perception in, 184–185
    as wholeness, 45–46
Schafer, Roy, 30, 71–72, 74, 75
schizophrenia, 2, 122, 142, 148
Scholem, G., 2, 21
Schopenhauer, Arthur, 3, 9, 40, 133
self-centredness, 1, 212
serial-killer, 1
sex, 11, 51, 52, 128–129, 170
sexual drive, 50, 51
shadow-side, 59, 173
social sciences:
    as philosophy, 34
    species survival in, 50

theories of action in, 70–71
    and utilitarian view, 15
sociology, 10, 11, 34
Socrates, 61, 110
solipsism, 1, 2, 4, 12
Solitary Confinement (C. Burney), 109
Solovyov, Vladimir, 9, 49
"Song of Myself" (Walt Whitman), 25
space–time axis, 56, 74
Spencer, Joseph, 68, 69
Spinoza, B.:
    and nature of god, 99–100, 103
    ontology in, 30–33
Spirit of Man, The (Robert Bridges),
    64
struggle for survival, 49, 50, 54
Study of History (Arnold Toynbee), 13
subjective experience, 159
suicide, 52, 124, 153, 212
Suicide (Emile Durkheim), 10
Sullivan, Ann, 28
superego, 179
symbolism:
    and act of faith, 34–35
    as aspect of true god, 106–107
    basis of, 28
    and dual self, 57
    and unity of being, 213
symbols, 7, 34, 58, 129, 213
Symington, N:
    The Analytic Experience, 96
    Emotion and Spirit, 6, 49, 110
    "Fish in a Shoal", 83
    The Making of a Psychotherapist, 19,
        116
    Narcissism, 4, 10, 97, 135, 136
symptoms, 2, 9, 51, 199
Szasz, Thomas, 141

Teresa of Avila, St, 10
Textbook of Psychiatry (E. Bleuler), 8,
    122
theology, 9, 10, 11
Thought and Language (L. Vygotsky), 8
Thwaite, Anthony, 191
Times Literary Supplement, 191
Tolstoy, Leo, 5, 10, 77, 208
Torah, 100
Toynbee, Arnold, 12
Trinitarian doctrine, 63

transference, 58, 96, 117, 201–202
trauma:
    analysis of, 131–140
    autism as, 2
    and chance events, 126, 211
    in childhood, 43
    as depression, 89
    envy as result of, 63
    in First World War, 54
    and fragmentation, 61
    and god, 108
    and guilt, 177–178
    and intensifiers, 82
    and narcissistic constellation, 157,
        205
Trollope, Anthony, 122
true self, 114n
Tustin, Frances, 8, 135, 136, 139
Two Sources of Morality and Religion,
    The (Henri Bergson), 66

unconscious:
    Ellenberger on, 9
    mourning as, 7
    and space–time axis, 60, 74
    unconscious decisions, 71
    unconscious knowledge, 41
uncreated projective action, 90
Upanishads, 99, 103–105
utilitarian view, 15, 51
Vico, G., 10, 67

Vickers, Sally, 206

"Virgin of the Rocks, The" (Raphael),
    38
Vygotsky, L., 8

War and Peace (Leo Tolstoy), 77
Weber, Max, 10
West (the), 8, 30, 42, 99, 103, 128
Whitman, Walt, 25
Winnicott, D. W., 8, 47, 114n
worm:
    and depression, 148
    and erotization, 190
    vs. god, 80, 195–196, 204, 209
    and hallucinations, 143
    isolation, sense of, 167
    and jelly, 82
    manifestations of, 152
    and narcissistic constellation, 157,
        202
    and negativity, 122
    and perversions, 128
    and principle of inclusion, 168
    and projection, 125
World as Will and Representation, The
    (Arthur Schopenhauer), 3
Wren, Christopher, 38
Wuthering Heights (Emily Brontë), 10

Yahweh, 100, 210–211

Zohar, 21
Zorba, 17
Zorba the Greek (N. Kazantzakis), 17